D1071720

# Okinawa: a tiger by the tail

# Okinawa: a

# tiger by the tail

M. D. MORRIS



Hawthorn Books, Inc.
Publishers New York

OKINAWA

 This book was manufactured in the United States of America and published simultaneously in Canada by Prentice-Hall of Canada, Ltd., 1870 Birchmount Road, Scarborough, Ontario. Library of Congress Catalogue Card Number: 68-10108.

First Edition: 1968

# Acknowledgments



For the three years prior to its publication, this book has been my personal tiger by the tail. Though it was conceived on Okinawa in 1946, serious writing did not start until 1965. It is the end product of a purely free enterprise. As such, I am truly appreciative of all help, great or small, I got along the line. If someone's name is missing, it is not out of ingratitude, but because of space.

Thanks go to my old C.O., now General L. B. Washbourne, USAF, Ret., for the assignment in Real Estate which enabled me to digest the Ryukyus in full dimensions; and to former Seabee Ralph Young for his aid in two capacities over two decades. And gratitude goes to Public Information Officers Lieutenant Colonel Edward Endres at New York, Lieutenant Colonel Robert Webb at Washington, and Mr. Montia Osborn at Naha for their broad vision, and Mr. Fred Kerner, all for recognizing the merit in this story. Most hospitably helpful for a base of operations in Okinawa was the entire Public Affairs Division of USCAR under seasoned newshawk Joseph S. Evans, Jr., and his staff: Major Thomas H. Farrington, Les Hardwick, Sam Mukaida, Sam Kitamura, Charles A. Dunn, the movie magnate; the ladies Catherine Vander Grift, Jane E. Clark, and Mary Nell Troxler. Hongo's photo files, Nadoyama's machinations, Liosnoff's liturgies, and Tanabe's tips were all helpful. John Palmer's data distillation was basic to the battle chapter, and the University of New Mexico Press provided several student statements. In Tokyo, my key blocks were set up by Masaki Yagi, Deputy, Press Section, Japanese Ministry of Foreign Affairs, and some by Yukio Higasheda of JiJi Press. Thanks, too, to Hank Gosho of the United States Embassy there, and Charley Tuttle.

Bouquets for the thousand pages of preliminary production typed out nights, Sundays, and holidays by Ruth Prindle, and reams of finished copy professionally polished off by my genial amanuensis, Nancy R. Flipping. Finally, to my severest critic and connubial chum Maureen Morris, for endless listening hours of "How does this sound *now*?", my affectionate kudos, but not the last word. That, with thanks, goes to the Ryukyuan people for being such magnanimous subjects—still.

M. D. Morris

New York City

TO THOSE WHO LANDED ON LOVE DAY—AND STAYED

PROSPERITY TO THE LEW CHEWANS,
AND MAY THEY AND THE AMERICANS
ALWAYS BE FRIENDS.

—Commodore Perry at a
reception in his honor at
Omiudun (the royal guest
house), Shuri, Okinawa, June 6, 1853

# Contents

# Introduction

## THE TIGER'S TALE

The rising sun in the east marks the beginning of the day. Wearily, women light fires under waiting teapots while their men get ready for the day ahead. Gulls unwind, stretch their feathers, and fly off. Presses turn to roll the morning edition at two local news plants, street vendors start to hawk their wares. Traffic swells avenues, which just a while earlier were damp and deserted. Buses carry drowsy workers to bakeries, stores, machine shops, hospitals, and the anthills of union and government offices. Reluctant children are bundled off to school.

This scene unfolds daily in Greater London and Los Angeles, Boston and Boca de Buenos Aires. It is also the start of any day in Naha, Okinawa, the city which in 1946 was a deserted, bomb-leveled pile of rubble without even a passable street. Today Naha boasts a quarter-million native population and enjoys a standard of living second in all Asia only to Tokyo, Japan.

As the site of the last battle of the Pacific phase of World War II, Okinawa was devastated by the fighting. The American forces stayed on and built up a fantastic, island-wide military establishment as well as the native commonweal. Although at one point the project was almost abandoned, this probably will not happen again unless the Japanese pursue to its ultimate an American agreement on "residual sovereignty."

Okinawa, a coral island and the largest of the Ryukyu chain, is located in the East China Sea at about the center of a triangle among southern Japan, mainland China, and northern Taiwan. Equidistant from each by fewer than five hundred miles (less than the distance between Buffalo and Chicago), it is comparable in size to Long Island and in shape to New Zealand. Since 1945, the Ryukyuan people have lived with the enigma of two worlds. These two distinct cultures were thrust upon the Ryukyuans in fewer than the last hundred years, while tens of centuries of their own heritage, including their language, have all but disappeared.

The Ryukyus were thoroughly "Japanized" following the Meiji restoration in 1871. They were superficially Americanized somewhat after the conquest of

1945 and more so after the United States refused in 1950 to absorb them legally.

Today the Okinawans speak, read, and write Japanese. They have Japanese names and have adopted Japanese religion and literature. On holidays they fly the Japanese flag. But they use American money—it is the island's only legal tender—buy goods imported from the United States, and ride in American vehicles fed on American petroleum products.

The neon-lighted Naha bars and bowling alleys; the Koza City juke boxes, electric guitars, and drive-in movies; the Nago beauty salons for coifing hair on women and poodles—all swallow up the same quarters, halves, singles, fives, and tens as they do in Milwaukee, Miami, Menemsha, or Malibu. But for a lapse of American foresight, the Ryukyuans might also have been speaking English.

An Okinawan who is the head of the Chamber of Commerce is also the kendo instructor at the local Police Academy. Commingled with karate, judo, sake, and steam baths are Rotary, Boy Scouts, the YMCA, and rootbeer. While tea ceremonies and koto concerts are only for festive occasions, yakatori and mizu-shiro appear in the daily diet as often as hot dogs and French fries.

But these Yankee delights are not what have Americanized the Ryukyus. They are by-products of the omnipresence of the American serviceman. Literally, there is no place in the islands where the ubiquitous soldier, sailor, marine, or airman—or his base—is not conspicuous.

The base is the heart of the native economy. The Yankee dollar and its fringe benefits support the uncommonly high local standard of living enjoyed by the majority of the Ryukyuan people, along with a good deal of freedom from responsibility.

Throughout the island's countryside, U.S. war machines dominate the landscape. Huge aircraft, small aircraft, and helicopters fill the sky day and night, and high-tension towers transmitting megawatts of electric power via scores of cables loom overhead like puppet lines of giant skeleton scarecrows.

Mountains of systematically stacked steel chemical drums and wood shipping crates range over square miles of depot areas fenced in by mesh and barbed wire. Acres of new vehicles sticky with cosmoline stand ready to be put into motion in convoy caravans. Tanks and amphibious vehicles wait in port areas, where fleets of ships daily bring more military stores for stacking, then take away from those same stacks for distribution and destruction in Viet Nam. Radio antennae fields stand along the shore, while radar and missile sites mushroom in the hills.

On the ground, giant steel pipelines carry endless gallons of diesel oil, jet fuel, lube oil, gasoline, and fresh water to thousands of machines. And stored below ground in massive shockproof, radiationproof, fireproof steel and concrete caverns, are reservoirs of petroleum products; magazines with megadeaths of munitions; and the billionth-of-a-second sensitive computerized control centers, the brain and nerve cells of this island bastion.

At many combat training areas in the north, jungle and village battle situations are simulated with deadly precision. Near the coast, periodic live-missile firing drills keep the troops alert—and their neighbors alarmed.

This military establishment, our largest outside the continental limits of the United States, requires a considerable housekeeping force to do nontactical, nonoperational chores. This labor market has become the prime pillar of the Ryukyuan economy. In addition to paying high wages to a vast native employee force, the United States pays rent to the Okinawans for all the land which it has pre-empted for the base. The thousands of Americans buy local industrial goods, and there is a large annual American aid to help the government of the Ryukyu Islands.

Interspersed among the defense installations through the countryside are native villages, farms, and plants. No land goes unused. Though there are many modern conveniences, rural people tend to live much as they did long ago. But cheap, frequent, rapid bus service and telephone networks leave no one isolated. Fishing communities are enjoying "progress" in a littoral life much improved from prewar days.

In the big cities, Naha, Nago, Koza, etc., large American-style and -stocked department stores sport the Japanese innovation of rooftop kiddie parks. Slides, carrousels, and Ferris wheels delight both Okinawan and American children while their parents shop. Further down the street kimono-clad women carrying infants in obuhimos on their backs stop at a shop front to chat while their husbands go inside to be fitted with Ivy League suits.

Though no resident Japanese are permitted into the Ryukyus officially, the Nipponese presence is strongly evident in the newspapers, magazines, radio, and in the new microwave transmission television, a vivid and effective remote-control influence.

Perhaps a dozen Taiwan Chinese reside in the Ryukyus in commercial, unofficial capacities, and the Filipinos are steadily going home. Europeans number only a handful. The Ryukyuan population approaches one million (about as many as Baltimore, Maryland, or Bogotá, Colombia), and there are over a hundred thousand American "residents," not including troops en route to or from Viet Nam and nearby combat areas.

The two ethnic groups break down into three categories each with subgroups. There are the Okinawans employed by the United States Government, and those living on the local economy. Of the latter, there are country people and city people. The Americans are in the military establishment or civilian employees either of the United States Government or private industry. And, of course, there are dependent wives and children.

Besides living with two competing cultures, the Ryukyuan people themselves are divided between the elders' preference for "tradition" and the teen-agers' for worldliness and conformity with Western and Nipponese youth. The desire for material comfort conflicts with the need for "national" identity. All this is mixed with the plea-for-peace and the demand-for-defense.

On the American side, the usual stumbling self-entrapment of United States foreign policy works at odds with the logical dictates of balance of power in Asia. While it appears to some as politically expedient to promise the reversion of Okinawa to Japan, can we sensibly do this in the face of mounting military commitments in Southeast Asia?

The oriental concern with face and the American preoccupation with image must join in common regard for economic and military survival. The "Two Chinas" are uniquely in agreement with each other and with Japan about an American departure. And while the United States promises to leave, it is planning to remain.

Nature, too, is in conflict with progress. The habu, the Ryukyus' resident reptile, perhaps a direct descendant of the one that allegedly disrupted the bliss of Eden, at night often climbs the high-tension towers and while slithering across the cables, short-circuits a whole community's electric power. Annually typhoons sweep up from the south, laying waste everything before them.

To solve most of these problems, the Ryukyuan people need a leader of their own. Unfortunately, they have always been a dependent people. The mainstay of their daily diet, the sweet potato, came back to them from China in a vessel returning from transporting gold for the Emperor's tribute. In the fifteenth century Ryukyuans developed a seafaring commerce which might have made Okinawa the Venice of the east, but they did it for Sino-Japanese overlords. In the nineteenth century, though steeped in five hundred years of Chinese cultural influence, the Ryukyuans surrendered their heritage, habits, and way of life to the Japanese Emperor Meiji in exchange for a subordinated citizenship and a meager but steady subsistence.

Plans for an early end to World War II made it necessary for the Allies to dislodge the Japanese from Okinawa. In this battle the best parts of the island were devastated, and nearly a third of the population made casualties. This was a consequence of a war which the Americans neither wanted nor enjoyed—but one they had to win.

Now, nearly a quarter of a century after the destruction, the Okinawan population has doubled and the life expectancy increased by a decade. Ryukyuans are relatively free of diseases—and responsibilities—their dignity has been restored, and they are prosperous. Wholly owned Okinawan industry runs into millions of dollars. Local private capital boasts a brewery, two newspapers, a radio and video station, soft-drink factories, a huge cement plant, a fishing fleet with markets, pineapple orchards and cannery, and sugar plantations and plants. All this evolved because the United States chose to retain control of a major military victory; a base on the perimeter of Asia, just six hundred miles from mainland China.

Suppose the American had left the Ryukyus? Would there now be so much prosperity? And would those who are still poor be any better off? Would Okinawans enjoy the same bountiful life as those in Tokyo?

In a conversation about the Okinawans, a prominent and knowledgeable Japanese frankly said: "They really don't want us, we can't ever hope to buy them what you people do. It's just that under it all they feel left out. You Americans have a cartoon of an infant (Linus) hugging a little warm blanket. The Japanese flag has become the 'security blanket' for the Ryukyuan people."

Not only is the Okinawan domestic picture complicated, the "foreign" view is also a tangle. Externally, it is a tangle in which the principal protagonists are the United States, Japan, and the object of their mutual attentions—the Ryukyu Islands. The mainland and Taiwan Chinas are only peripherally involved. Each principal contains groups, parties, and factions, and these in turn are made up of people, each having something else to say about the future of these islands.

The Ryukyu Island chain is the focus of a great deal of conversation and documentation on the part of knowledgeable people—who say only what is expected of them. Statements about Okinawa are, for the most part, either prudent, paraphrased, proper, popular, polemic, or political. The Ryukyus appear to serve as a vehicle for one or another person's, faction's, or nation's own gains.

To predict where the Ryukyus may go we must look at each element—from the surface and from the depths.

*The Surface:* The Chinese People's Government at Peking, in rare concert with the Taiwan Chinese, supporting Asia for the Asians, advocates the return of the Ryukyus to Japanese residual sovereignty.

*The Depths:* Mainland China has found it impossible to substantiate or even generate a grain of support for its long-forfeited "Chinese rights" to the Ryukyus. Consequently, it feels that it might possibly be able to gain a toe hold by remote control. The Okinawa Socialist Party is not an independent party in the Ryukyus, but lists itself as the Okinawa Prefecture Branch of the Japan Socialist Party. The Chinese originally hoped to gain influence in Okinawa by influencing the J.S.P. in a strange chauvinistic alliance with the Japan Communist Party, because all Japanese political parties agree on the Ryukyus question. China wants the Americans out from a nuclear spearhead so close to its own unbuffered home coastline.

*The Surface:* The Chiang Kai-shek regime on Taiwan has worked itself around to an uncommon agreement with Peking on the reversion of Okinawa to Japan, on the grounds that the problem is an Asian matter.

*The Depths:* Nationalist China, equally unable to make a single point on the same ancient "claim" to the former Loo Choo Islands, felt it better to support the Japanese claims, hoping to gain face, stature, and influence post factum. But the two problems Japanese sovereignty of the Ryukyus poses to Taiwan are major. The U.S. naval strength (which until now has provided Taipei with the impregnable outer defense ring behind which it has done all its strong talking) will be gone for lack of an operations base. Deeper, even, politically is the inescapable fact that Chiang's government, his army, and his people, replete with their highly viable economy, are now a tenant nation. They live on an island which (though once Chinese) was, like Okinawa, "Japanized" by the armed force of the Meiji Restoration, along with the neighboring Pescadores Islands in 1895. If the Ryukyus set a precedent for returning conquered islands to Japan without, in turn, requiring Tokyo to make restitution to the nation from which the islands were originally taken, then should Japan also decide to want a Formosa reversion, Chiang's position would indeed become interesting.

*The Surface:* Japan has relentlessly, though tactfully, pursued its alleged "right" to "residual sovereignty" over the Ryukyus as provided in the Peace Treaty of 1952 which officially ended World War II. Every Japanese government, regardless of other issues, has held that the Ryukyus are "Japanese home islands."

*The Depths:* Japan is well off, despite having lost the war. Within twenty years after the surrender, the American victors have insured Japan's prime objective of the war—the Great East Asia Co-Prosperity Sphere with Japan on top. To all this then, Tokyo wishes to add the territory lost in the war.

The Japanese islands are volcanic; the Ryukyus, coral. Fossils found by paleontologists in both places show different ties to the Asian land mass. Both the prevailing winds and the ocean currents flow northward from Okinawa toward Japan. Present ethnic traces all indicate that the Ryukyus were never, in antiquity, a part of Japan. Nippon absorbed them with a superior military force in 1871 and kept them behind a closed door until the Allied invasion of 1945.

Through co-operative action, money, educational materials, literature, communications, and tourists, the Japanese Government has expressed overtly firm interest in regaining control of the Ryukyus (all after they were repermitted any influence in 1952).

Today, Japan enjoys a privileged position; it has been relieved of the responsibility of defending itself. The United States does this for them from bases—in Japan, but mainly from the forces at Okinawa. Were the Americans ever to withdraw, the Nipponese would be obligated to defend themselves as well as "their" Ryukyus Islands. And since the Okinawan economy is not self-sustaining, the Japanese treasury would have to contribute more in subsidizing their acquisition than they would expect to receive in taxes. How would the Japanese cope with the grumblings of a provincial population who might find themselves with a standard of living below their present one?

*The Surface:* Some people feel that, in the interest of preserving the American image in Asia, and to foster better U.S. relations with Japan, we must keep our word and return Okinawa to the Japanese. Others insist the United States cannot afford to move a man from Okinawa as long as the world situation remains what it is. The Pentagon Press Director: "Okinawa is closed!" The general public: "What's Okinawa?"

*The Depths:* Okinawa is one of the only two occupied areas of the world left residue from World War II. Unlike the other, the divided city of Berlin,

Okinawa has so many U.S. military installations that it is nearly all base. Over the past twenty years, America has poured billions of dollars into plant and hardware for the base, while also contributing to the socioeconomic improvement of the area. The United States does not like to be considered a "meddler" or other more strongly worded Asian accusations. Also it would like to be relieved of the expense of a hundred thousand-man military establishment replete with full equipment and fringe benefits, and the expense of subsidizing a high-level, although baseless, economy. These cost hundreds of millions of dollars annually. But even *if*—and this is highly unlikely—the United States were ever to work out an arrangement whereby American forces would remain on bases which were enclaves on a Japanese home-administered Okinawa, and if in response to a "red alert" the flyers made the three-minute scramble, no U.S.A.F. craft could ever take off from Japanese territory without the express permission of the Nipponese Prime Minister. Or in case of direct attack on Okinawa itself, no defensive missile might be fired from any silos in "Japanese homeland" until Tokyo gave the word. And can the Japanese nation, now constitutionally dedicated to peace and outlawing war, say "Go"?

*The Surface:* Ryukyuans of all parties and all walks of life outwardly agree only on the single issue of reversion to Japan. Virtually no one, except a minute and radical fringe group, is even remotely interested in independence for the islands. Americans are, by and large, regarded as "gai jins," the "outside country men," the friendly invader from whom the trouble and money come. But those who really know, hold the respectable Americans in genuine high regard, without ever diminishing their espousal of Japanese residual sovereignty.

*The Depths:* The Japanese flag is now flown on Okinawa at all oriental holidays. The Japanese language, customs, and culture are again taught in the native schools, operated at American expense. Ryukyuans do have autonomy. The socioeconomic life of the islands is directed by elected Ryukyuans through the Government of the Ryukyu Islands (GRI), though under the careful aegis of the United States. The postal system, the police, and many other public services are local (also generally patterned along Japanese lines). But the coin of the realm is U.S. dollars and cents. Okinawan manufacturers demand tariff protection against Japanese imports and internal tariff assistance so their goods can be sold in the United States. Yet Ryukyuans clamor for Japanese technical and commercial advice so it will be easier to integrate "when reversion comes." But would they want to compete with Japanese home industry?

Would a people once second-class citizens, later nearly devastated by a three-month all-out war, who were in twenty years pulled up and inflated to gainful employment, political stature, reasonable prosperity for the majority, and filet mignon for some, ever want to go back to eating canned fish heads and rice?

Okinawa has had a history of internal strife, Japanese incursions, Chinese absentee domination, ethnic mutations, administrative cross purposes, and political intrigues. Even the weather plays havoc with its climate and soil. Still

Okinawa is at present somewhat better off than several other areas which have chosen to become "emerging nations."

In 1950, Okinawan leaders pressed for legal absorption by the United States. When this was refused, they redirected their energies toward the only other place they knew. Today they talk, write, demonstrate, but under it all they do not seek freedom from American influence. They are ambivalently pro-Japanese, yet are reluctant to see the day the last Yankee sails away with his green beret and his green dollar.

Indeed, Okinawa is a tiger by the tail for every government even remotely concerned with it. Each strives to maintain a firm grasp on a vital situation from which it would truly rather be free. It cannot let go because of vested interests and national "face."

PART I

# The Kokubokan and the Iceberg

# CHAPTER 1

# Kokubokan, the Prelude

The Poland of the Pacific, Okinawa has been a battleground from the beginning. It has been repeatedly invaded and drained by China or Japan or by their combined forces. And, internally, Okinawa has suffered feuds comparable to any Shakespearean tragedy.

In the 692 years of recorded history under five dynasties up to 1870, Okinawa was a semi-independent kingdom. But it was never left in isolation.

Okinawa was never able to defend itself against its invaders. Most of the Ryukyuan military history prior to the 1187 unification by Shunten and in the weak era between 1337 and 1429 has consisted of internal wars between kings.

Toward the end of the thirteenth century, Kublai Khan wanted the Ryukyuans to provide him with both manpower and a staging area for his planned invasion of Japan. Fortunately, other things distracted the Mongol Emperor. The consequent Okinawan landings were minor and the Japanese phase aborted.

Seven and a half centuries later, in 1945, this very same plan for attacking Japan from a Ryukyuan stage was reconceived by the United States, this time to crush Nipponese aggression. Again the plan to invade Japan was not carried out.

Okinawa fared better in the Mongol skirmishes than in the utter devastation by the Allied armada. Moreover, this reversal of historical initiative which resulted in the 1945 fall of Japan and concomitant destruction of Okinawa was brought about by Japan itself in a seventy-one-year headlong race to ruin. Japanese military history determined Okinawa's fate.

On Monday, December 8, 1941, radios in Japan announced an event which, due to the international date line, had occurred some hours earlier, some three thousand miles to the east in the Pacific. Radios in the United States carried President Roosevelt's address before a joint session of both houses of Congress:

"Yesterday, December 7, 1941, is a date which will live in infamy. The United States of America was suddenly and deliberately attacked by Naval and Air Forces of the Empire of Japan. The United States was at peace with that nation, and at the solicitation of Japan was still in conversation with its Government and its Emperor, looking toward the maintenance of peace in the Pacific. Indeed, one hour after Japanese air squadrons had commenced bombing in the American Island of Oahu, the Japanese Ambassador to the United States and colleagues delivered to the Secretary of State a formal reply to a recent American message. While this reply stated that it seems useless to continue the diplomatic negotiations it contained no threat or hint of war or of armed attack."

The President further told the nation of several other American areas then under attack by the Japanese in the Pacific. He concluded with a request for a formal declaration of war, and warned of the sacrifices which would lie ahead:

"Hostilities exist. There is no blinking at the fact that our people, our territory, and our interests are in grave danger. With confidence in our armed forces, with the unbounding determination of our people, we will gain the inevitable triumph, so help us God. I ask that the Congress declare that since the unprovoked and dastardly attack by Japan on Sunday, December 7, 1941, a state of war has existed between the United States and the Japanese Empire."

The most important date in this full-scale struggle over the control of the western Pacific and for the very existence as a nation became December 7, 1941. To show how this inevitable moment came about I turn to a similar date nearly a century earlier.

On December 7, 1857, Townsend Harris arrived in Yedo (Tokyo) from Shimoda Port to present to the shogun (whom he called the Tykoon) his credentials as United State Ambassador to the Japanese islands. The shogun was interpreted, according to Harris, as having been "pleased with the letter sent with the Ambassador from a very distant country, and likewise pleased with his discourse. Intercourse shall be continued forever." Thus eighty-four years before the "day of infamy," Townsend Harris officially consummated formal relations between the Japanese Empire and the United States. Commodore Perry had initiated this more than four years earlier, on July 8, 1853, when he sailed into Yedo Bay with the first steam vessels ever seen by the Japanese. Later, on his second arrival in Japan, Perry signed a treaty of peace and amity in Shimoda with the Tokugawa Shogunate March 31, 1854. For the first time, Japan entered into a treaty with a nonoriental power.

Perry opened the way with his treaty, but it remained for Harris to place our relationship with Japan on a firm basis. The Japanese had given in to Perry reluctantly, hoping to evade fulfilling the treaty once Perry sailed away. Harris's patient, diplomatic labor eventually overcame the traditional Japanese hatred of foreign infidels. Harris did this, of course, without Perry's show of force which had so impressed the Japanese earlier. His two years of effort were rewarded with the signing of a second treaty with Japan on July 29, 1858. This was a workable treaty of commerce which remained in force for forty years and actually formed the basis of our relationship with the Japanese until World War II.

In the Japanese language, *sho* means "to lead" and *gun* means "army." Ergo, shogun means the leader of the Army, a title given in old Japan to the chief of the Emperor's Army, or generalissimo, who was also the major-domo in the Imperial Palace. About the middle of the sixteenth century a shogun named Tokugawa seized the powers of the Emperor from the incumbent and made himself the ruler of Japan. This was what we call today a military coup. For nearly three hundred years, through the middle of the nineteenth century, descendants of the Tokugawas passed the shogunate down via primogeniture. Because the Japanese believed in the divine right of the Emperor (he is the Son of Heaven), Tokugawa did not overthrow him. The Emperor became a figurehead, in regal exile in Kyoto. This condition existed at the time of Perry's arrival.

The decade or so which followed, until 1868, saw the worldly wakening of the Japanese and the disintegration and eventual demise of the shogunate. Ironically, the treaty with the United States, the greatest thing the shogunate did for Japan had, within ten years, led to its own collapse and to the restoration of the monarchy.

The incumbent, Emperor Meiji, was able to seize and use an opportunity. He reclaimed what he felt was the divine right of the Imperial house from a pseudo "regal" line of army leaders. His first act was to abolish the position and title of shogun, doing away with the Tokugawas. He restored full authority to the Emperor. In all the treaties Japan had signed, the title "Emperor" had to be substituted for that of "Tykoon."

Of course the restoration brought about a complete transformation of Japan. All the feudal clans were abolished and the empire was divided into areas called prefectures; thus ended the strangle hold of the feudal lords. A parliament or Diet was created, and Japan was then thrown open to all outsiders. Some foreign envoys were received at court, and Nipponese embassies were created in capitals abroad. Japan then underwent a thorough modernization in such things as education, building architecture, street dress, religion, industry, public works, business, finance, and, to aid this, they built railroads.

In the three years between 1868 and 1871 the Army of the Two-Sworded Men, the ancient Japanese samurai warriors, disappeared. They were replaced by a modern army and the beginnings of a navy. The need for a strong military was apparent when Perry's armada arrived, awakening a fear of invasion from overseas. Clearly Japan was at that point completely unprepared to meet any serious foreign challenge and shipbuilding was forbidden under the shogunate.

The Japanese adopted the French system of drill to train the old feudal Army. (French Lieutenant Colonel Marquirie became Japan's first military adviser in

1871.) In 1872 a conscription law was enacted, but met with a great lack of public support. Although the people wanted to see Japan emerge as a power, they felt war was the business of the feudal lords and their retainers, not the general populace. Despite the popular apathy, the military establishment emerged in strength.

Unlike the army, the navy took somewhat over twenty years to become strong enough to wage a full-blown war with another nation—the 1894 war with their ancient rivals, the then crumbling mainland empire of China.

The Japanese military encroachments began back in 1875, when the Army went north and annexed the Kurile Islands. The following year they went east and took the northern Bonin Islands (Ogasawara group). In 1879 they annexed Okinawa and the Ryukyus, all of Nansei Shoto, and in 1891 they went back and took the southern Bonin Islands, making that conquest complete. By then Japan felt strong enough for its first full-scale conflict. This war set the standard pattern for Japanese aggression: attack first, declare war later. For war, a situation was trumped up over the administration of Korea which, at that time, was allegedly independent but was in truth under the domination of the corrupt Chinese Empire. The Japanese Army quickly occupied Seoul without resistance and then defeated a Chinese army at what is now Heijo (Pyongyang) in northern Korea. Simultaneously, the Japanese Navy destroyed whatever Chinese fleet there was off the Korean coast.

The Treaty of Shimonoseki brought Japan's first modern war to a close within two years. Nippon gained confidence from a victory over an allegedly much greater power. It also achieved "autonomous independence" for Korea. Japan won territory too—the Liaotung Peninsula, all the islands of Formosa, and the Pescadores (which lie between Nippon and the Chinese mainland)—and forced open great areas of China previously forbidden to Japanese trade.

Japan at that time was not quite strong enough to resist the diplomatic pressures of France, Russia, and Germany to renounce her claims on the Liaotung Peninsula—this smoldered within the Japanese warlords and eventually brought about the Russo-Japanese War a decade later. By then a second aggressive pattern had developed: move in a major direction once each decade.

Korea, which earlier posed the excuse for the Sino-Japanese conflict, also triggered the Russo-Japanese War of 1904. The Japanese fleet attacked the Russian squadron at Port Arthur simultaneously with the Japanese occupation of Seoul. A formal declaration of war came two days later. The treaty of Portsmouth mediated by President Theodore Roosevelt ended the war. Imperial Russia suffered a disastrous and humiliating defeat. Russian armies went the entire eight-thousand-mile length of the Trans-Siberian Railway—only to get out into the field with ammunition that was not the same caliber as the rifles. The Russian-Asiatic fleet was destroyed at Port Arthur by the Japanese. And, finally, Admiral Rozhdestvenski, after coming halfway around the world from the Baltic Sea, saw his forces devastated in the battle of Tsushima Straits. The result was world acknowledgment of Japan as a new and major naval power just thirty years after she began to build a navy. Nippon also established itself as a nation to be reckoned with, having humbled one of the major world powers.

In addition, Japan received Karafuto, the southern half of Sakhalin Island, from the Russian Empire. The Nipponese also made a protectorate out of Korea, gained Kwantung, and finally got the Liaotung Peninsula, denied to them only ten years earlier. Thus the Japanese had evened the score with the Russians, and there remained now only the Germans and French with whom to reckon.

Russia was also required to lease to Japan the South Manchurian Railroad running from Port Arthur to Changchun, which from that moment became the vehicle for Japanese exploitation of the Manchurians. This gave Japan an artery into the province it was to pursue and ultimately absorb. In 1910 the Japanese annexed Korea, their so-called "protectorate."

Although the Anglo-Japanese alliance had been in effect since the turn of the century, the Japanese did not try to use it in the war with the Russians because of pride and a desire for a major field trial. However, this alliance (which was abrogated by mutual consent at the Washington Conference in 1922) was the main reason for Japan's involvement in World War I as a British ally. This was a politically expedient gamble. While betting on what appeared to be a sure thing, the Japanese still preserved the chance to settle with France at some future date they knew would come. Japan participated in World War I by occupying Tsingtao to drive off a German foothold in China, and later by occupying three sets of German-held islands in the Pacific: the Marianas, the Marshalls, and the Caroline Islands. In 1919 the League of Nations gave these islands to the Japanese as trust territories on the condition that they would not arm them—but they did. These islands were key posts in the Pacific phase of World War II. With this World War I maneuver, Japan evened its score with the Germans over Liaotung, while gaining considerable territory. It was an easy war for the Japanese. Unlike World War II, the total Japanese force participating amounted to only eight hundred thousand men. There were 300 killed, 907 wounded, and just three reported prisoners or missing. With such statistics, the Japanese home front scarcely paid attention to the war. It became an attractive milestone in the march toward the divine destiny of the Great East-Asia Co-Prosperity Sphere.

Nippon's occupation of Tsingtao on the Chinese mainland lasted until 1923. It was difficult to get them out. Also, in 1918, Japan joined with the allies against the Bolsheviks in Russia and went with an international force to Siberia to try to quell the October Revolution through the back door. But the predominance of Japanese in this international band disturbed the others. The Japanese force would not withdraw from Manchuria until 1922.

Emerging from World War I as one of the Big Five at the Versailles treaty conference, Japan gained a permanent seat on the council of League of Nations and participated in all kinds of European affairs. She joined with the United States, France, Great Britain, and Italy in reducing their navies and aircraft carriers (kokubokan). She adhered to a ratio of 5-5-3 for the United States, Britain, and Japan, respectively, on capital ships, and further co-operated by joining the London Conference in 1930. However, the Third Naval Conference in London in 1934 fell apart when the Japanese demanded naval parity. Instead of 5-5-3, they wanted 5-5-5, which would have given them undisputed supremacy in the Orient. After the failure of the Conference, Japan denounced the Washington Naval Treaty, and began a secret naval building program.

In 1931 a concocted incident at Mukden along the South Manchurian Railroad gave the Japanese an excuse to conquer the Chinese Province of Manchuria. Japan then set up the regime of Henry Pu-Yi, the former boy Emperor of China, who became puppet Emperor of the land renamed Manchukuo. In 1932 the Japanese Army moved in and occupied Shanghai, then the second largest city in the world and largest city in the Orient. In 1933 the Japanese Army moved to conquer Jehol (the province of China which sits north of Korea and south of Manchukuo), thus enlarging Japanese influence on the mainland.

Feeling strong enough by 1937 to take on China again, the Japanese began making incursions into the mainland. They believed Chiang Kai-shek was occupied with internal problems. But the Chinese were more desperate than Japan had calculated. They undertook a defensive war against the Japanese invaders, more out of patriotism to their land than to the Kuo-Min-Tang government. There were many separate Chinese factions fighting the Japanese, all in disarray and disorder; and all ultimately were defeated. But the fighting took its toll on the Japanese Army. Two years later, in 1939, the China Incident was still going on and had by then become a war of attrition. The Japanese went south and occupied the large offshore island of Hainan, and then went still farther south and annexed the Spratly Islands (listed as French); actually just a large coral reef such as Midway or Wake Island. They were in an important strategic position vis-à-vis Indo-China and the Dutch East Indies.

To gain time the Japanese made a "friendship treaty" with Thailand in 1940, permitting them influence in the area without fear of reprisals. The British, deeply involved in World War II and their treaty with Japan long ended, did nothing to block this move. The Japanese, although tied to the Axis cause by sympathy and by the Anti-Comintern Pact, were not yet at war with the Allied powers. German victories in Europe caused the withdrawal of British forces from both Shanghai and north China, enabling the Japanese to fill the void unopposed. Then the fall of France to the Germans enabled the unhampered Japanese to take French Indo-China as an occupied territory. The complete score over the Liaotung Peninsula incident was at last settled. But, far more significantly, France's inability to keep the hated Japanese out of Indo-China smoldered; then made the French postwar return a devastating holocaust which, as late as the mid '60's, burned the U.S. in Viet Nam.

After the fall of the Netherlands the Japanese moved in and took the Netherlands East Indies, rich in needed natural resources (oil and rubber). They also had the military and naval bases Japan needed. Finally, on September 27, 1940, Japan made a military alliance with Germany and Italy, who recognized her leadership in Greater East Asia.

These developments disturbed the United States, which, during the Chinese campaign of attrition, aided the Chinese with military supplies, money, engineering assistance, and manned fighter planes. The United States also ceased exporting iron and aviation gasoline to Japan and began negotiations with the Nipponese leaders, hoping to persuade them to return the seized territory and give up their policy of aggression. This was unrealistic on the part of the United States, as was—and still is—much of American Far Eastern policy.

Encouraged by the alliance with Germany and Italy, Japanese Foreign Minister Matsuoka said, "I fling this challenge: If she is going . . . to stick blindly and stubbornly to the status quo in the Pacific, then we will fight America."

The United States, at last aware of Japanese intentions, stepped up its aid to China. General Claire Chennault was allowed to launch his Flying Tigers (an American volunteer fighter pilot organization) by intercepting the Japanese in China skies. The United States was still seeking to avoid war, although they knew eventually they would have to take a firm stand in the Pacific.

As early as March 1941 talks began between Admiral Nomura, the Japanese Ambassador to the United States, and the State Department in an attempt to find some common ground. These dialogues continued into the fall of 1941, but the Japanese refused to surrender their seized territories, or give up their Great East Asia ambitions. Saburo Kurusu, a special envoy from the Emperor, came to assist Nomura. When Kurusu arrived in San Francisco he expressed hope that he would "make a touchdown" in his talks with U.S. Secretary of State Cordell Hull. General Tojo's government continued to propound Japan's peaceful purposes while claiming its divine right to Great East Asia. Tojo said the United States then had a "last opportunity to make amends for her past aggressions." All the while, a Japanese naval task force under radio blackout was inexorably en route to Pearl Harbor.

To find the tap root of such planning we must look back to 660 B.C., when, according to legend, Jimmu Tenno, the first Emperor of Japan, issued an Imperial Rescript which translated roughly from the old calligraphy asserts: "We shall found the Empire and cover the whole of that which is under the heavens." This view of Japanese destiny has been reiterated by Nippon's leaders for twenty-six hundred years.

President Roosevelt sent a message to the Emperor from Washington at 9 P.M. on December 6, 1941, which was received in Tokyo before the actual Pearl Harbor attack but after the die had been cast. Although the order already had been given, the Emperor still had the option of reading Mr. Roosevelt's detailed message, which concluded: "I address myself to Your Majesty at this moment in the fervent hope that Your Majesty may, as I am doing, give thought in this definite emergency to ways of dispelling the dark cloud. I am confident that both of us, for the sake of the peoples, not only of our own great countries, but for the sake of humanity in neighboring territories, have a sacred duty to restore traditional amity and prevent further death and destruction in the world."

The F.D.R. plea was ignored. On the morning of December 7, 1941, Japan struck at the United States by hurling a powerful bombing attack against eighty-six ships of the Pacific Fleet at the strategic American base in Pearl Harbor. Every battleship and most of the aircraft in the Hawaiian area were disabled. Other naval vessels were destroyed and most shore facilities were damaged. Human casualties were high. Fortunately two task forces were saved because they were at sea, as were all the aircraft carriers of the Pacific Fleet. Per pattern, three hours after the first attack, Japan declared war against the United States. The other Axis powers followed suit later in the week.

Thirty minutes after the attack, Ambassador Nomura delivered to Secretary Hull's office a letter which revealed Japan's true objectives. This letter concluded, "Obviously it is the intention of the American government to conspire with Great Britain and other countries to obstruct the Japanese effort toward the establishment of peace through the creation of a new order in East Asia, and especially to preserve Anglo-American rights and interests by keeping Japan and China at war. This intention has been revealed clearly during the course of the present negotiation. Thus, the earnest hope of the Japanese government to adjust American-Japanese relations and to preserve and protect the peace in the Pacific through cooperation with the American government has been finally lost . . ." Japan optimistically approached the American challenge as its final obstacle to domination of all East Asia, and all of the Pacific.

It takes a surprise move to unhinge the Japanese war machine. The Japanese are careful, meticulous planners and organizers. They set out checks and balances to cope with any situations they can envision. But the slightest unexpected occurrence upsets everything. And this has been the situation vis-à-vis Japan's dominance of East Asia. From 1871 through 1941, what had appeared as Japanese invincibility was a combination of the inertia of their war machine coupled with the inability of any foe to plan an effective countermeasure. Japan also expected all defeated peoples to remain subservient.

The Japanese citizen, once in military uniform became imbued with the feeling that he was a personal representative of the Emperor, the descendant of the Son of Heaven. This consequently gave him all the power and self-confidence he needed to win a psychological duel with an opponent even before actual combat began. Most Japanese soldiers came from peasant stock and were hardy souls used to long hours of hard labor and much privation. On November 15, 1944, the U.S. War Department Military Intelligence Service issued a *Soldiers' Guide to the Japanese Army* which advised:

"In combat the Japanese soldier is strong and hardy. On the offensive he is determined and willing to sustain sacrificial losses without flinching. When committed to an assault plan, Japanese troops adhere to it unremittingly even when severe casualties would dictate the need for abandonment or modification of the plan. The boldness and courage of the individual Japanese soldier are at their zenith when he is with his fellows and when his group enjoys advantages of terrain or fire power. He is an expert at camouflage and delights in deceptions and ruses. Japanese troops obey orders well, and their training and discipline are exemplified in night operations. On the defense they are brave and determined. Their discipline is good, their fire control excellent. In prepared positions the resistance of Japanese soldiers often has been fanatical in its tenacity.

"Surrender is considered a great disgrace, not only to the soldier but to his family, and his religion teaches the Japanese soldier that it is the highest honor to die for the Emperor. There have been a number of instances where numbers of Japanese troops, in hopeless positions, having fought to the last, begged to be killed to avoid the ignominy of capture. 'Fight hard,' the Japanese soldier is told. 'If you are afraid of dying, you will die in battle; if you are not afraid you will not die . . . Under no circumstances become a straggler or prisoner of war. In case of becoming helpless, commit suicide nobly!"

Propaganda emanating from Tokyo emphasized the contention that Americans are individualistic, whereas the Japanese have the advantage of selflessness. Officers and enlisted men have both shown their willingness to die for the Emperor. The most famous case of suicide occurred on the death of the Emperor Meiji. General Nogi, the national hero of the Russo-Japanese war, committed hara-kiri to be with his Lord.

This is what the American citizen soldier had to cope with in his uphill march from the bottom of the bay at Pearl Harbor to the top of the Yusa Dake Hills on Okinawa. The American countermeasures to all the Japanese military attributes were the ability to improvise, the firm and compulsive desire to stay alive, and the belief that the United States was in the right. Even on December 7, 1941, America knew it was not down for good and thus began its long trek back.

Since the outbreak of the Manchurian Incident in 1931 Japanese military forces have fought virtually every type of action under the widest variety of terrain and climatic conditions. Their experiences taught them that a simple plan, carried out with power, determination, and speed, will disrupt the plans of hostile forces and lead to a quick Japanese success. Japan followed Pearl Harbor with invasions of Thailand and Malaya on December 8, and an invasion of the Philippines on the tenth. On the same day, the British battleships *Repulse* and *Prince of Wales,* sent from Singapore to destroy Japanese convoys landing troops, were both sunk by Japanese aircraft off the Malay coast. On the thirteenth, Guam fell to the Nipponese; on the seventeenth they landed in Borneo;

on Christmas Eve they captured Wake Island, and on Christmas Day the British surrendered Hong Kong. So ended 1941.

New Year's Day of 1942, Sarawak on Borneo was occupied by the Japanese. Next day, Manila fell to them. On the eleventh the Dutch East Indies were invaded; by the twenty-third they had made landings at Rabaul and Balik Papan. January twenty-fourth saw the Battle of Macassar Straits and landings on New Ireland, and by the end of January Japan had seized Amboina. The only retaliation the United States made during this period was a pair of raids on the Marshall and Gilbert Islands. In February 1942 the Japanese landed on Papua and New Britain—on the ninth and on the fifteenth. Singapore fell to them on February twenty-third. Santa Barbara, California, was shelled from the sea by a Japanese submarine. The day after, the U. S. Navy made a raid on Wake Island, and on the twenty-seventh the Battle of the Java Sea began; the following day the Japanese landed on Java. By March 7th the British had evacuated Rangoon, Burma; and all the Netherland East Indies had fallen to Japan—by then enjoying complete control.

For the first three months after Pearl Harbor Japan clearly held the initiative and set the pace. But they were forced to drive fast and furiously. Time would eventually become an ally of the Allied powers, yet none of them could afford to sell space for time because they realized in the long run they would have to buy it all back at a high price in manpower. After the March 9, 1942, conquest of the Netherlands East Indies (now Indonesia), the Japanese, on March 16, made a full-scale raid on Darwin, Australia. On the twenty-third they occupied the Admiralty Islands. By April 6 Japanese fliers raided India, and on the ninth the "battling bastards from Bataan" finally had to capitulate completely, almost ending U.S. resistance in the Philippines. However, Americans gained some hope when Tokyo was raided by carrier-based bombers of the U. S. Air Corps. This was followed on the twenty-fifth by an occupation force of Americans on New Caledonia Island. But on April twenty-ninth the Japanese cut off the Burma Road and thereby closed the back way to any resistance from the south which American and Chinese forces might have made on the Chinese mainland.

May 4 saw the beginning of the Battle of the Coral Sea. The next day the Japanese closed the Burma-Chinese border and started to enter China from "underneath." On the sixth Corregidor, the last remnant of the Americans in the Philippines, gave up. By June 3, Japanese carrier-based planes attacked Dutch Harbor, Alaska, foreboding the beginning of Japanese attacks on the Western Hemisphere. Next day, the U. S. Navy began a battle off Midway Island attempting to recover it. On June 7 the Japanese landed on Attu and Kiska, two islands at the end of the Aleutian chain, Alaska (U.S. mainland territory), which by the twelfth were then occupied completely. On June 20, 1942, Vancouver Island off the coast of British Columbia was shelled by a Japanese vessel. The very next day the same vessel shelled the Oregon coast, and on June 27, the United States raided Wake Island again. Japanese successes in the early phases of the war were largely due to their troops' being specially prepared and trained for operations in jungle terrain. The weakness of their artillery and their comparative lack of motorized transport did not count as decisively against them as would have been the case if operations had been conducted in open country. The ability of Japanese troops to live off the countryside compensated, to some extent, for weaknesses in their army supply (intendance) system.

August 7, 1942, American forces attacked Guadalcanal and Tulagi in the Solomon Islands. This battle ultimately became an Allied success. In spite of fierce Japanese counterattacks the U.S. control was firmly established over the southernmost Solomon Islands, including the harbor of Tulagi. Another attack relieved Port Moresby and finally cleared all Japanese out of Papua. By the end of the summer of 1943 the Japanese had been cleared from New Georgia in the Solomons, where the saga of Roger Young unfolded as the Allies moved closer to the Japanese bases at Rabaul.

The Japanese built air-force runways and hangars in their two held islands of Attu and Kiska in the western hemisphere. However the forces of General Simon B. Buckner, Jr., defeated them here and later defeated them again on Okinawa, in the last battle in the Pacific. Attu, the easternmost of the Aleutians, was recaptured from the Japanese in June 1943 and Kiska, Japan's last outpost in that area, was recouped in August 1943.

In China the Japanese continued to make casual but costly headway. Back in May of 1943 they had started a new drive toward Enshih and Chungking. Later in May they were routed south of Ichang. Early in June, Japan announced the conclusion of the Yangtze drive. In September 1943 the United States raided Marcus Island, and in the middle of the month took Salamaua and Lae. Early in October the U.S. Navy again raided Wake Island.

The Soviet Union was the only Allied nation in the unenviable position of bordering directly on both Japan and Germany. A five-year nonaggression pact with Nippon permitted the Russians to devote their major attention to the defeat of Nazi Germany, which the Allies all agreed was the stronger land force requiring more important concentration. However, the existence of Russian troops of the Red Banner Army in Siberia was considered by the Japanese a great potential danger, which kept hundreds of thousands of Japanese troops immobilized along the Manchurian frontier watching it. That pact also made it possible for Soviet airplanes and ships to carry lend-lease goods safely from the U. S. Pacific ports to Siberia for transport by rail to the Eastern Front and use against the Germans. This saved considerable time and shipping space in U.S. aid to Russia while relieving much pressure on transport across the Atlantic, and up the northern route to Murmansk. Also, the Soviets' "neutrality" with the Japanese aided the Allied cause, since the Russian military concentration had not been divided on a two-front war. Thus the Germans had much more pressure in Eastern Europe, which helped in their ultimate defeat. The Allied victories were accomplished not only by effort and superior forces but also by the lessons learned from the earlier Allied losses. The defensive was extremely distasteful to Japanese commanders. When forced to this position, they regarded it as merely a passing phase in combat. The Japanese tried to inflict heavy losses on a temporarily superior hostile force in order to regain the offensive.

Japanese commanders believed that the fundamental purpose of defense was just to await the moment when the Allied forces were so disorganized that a quick and decisive counterblow could be delivered. In almost every situation the defensive forces then had to counterattack. Every defensive plan would include directions for the conduct of such maneuvers. Japanese counterattacks usually were directed against Allied flanks and ordinarily were quick and valiant. Often major counterattacks would develop from a series of local attacks. In some cases Japanese troops forced out of defensive positions had counterattacked without proper preparation and were annihilated. Between October 1943 and April 1944 the U.S. forces successfully regained Bougainville and the surrounding islands, the Caroline and Mariana Islands and Roi Namur in the Marshalls, Kwajalein, and the Admiralties. Then followed Admiral Lord Louis Mountbatten's description of the triumphant Allied operations in west Burma as a "complete victory." In February 1944 American infantrymen under the command of General "Vinegar Joe" Stilwell were co-operating with Chinese troops fighting the Japanese in Hukawng Valley in north Burma. Later in the year, Stilwell's troops routed the Japanese forces from that area. Nippon also tried unsuccessfully to capture India through Manipur. General Stilwell, who later ended a distinguished active career as Commanding General of the forces on Okinawa, maintained the pressure on the Japanese in conjunction with General Claire Chennault's Flying Tigers and Generalissimo Chiang Kai-shek's seasoned Chinese regulars. This sealed the fate of Japan, which had some time earlier been foretold by Prime Minister Winston Churchill: "In ashes they must surely lie before peace comes back to the world."

# CHAPTER 2

# Iceberg, the Action

It was abundantly clear to all the Allied powers that the only way to end both the war and the compulsion for the Great East Asia Co-Prosperity Sphere was to land in Japan proper. In all Japanese history no foe had ever conquered them at home. Only once, a thousand years before, was a landing even attempted —this, unsuccessfully, by a Chinese coastal clan.

In the early years of World War II, perhaps even as late as 1943, the Allied long-range master plan indicated the possible counteroffensive routes as being light feints across the Pacific from Hawaii, and down along the Aleutian-Kurile chains. But the main thrust was to have come from the India-Burma sector, across mainland China, broadside to Japan's west coast.

As time went on, the most logical plan for assaulting the Japanese home islands appeared to be a feint at the coasts and an actual attack on the south end, moving northward between the shore lines. To do this, the United States and its Allied forces would need a staging area large enough to accommodate all the troops, stores, and matériel necessary to mount such an attack, neither too far away nor so close that a possible Japanese counteroffensive would be overwhelming.

The only location even close to the specifications, for the most part, was Okinawa. A plan coded as "Operation Iceberg" was then formed for the acquisition of this staging area. The Operations Division of the War Department General Staff officially listed Operation Iceberg as:

*MISSION:* To assist in capture, occupation, defense, and development of Okinawa Island and establish control of sea and air in the Nansei Shoto area, with the eventual aim of expanding control of Nansei Shoto by capturing, defending, and developing additional positions.

*Phase I*

(a) L-6 Day: capture the islands of Kerama Retto for use as an advance naval anchorage and seaplane base.
(b) L-1 Day: capture the Keise Islands and emplace heavy artillery thereon for operation against Okinawa.
(c) L Day: land on western shore of Okinawa with XXIV and III Amphibious Corps abreast.
(d) L and L+1 Days: feint a landing on southeast shore of Okinawa by one reserve division.

*Phase II*

Seize Ie Shima and remainder of Okinawa on W Day (Estimated L+30).

*Phase III*

Seize and develop additional islands in the Nansei Shoto.

U.S. FORCES: Tenth Army—CG, Lt. Gen. Buckner

XXIV Corps—Maj. Gen. Hodge
7th Infantry Division
96th Infantry Division

III Amphibious Corps—Maj. Gen. Geiger, USMC
1st Marine Division
6th Marine Division

Reserve:

27th Infantry Division
77th Infantry Division
2nd Marine Division

Supported by:

Central Pacific Force—Adm. Spruance
Amphibious Force—V. Adm. Turner

ENEMY FORCES: Estimated 70,000 enemy with Headquarters, 32nd Army at NAHA, two Infantry Divisions (24th and 62nd) plus miscellaneous units and Navy shore-based personnel.

Lieutenant General Simon Bolivar Buckner, Jr., the soldier the General Staff had selected to be Iceberg's over-all commander, was a natural choice. When he was awarded the distinguished service medal for the campaign in Kiska and Attu (1943), the citation read:

"For exceptionally distinguished and meritorious service in a position of great responsibility . . . General Buckner successfully organized the defenses of Alaska and limited the enemy's encroachment on that territory to footholds of little strategical importance and personally supervised the establishments of new bases in the Aleutian Islands, from which attacks were launched that led to the defeat of the enemy and his expulsion from the Western Hemisphere. In the face of a difficult climate, a rugged terrain, and conditions of extreme isolation, General Buckner, by his personal example and fortitude, inspired his troops to overcome severe hardships and maintained a high state of morale and military efficiency. . . ."

S. B. Buckner, Jr., of Munfordville, Kentucky, was graduated from the U. S. Military Academy at West Point and commissioned a second lieutenant in February of 1908. From his first assignment with the 9th Infantry at Fort Sam Houston, Texas, until he was ordered to assume command of all U.S. troops in Alaska, his regular army career was exemplary. He rose regularly in rank to brigadier general in September 1940. By May 1943 he was a lieutenant general. In August 1944 he was sent to command the Tenth Army assigned to the Pacific area, destined eventually for Okinawa. Buckner had taught at West Point and had seen World War I service in Luzon, Philippine Islands, while the Japanese were then our co-belligerents. General Buckner was an esteemed tactician, well liked by the enlisted men, and a responsible commander. But most important he was a man with experience in combating and defeating the Japanese forces in the field. His four subordinate commanders were also men of superlative achievement and talent.

But the Staff's planning of its timetable for Operation Iceberg was misjudged. The difficulty lay in a lack of complete intelligence. There simply wasn't much up-to-date information about Okinawa and the rest of the Ryukyus for the General Staff to be absolutely certain on all details.

In the invasion of Italy and the Normandy beachheads, a full intelligence "book" was obtained by G-2 with the aid of Italian and French natives, but Japan had kept Okinawa under cover since 1879, and there was none. The lack of firsthand knowledge of the Ryukyu Islands, its occupiers and its occupants can be seen in the contrast between the plan layout and the summary data of Iceberg: "Phase II. Seize Ie Shima and remainder of Okinawa on W Day (estimated L+30)." Actually the fighting ended at L+82! This fifty-two-day miscalculation might relate closely to the "Estimated 70,000 enemy . . ." vs. the closing figure of 110,071 Japanese killed and 7401 (including wounded) listed as captured. These "spy" errors were not the complete fault of G-2. There were no prewar Americans who had vacationed on Okinawa's beaches—no Britons who had wintered at a Ryukyuan Riviera; no Katchin Hanto counterparts of Maqui French to give the planners a "case" on the coves, the tides, and the short cuts. Save for a few scant facts, General Buckner might just as well have been assaulting the planet Mars.

The limited knowledge of the Ryukyus was further brought home by a book called *The Pacific World,* published originally in 1944 and later reprinted by the *Infantry Journal* in June of that same year—just nine months before the invasion. This volume was edited by thirty men from several eminent institutions of higher education and was doubtless the best information at hand. In the Foreword the editor, Fairfield Osborn (then president of the New York Zoological Society), wrote, "The information presented here has been gathered together by the men of seven educational and scientific institutions. We need make no excuse for presenting so vast a subject is so small a book. It is at best but a general picture, one, we hope, which will give to those in our Armed Services and to their families and friends at home a clearer idea of this great area of the earth's surface from which we cannot turn our faces."

The best that these authors compiled on the Ryukyus, the area in question, appears on less than one page (142). I quote this section verbatim only to illustrate the lack of substantial working information available as late as 1943:

"THE LUCHU ISLANDS OR THE RYUKYU ARCHIPELAGO"

"The Luchu Islands formed stepping stones from Japan proper south to Formosa. They are divided into two groups: the Okinawa, northern, and the Sakishima, southern.

"The Luchus are mountainous and composed mainly of elevated coral reefs formed into tablelands and isolated hills. Near the northern end of the Luchus are two islands with active volcanos, Nakano-shima (3500 feet) and Suwanose-shima (2700 feet).

"The archipelago of 55 islands, with a land area of only 935 square miles, has a population of more than 577,000. The climate is semi-tropical with very heavy summer rainfall. The summer is not too hot, owing to prevailing southerly winds. The maximum temperature reaches 96° F. and a minimum 38° F. In spite of the unfavorable climatic and physical conditions, the islands are heavily populated and every available piece of land is under cultivation. Sugar cane and sweet potatoes are the chief crops. Pineapple, bananas, indigoes, and vermilion lacquer are also produced.

"Okinawa, the largest island of the two groups, is 268 miles in circumference. On it are two cities: Naha, the capital and principal harbor with a population of 65,000, and Shuri, 3 miles from Naha. From Naha a small railway runs to Yonabara and a branch line to the famous fishing village, Ichuma. Ichuma is of interest because here the women enjoy equal rights with the men, a thing unheard of anywhere else in the Orient until fairly recently, when China incorporated 'equal rights' provisions in some of its civil codes.

"Up to the 17th century, when the northern group was conquered by the Japanese, the Luchu Islands were under Chinese rule. In 1879 the Luchu king was deposed and sent to Japan, where he was given a noble title and no responsibility. In this way, all the Luchus became a province of Nippon."

Their information was so incomplete. The northern group of islands is Amami, and Okinawa is generally referred to as the "southern Islands." There are also seventy-two islands, forty-eight of which are inhabited. It does not rain all summer long. The circumference of the island of Okinawa is of little value, since it indicates nothing about its shape or dimension; there were many more cities than Naha and Shuri. Shuri was the traditional capital. The railway ran north along the west coast to Kadena. The short spur which ran down to the little fishing village of Itoman was horsedrawn. Women enjoyed equal rights along with the rights to have more than one husband. The islands were never under Chinese rule but always were considered as tribute territory. Current information was sorely lacking and it still is. In 1946 (a year after the battle ended), I had to locate sites for new troop housing by using a U.S. Coast and Geodetic Survey Chart, which still indicated areas of Motobu Peninsula (and of the northern third) as "unexplored."

During the summer of 1946 I spent many evenings in the select confines of the Officers' Mess and Club of the Naval Operations Base at Tengan (White Beach), absorbing ten-cent scotches and war stories. There was an undenied rumor that long enough before the campaign the Navy (by some guile) had put a flier ashore on Okinawa to collect intelligence. He was ordered to gather a "book," keep himself safe and sound, and a month later meet a pin-point rendezvous with a submarine which was to have taken him back to Hawaii replete with his "information." This story rang a bell with me even then; particularly because a little over a year earlier I had heard a radio broadcast following closely the same concept but set in a somewhat different form.

Through most of 1945 the National Broadcasting Company, in co-operation with the University of California at Berkeley, broadcast a series of public information dramatic documentary programs called the "Pacific Story." Coincidental with the Love-Day landings, the episode for Sunday evening, April 1, 1945, was about Okinawa. Allegedly the fictitious concoction of writer-director Arnold Marquis, the radio play unfolded the tale of one "Lieutenant Reid," a carrier-based navy dive-bomber pilot shot down over Okinawa. "Joe," his enlisted gunner, died in this action and was buried on a sandy beach by Reid and a "Father Fénelon" * (an old French missionary priest who saw their rubber boat come drifting onto the beach although the Japanese did not).

Father Fénelon took Reid to his house where he hid and fed him until he was well. All the while the priest jollied the Japanese along when they came to inquire about an American flier believed to be on the island. He did not turn Reid

* François de Salignac de la Mothe-Fénelon (1651–1715) actually was a French ecclesiastic and writer.

in because he was "not concerned with who rules these islands." He was "concerned with the soul of man."

As Reid grew stronger Fénelon became more friendly. He drew him a map of Okinawa which Reid must surely have seen during his target-briefing sessions. Fénelon, from his thirty-five years in the Ryukyus, told Reid of Naha and its 65,000 inhabitants just five miles west on the other coast of this island "some sixty miles long" which "varies from two miles to sixteen miles wide." In their after-dinner chats the priest told the flier there were 800,000 people on fifty-five islands in the chain over an area of 935 square miles. Half the Ryukyuan people lived on Okinawa. Reid carefully posted everything in his notebook, from the time he crash-landed until the episode ended. He included an account of two breath-taking close calls when Japanese soldiers made surprise visits to Fénelon's house during the missionary's absence.

Fénelon's Japanese hosts obviously had told him nothing about any of the United States victories or the Americans' return to the Philippines. (This item would then fix the time of this incident as at least late 1944.) The Japanese did, however, allow Fénelon freedom to come and go without his being attached to any church. Father's background information from an ancient "Manuscript History" is also fairly accurate, tagging the U.S. Government with having "lost her opportunity" at the Ryukyus by not having "listened to" Commodore Perry. (Kerr, in his book, says just the opposite.)

Reid learned of the local produce, but he longed to know the enemy's troop strength. He made a clandestine trip to Naha, where, while inventorying the Japanese ships and port facilities, he was caught in a nine-hour U.S. Naval Air Force bombing raid. He made a survey of roads, railroads, supply depots, anti-aircraft batteries, et al., while living off the land and keeping himself well sequestered. The lieutenant returned to Father Fénelon for help in getting off the island with his notebook. The priest told him he could not survive even if he did get off. But Fénelon himself would try to get Reid's notebook out—and send along his own. Lieutenant Reid gave his notebook to Father Fénelon. "Perhaps he can get it out, and with it his own notebook, which should be of more value than mine. . . . Perhaps eventually this information will be brought to the attention of the right people." The program ended, and we can only guess that the missionary never turned the notebook and the flier over to his Japanese hosts. Apparently Fénelon must have gotten his contraband to the "right people" but without troop-strength figures. Actually writer Arnold Marquis was reasonably well informed, except for a few small items like wild boars in the south end, a big airfield *just* east of Naha, and how possibly one could drift along the east coast from the north end to Nakagusuku without having to circle Katchin Hanto peninsula and the small outer islands.

Now, a radio program of this type normally takes at least a month from conception to airing, and facts like those contained therein were considered classified. Where did Marquis get all *his* information? Why was Sunday evening,

April 1, 1945, selected for a program about Okinawa? Was there really a Father Fénelon? Was ever a "Lieutenant Reid" put ashore by accident or by master plan? No one is truly willing to say. But planning had to be done in 1944. I am certain there was basically enough usable information or G-2 never would have mounted the expedition in the force and magnitude with which Iceberg was done.

Japan was beginning to feel the pressure early in 1945 and was apparently contemplating a counteroffensive of its own. Japanese Navy order no. 37 disseminated January 20, 1945, concluded: "In view of the acute turn of world events the Imperial Army and Navy should aim at defeating the invading U.S. forces, the principal enemy, by crushing the enemy's fighting power everywhere in depth, and securing those areas vital to the prosecution of the war. In this way they will undermine the enemy's fighting spirit and promote the attainment of the objectives of the war." In 1945 the Japanese were still undaunted, never expecting an attack on Okinawa. But America knew that it was necessary for the ensuing battle for Okinawa to happen when and as it did.

The Ryukyu Islands were defended by the Thirty-second Japanese Army under the command of Lieutenant General Mitsuru Ushijima. The principal Japanese defenses were in the rugged ground north of Naha. The forward Shuri defenses were along a natural barrier running east and west from Machinato to the Yonabaru airfield, and the well-fortified defense zone extended south from this line for five miles. Caves, pillboxes, and gun emplacements were connected by tunnels. In an effort to trap and destroy rather than drive off the American invaders, Ushijima planned to offer no initial resistance but would depend upon the Japanese surface fleet, kamikaze planes, and suicide boats to destroy the American supply lines. Then he hoped the Thirty-second Army would push the Americans back into the sea.

The invasion of the Ryukyu Islands was the responsibility of Lieutenant General Buckner, Commanding General, Tenth U.S. Army. "Softening up" the beaches started in October 1944 and was continued by carrier-based aircraft until the actual assault in April 1945. Six days prior to the main invasion the first landings in the Ryukyus were made on the Kerama Retto, centered fifteen miles west of southern Okinawa.

At 0930 March 25, troops of the 77th Division were ashore on the islands of Aka, Kerama, Hokaji, and Zamami. By the evening of March 29 all the Kerama Retto was in American hands. The stunning speed of the invasion frustrated Japanese hopes for a whirlwind suicide boat attack on the American fleet. With the securing of the Keramas, two dozen 155-millimeter guns were emplaced and trained on Naha, Shuri, and the invasion beaches eleven miles eastward. On April 1, 1945, the greatest invasion effort of the Pacific campaign got underway as the bloodiest battle of the Pacific War had begun. Over thirteen hundred major naval units converged on Okinawa carrying six reinforced army divisions with supporting units, supplies, and equipment for the campaign.

The initial assault wave consisted of two Army and two Marine divisions. While this force made landings along the Toguchi beaches, the 2nd Marine Division feinted along the southeast coast above Minatogawa, hoping to pin down enemy reserves. The heaviest concentration of gunfire ever to support a troop landing began at 0530, April 1, * Carrier planes struck with napalm as the invasion force waited offshore, watching shells hitting the invasion beach. H-hour was 0830. The landing was made entirely unopposed! Correspondent Ernie Pyle reported, "We were on Okinawa an hour and a half after H-hour, without being shot at, and hadn't even gotten our feet wet." But Ernie Pyle and his comrades were soon to discover that what had begun as a picnic would end as the bloodiest battle of the Pacific war. In one day the beachhead was established plus the capture of Kadena and Yomitan airfields. By the second day, the 7th Division had completely bisected the island in a drive to the east coast. By April 6, the XXIV Corps, comprised of the 96th, 7th, and 27th Army divisions, formed a battle line to the south. At the same time, the 1st and 6th Marine Divisions of the III Amphibious Corps began their push toward the north end of Okinawa. The Marines encountered only slight resistance. On the night of April 5, some thirty Japanese blundered into their lines and were killed or driven off.

The Marines moved onto the Motobu Peninsula where fifteen-hundred-foot-high Yae Dake was the critical terrain feature. The Japanese still avoided contact, hoping to delay the Americans further with guerrilla resistance rather than try to destroy them. On April 14, three U.S. battalions attacked east toward Yae Dake to secure the crest: the defenders were dead or had disappeared. The main Japanese defenses to the north of the invasion beaches had been broken, but enough Japanese remained to participate in guerrilla warfare. While the III Amphibious Corps had moved north, the XXIV Corps began its drive to the south. Scattered Japanese defenses gave way until army units reached the first prepared Japanese defenses on the Machinato line, running from the north end of Yonabaru Airstrip to the northern end of Machinato Airstrip. Kakazu and Hacksaw Ridges were located along this line. It was at Kakazu and Hacksaw that the Americans found what had been waiting for them on Okinawa.

One regiment of the 96th Division was ordered to seize and hold Kakazu. Almost immediately the regiment was pinned down under intense artillery, mortar, and machine-gun fire. It was forced to withdraw. After this failure, two regiments were ordered to seize Kakazu. Again the Americans were unsuccessful, and the battle resulted in a stalemate.

Meanwhile, ahead of schedule, the 77th Division began to work on phase two of the campaign by striking at the Japanese airfields on Ie Shima, the small island just west of Motobu Peninsula. Some of the hardest fighting of the entire battle occurred at Bloody Ridge and Government House on Ie Shima. Four

* Because Sunday, April 1, 1945, was Easter Sunday, it was called Love-Day, not D-Day.

thousand Japanese soldiers were hidden in a 600-foot-high point, perfect for observing advancing American troops, which the Japanese called the Pinnacle and the Marines called "Maggie's Tit." There were many banzai charges, often with the enemy carrying only wooden clubs. These were local Okinawans, untrained and pressed into service. The little island was secured after five days of intense close-in fighting. Ie Shima is now world-famous as the place where American war correspondent Ernie Pyle died. Ernie landed with the troops on Love-Day. He would spend all day of every day ashore with them, moving up with them, recording for the home front their actions and their feelings. Nightly he would return to his quarters aboard the command ship *Panamint* to rewrite and file his stories, and then get briefing talk from the planners. Pyle decided to go with the 77th to take Ie Shima and, departing from his pattern, passed the night of April 17 on the beach with them.

Early next morning, the second day of battle on Ie, he went in a jeep with Lieutenant Colonel J. B. Cooledge and two soldiers to locate a new command post for the 305th Regiment. They were exposed and forward in questionable territory. Near a road junction a Japanese machine gun opened fire on the jeep, but everyone hit the ditches unscathed. Perhaps had he kept his head down, a shell from the second machine-gun burst would not have hit him, as it did—in the left temple just below the helmet. Ernie Pyle died among the men with whom he lived and worked. The Army buried him about 300 yards west of the spot in a small military cemetery. The plain white cross I saw shortly thereafter read simply, "E. Pyle, Civilian." In 1947 his body was removed to Okinawa and thence to a more elaborate final resting place in the Hawaii Punch Bowl. On Ie Shima today still stands the monument which, since its erection in 1945, has carried the mute tribute, "At this spot the 77th Infantry Div. lost a buddy, Ernie Pyle, 18 April 1945."

The other newsman to die on Okinawa was John Cashman. Losing his left arm in the Navy in 1942, he joined International News Service and was soon again back to the war fronts, this time as a noncombatant. Killed in a crashed Liberator bomber, Cashman is remembered along with Pyle on the memorial plaque in the New York headquarters of the Overseas Press Club.

On the southern front of Okinawa, the 7th, 27th, and 96th divisions were still held tight on the Machinato line. In addition to the stalemate at Kakazu Ridge, intense fighting centered around Item Pocket and the Machinato Inlet area. On this line, objectives of small units were named after the company commanders, such as Brewer's Hill and Ryan's Ridge. It was here that the Americans for the first time lost more men than the Japanese. Finally, with the capture of Ryan's Ridge, the tide changed to the Americans' favor. A 27th Division combat team broke through the defenses of Kakazu, Item Pocket, and Skyview Ridge, and a regrouping of American forces was accomplished.

From the crest of Hacksaw Ridge, soldiers of the 77th used cargo nets and grenades in hand-to-hand battles. Japanese resistance there was cremated with burning gasoline and flame throwers. Then the main element of the Japanese forces withdrew to the most formidable defenses of the island, the Naha-Shuri-Yonabaru line. Jubilant over their success at holding the Americans, the Japanese issued attack plans for May 3, still hoping to drive the Yankees into the sea. The objective of the attack was an east-west line at Futema (site of the 96th Division command post), which the Japanese mistook for General Buckner's Tenth Army Headquarters.

At dusk on May 3, kamikaze planes struck at American shipping. In an hour, the *Aaron Ward* was fired, and the *Little* sunk. During the night Japanese soldiers on both coasts attempted a flanking action with barges, assault boats, and Okinawan canoes. Flares illuminated the scene as U.S. shore artillery destroyed all the boats and most of the troops: this effort ended in still another disaster for the Japanese. Next, the Japanese artillery opened fire with the heaviest land barrage yet encountered in the Pacific war. Just before dawn on May 4, they attacked and were stopped all along the line. During the day, Japanese artillery, brought out from concealed cave positions for the first time, enabled American forces methodically to search out and destroy the finally exposed guns.

On May 5, American artillery demolished another Japanese assault. Three hours later, the Japanese attacked again, this time supported by tanks. Losing six of them, the enemy pressed through and engaged in hand-to-hand combat. While the fighting was going on, a Japanese battalion infiltrated and occupied the town of Tanabaru and Tanabaru Ridge. A behind-the-lines battle raged for three days, until the intruders were annihilated. By midnight May 5 General Ushijima knew that his May 3 offensive had failed. With no help from home, having suffered tremendous casualties, he reverted to defensive warfare. From west to east, with the 6th Marine Division, the 1st Marine Division, the 77th Army Division, and the 96th Army Division occupying successive positions on a line facing Shuri, General Buckner ordered a co-ordinated Tenth Army attack on May 11. Working toward the attack date, the 7th Division on the east flank was advancing doggedly, although tired and undermanned. When relieved by the 96th Division, the 7th had its hold on Kochi almost complete.

In the center of Okinawa, the 77th Division took Maeda Ridge, then made slow, step-by-step advances along Route 5 toward Shuri. By May 11, the XXIV Corps had eliminated many enemy positions in preparation for the all-out drive. At a cost of fifteen thousand casualties the American forces had extended their line at Maeda, Kochi, and Awacha, providing more favorable ground for the major southward push by the entire Tenth Army.

Promptly on May 11 the attack began. For each attacking division the battle for Shuri took the name of a different terrain feature. Conical Hill dominated the front of the 96th Division. The 1st Marines attacked Wana Draw, and the 6th Marines had the capture of Sugar Loaf as their goal. On May 12, G Company, 22nd Marines reached the crest of Sugar Loaf but withdrew with heavy casualties. The next day, the 3rd battalion, 29th Marines entered the fight with naval and air corps fighter support. Again the attack was stopped. On the evening of May 14, Major Henry Courtney and a small group from G Company reached survivors on Sugar Loaf and managed to maintain their position all night, but were again forced to withdraw. It wasn't until May 19th that Sugar Loaf was finally secured. All along the Shuri line the fight was the same yard-for-yard struggle.

In the center of the line the 77th Division fought at Ishimi Ridge. On the east, the 96th Division attacks on Conical Hill were unsuccessful. Seven weeks after the unopposed U.S. landings, the heart of the Shuri defenses were still intact. Then, during the last week of May, a continual downpour drenched the entire front. Wana Draw was a torrent of mud and water. Tanks bogged down. Amphibian tractors could not get through. All supplies and the wounded had to be hand-carried over areas swept by the enemy fire. Weapons became dirty and wet. Mortar shells which had taken half a day to deliver to forward positions were rendered useless in seconds. The entire front was engulfed in a sea of mud. One man jestingly complained of webbed feet. As living conditions worsened, the strain took a rising toll of men. While the ground forces were bogged in the mire, the kamikazes continued to shower their air attacks on the Navy. From May 24 to May 28 alone, over 200 kamikazes struck, scoring hits on 22 ships.

Then the rain stopped. The 96th Division immediately secured the eastern slope of Conical Hill. It looked as if the Army's 32nd Infantry might be able to make a dash across the soggy Yonabaru-Naha Valley and seal the Shuri defenders into their positions. Fatefully, as the attack started, the rains resumed. Spearhead tanks and heavy assault guns again wallowed in the bog, leaving the 32nd unprotected in its slogging drive across the island. Automatic weapons fired from Japanese positions killed too many Americans. The bold Yankee gamble was defeated by the weather.

By this time, the continuing pressure on both flanks and in front of Shuri forced the Japanese command to start ordering withdrawals to the south, though some American staff officers believed Shuri would remain defended. The main movement of the Japanese Thirty-second Army units was conducted under cover from May 26 to May 28, although enough troops were left on the Shuri line to give the impression that defensive positions were still fully manned. However, in withdrawing, the Japanese somehow left one section of the Shuri line vacated. A small group of marines from the 1st Battalion, 5th Marines, was quick to cross corps boundaries and occupy Shuri Castle on May 29. They held their positions within the castle as the entire Shuri perimeter crumbled. On May 31 the 77th Division walked into Shuri as the XXIV Corps and the III Amphibious Corps joined forces south of what had been until then the Japanese strong point on Okinawa. The Shuri defense had finally been breached by the relentless Americans.

Japanese resistance, with the exception of naval forces, had been forced to take positions in the Yuza Dake hill mass. American troops started pursuing the enemy to the south, relatively unhampered by any unified defense. General Buckner spoke optimistically when he said, "It's all over now but cleaning up pockets of resistance." He could not know that his Army still faced three more grueling weeks of organized fighting; that the Japanese would set up another defensive line; and that there would be over fifty thousand more combined dead before the end of the month, including himself.

Okinawa was considered a Japanese "home island" only nine hundred miles from Tokyo and just four hundred from Sasebo. The Americans had to come clear across the mid-Pacific to make their landings. Yet ironically Japan was unable to penetrate the wall of ships with which the United States had enveloped the island. Although kamikaze planes and suicide boats destroyed much of the American fleet, not one Japanese soldier or single matériel item was brought through to the hard-pressed Okinawan garrison to reinforce its dogged dooryard defense. And all the while American men and supplies came and went at will.

The Oroku Peninsula, site of Naha Air Base, was defended only by chance. Some three thousand poorly trained naval troops were there under the command of Admiral Minoru Ota. Although the peninsula was heavily fortified, this naval unit was ordered to join the Thirty-second Army in its retreat from Shuri. Prior to the retreat, they destroyed their heavy guns. When Ota's men reached their new positions two days ahead of schedule, they were very dissatisfied. The younger officers coerced the Admiral into returning to Oroku. Foolishly, this return was accomplished without notifying General Ushijima; moreover, there were then no heavy guns to aid the defense of their location. The Japanese mined the area heavily and took machine guns and 20-millimeter cannons from disabled aircraft to bolster their positions. The American forces tactically elected to make a shore-to-shore amphibious assault on the peninsula. Two days after the landings, heavy fire was still encountered from well dug-in Japanese positions. The 1st Marine Division and eight battalions of the 6th Marine Division with heavy tank support cut across the base of the peninsula. Trapped here without their big guns, the Japanese opposition was crushed, ending a tedious ten-day battle. Admiral Ota and his brash staff were found in an underground chamber: each had committed suicide by cutting his own throat.

Now the Americans were set to move into position for the final phase of the operation. As the rainy period ended, troops of the XXIV Corps on the eastern front and the III Amphibious Corps to the west faced the Yuza Dake hill mass. The only break in front of the XXIV was a short narrow valley running south through Nakaza. But this approach was also open on both sides to observation and flanking cross fire. With replenished dry supplies, the American began massed artillery fire supported by air strikes. Lengths of flexible hose were attached to flame-thrower tanks and carried into caves which the tanks could not reach. The eastern end of the Japanese line was the first to crack, but on the western side of the island the Japanese fought the Americans to another stalemate. Kunishi Ridge became the site of the most frantic and costly battle fought on the southern end of Okinawa. The Japanese had the advantage of a detailed artillery fire plan for the valley leading to the high ground. In addition, the area was subject to bands of machine-gun cross fire in which the 1st Marine Division lead element was cut off and suffered heavy casualties. As the fighting continued, five other U.S. companies were cut off from their lines.

Tanks were called in to spearhead the offensive. Flame-throwing and regular tanks moved out into the cutoff sector, bringing in supplies, firing on the Japanese, and carrying out the wounded. Five days later the ridge fell to the Americans. The Japanese Thirty-second Army was compressed into an area smaller than eight square miles. With its back to the sea, it could only hold its positions during the day and make futile attempts to recapture American-held ground by night. Drained by nearly eighty days of continuous combat with neither relief nor reinforcement, the Japanese forces collapsed on June 17. The Thirty-second Army had been broken completely. General Ushijima's final formal order to his men was to infiltrate American lines and return to the rugged north end of Okinawa to fight on as guerrillas. The Japanese general refused General Buckner's invitation to surrender.

Sensing success, on June 18, General Buckner visited a forward observation post of the 8th Marine Regiment, 2nd Division. He was inspecting battle progress when a shell from a Japanese gun exploded directly overhead. A fragment struck him in the chest, killing him at the threshold of the most glorious victory of the Pacific war. The Army was stunned at news of General Buckner's death and the subsequent killing (the following day by a Japanese machine gun) of Brigadier General Claudius Easley, assistant commander of the 96th Division. The final phase of the battle continued under the command of Marine Major General Roy S. Geiger.

On June 21, Japanese generals Ushijima and Cho, ultimately realizing that the end had come, made ready for death. The two men shared a large meal and drank sake toasts of farewell with their staff. Then at 0400 on the morning of June 22, the two generals sat on a quilt covered with a white sheet and bowed in reverence to the eastern sky as the adjutant presented each a sword. American troops, only a short distance away, sensing movement in the cave below, lobbed down several grenades. Hastily, a shout, a flash of sword—and another—and both generals had fulfilled their ultimate duty to their Emperor.

This ceremonial double hara-kiri postponed but did not prevent the inevitable surrender of Okinawa to the U.S. forces. It did, however, mark the end of the organized fighting. Okinawa—the last battle in the Pacific—had three additional, reprise endings: a second, when the island was "officially secured" July 2, 1945; a third, in the formal surrender some two months afterward; and, finally, the snuffing out of the guerrilla action in the north over the following eighteen months.

Later in the day, June 22, 1945, Island Command Headquarters became alive with the short ceremony for which the triumphant survivors had strived from April 1. Since field positions had still to be maintained, only token formations from the Tenth Army, the two corps, and all the divisions stood on parade as a band played the "Star-Spangled Banner" and a color guard raised their flag. Near the top of the pole a sudden breeze caught up the cloth and the victorious American flag billowed free against Okinawa's now blue and silent sky.

PART II

# Wayside Aftermath

# CHAPTER 3

# Post Partum Depression

The "Iron Typhoon" was over. In its wake nearly one hundred thousand Okinawans died. Almost all survivors were left destitute and/or homeless. It was again their lot to have to pay for both their geographic location and their national weakness. Ryukyuans, throughout their history, have been made to suffer the ills of their stronger, greedier neighbors. However, their oppressors have had to pay a good price for keeping the Ryukyus.

The Empire of Japan formally gave up its "cause" and the war. Oddly, the formal surrender document did not include the Ryukyu Islands. At the end of hostilities on Okinawa there was no Japanese officer of record still living and empowered to sign a formal document. Besides, General Ushijima issued a "no surrender" edict. It was necessary though that a surrender formality take place. Therefore, by prior arrangement, on a bright sunny day, September 7, 1945, seventy-seven days after the battle and five days after the total surrender, a white Japanese aircraft with green-cross markings landed at Kadena airstrip. The Japanese surrender party had come down from the northern Amami Islands to complete the formal surrender. This occurred before a parade of U.S. forces but was an extremely simple ceremony. The laconic document, so historic yet so brief, was drawn up by General Stilwell himself.

The Japanese commanders immediately returned to their stations at Amami, and later to Japan. The surrender location is now known as Stilwell Park, a part of the Kadena Air Force Base. As the commanding officer of the Tenth Army, occupying the Ryukyus, General Stilwell accepted the Japanese surrender, though more than a month earlier on July 31, 1945, he assumed the

# Headquarters Tenth Army

7 September 1945

## Surrender

The undersigned Japanese Commanders, in conformity with the general surrender executed by the Imperial Japanese Government, at Yokohama, on 2 September 1945, hereby formally render unconditional surrender of the islands in the Ryukyus within the following boundaries:

30° North 126° East, thence 24° North 122° East, thence 24° North 133° East, thence 29° North 131° East, thence 30° North 131° 30' East, thence to point of origin.

[signed] Toshiro Nomi
Lieutenant General
Commander Japanese Forces
Sakishima Gunto

[signed] Toshisada Takada
Major General
Commander Japanese Army Forces
Amami Gunto

[signed] Tadao Kato
Rear Admiral
Commander Japanese Navy Forces
Amami Gunto

Accepted:
[signed] J. W. Stilwell
General, United States Army
Commanding

title of Military Governor of the Ryukyu Islands, which included *all* the islands in the chain.

And so title to Okinawa passed from Japan to the United States by right of conquest. With the surrender, Japan lost what it had once gained so easily. The Ryukyus were never "in fact" Japanese until the Meiji restoration made them so in 1871.

Hostilities, along with the Japanese domination, ended officially when General Stilwell's short document was endorsed: "The undersigned Japanese Commanders . . . hereby formally render unconditional surrender of the islands in the Ryukyus . . ." But seventy-eight days earlier, the June 22 cessation of organized hostilities had presented a wayside aftermath which could have posed an impossible situation to a lesser commander than General Stilwell.

It was his task to make order out of the chaos on the island, attempt to provide security, and begin immediately some form of Military Government. Stilwell had to try to end all the resistance from the isolated Japanese guerrillas and consolidate the American position. Also he had to gain the confidence and trust of the Okinawan people, while keeping them contented and unrebellious. General Stilwell negotiated the surrender with minimum ceremony and maximum efficiency, without subjecting the Japanese to indignities, and then proceded to piece together a shattered land for a bewildered people.

After graduating from West Point in 1904, Palatka, Florida-born Stilwell was assigned to the Philippines until his World War I service in France with a U.S.-British joint command. In 1919 Stilwell was sent to Chinese language school at Berkeley, California, then on alternating tours in Peking and command school. On Stilwell's forty-ninth birthday, Generalissimo Chiang Kai-shek placed him in command of the Fifth and Sixth Chinese Armies and later made him chief of staff. Eventually he became Deputy Supreme Allied Commander of the Southeast Asia Command and commander of allied ground forces in North Burma. During one of these tours of duty, "Vinegar Joe" personally led a retreat through the back door of China to Burma, a successful march of many days.

Unfortunately, a conflict of personalities developed between the general and Chiang Kai-shek. Shortly after, in November of 1944, President Roosevelt recalled Stilwell to the United States. Then after the sudden death of General Buckner on the Okinawa firing line, General Stilwell was ordered to Okinawa June 23, 1945, to take active command of the Tenth Army. He was liked and respected by the troops. A wry facet of his personality was his venerable campaign hat, a relic of the old regular Army, which he wore at all times except on formal occasions. Once, while inspecting part of the island from a reconnaissance plane, the hat blew out a window and disappeared below. Quickly he posted a reward of $25 to the soldier who would return it to him. Almost immediately, everyone on the island wanted to find it. He *did* get his campaign hat back.

June through December of 1945, the period of General Stilwell's command tenure on Okinawa, was a busy time. There were five specific official changes in the order and designation of his command and as many separate changes in the order and designation of the military government (MG).

On July 20 a congressional committee visited Okinawa and, on July 26 the *Uruma Shimpo,* an Okinawan newspaper, was established by MG, although its first issue as a weekly was not published until August 28, "by authority of the U.S. MG." In August an Okinawan museum was established at Higashionna. Later that month, the Army Forces of the Western Pacific was delegated as authority to approve marriage applications (this did not include marriages between Americans and Okinawans, which were banned). Grass roots progress was made when about one hundred local representatives of various districts gathered at Ishikawa to discuss the establishment of an Okinawan Advisory Council. Five days later, fifteen members of this advisory council, including one Koshin Shikiya and two compatriots, were elected by other representatives to chair the group. In September the final surrender of all the islands was the big event, shortly followed by the division of the islands into sixteen political districts. All men and women over twenty-five years of age and of Okinawan nationality were given the right to vote, and elections for councilmen were held.

By the end of September there were elections for the sixteen district mayors, quickly followed by meetings at Ishikawa among the newly elected mayors, the MG political affairs officers, and the MG department advisory council people to consider and settle details of standard local government organizations in all sixteen MG districts. October saw the arrival of the first U.S. forces for military occupation of Yaeyama, solely to destroy Japanese military supplies. Later that month General Stilwell took part in ceremonies dedicating a memorial south of Itoman at the site of General Buckner's fall. On October 14 there was an order to begin repatriation of Japanese from the Ryukyus, after which no Japanese were permitted to enter the islands to stay, nor were they permitted to trade. Visits were restricted to Japanese physicians needed for health services. On October 17 General Stilwell named as military governor Brigadier General Lawrence A. Lawson to direct the establishment of central responsibility in the Okinawa administration, an appointment which released Stilwell to his military duties. On November 6 a U.S. Army team first visited Miyako to accomplish surveys for repatriation. The Army also sent a Northern Island MG unit to Amami Oshima, and shortly thereafter sent a large quantity of relief supplies.

Early in December 1945, the Mura (township) was made the basis for local administrative reorganization to be effective after the first of the following January. There was a directive for the preservation and assembly of all land records, but unfortunately none were ever found. And the repatriation of all Japanese prisoners of war from Amami was completed.

The most serious of General Stilwell's projects was establishing a relationship between the American occupation forces and the native Okinawans. Prior to the invasion the natives were told by the Japanese Army that Americans would be thoroughly cruel and heartless. Americans, they were warned, would bring nothing but death and devastation. Therefore most Ryukyuan people who survived showed little trust for the victors. Much was left to the empathy and understanding of the American foot soldier; and each in his own way, as best his conscience would guide him, did attempt to make his own peace with the local people. Sometimes it would take, again it would not. Two interesting and diametrically opposed stories stand out from hundreds of extant similar tales. Both men who reported their experiences were young Okinawans pressed into Japanese military service, were wounded in the fighting, treated by the Americans, recovered, and by 1966 were working pressmen at home, each nurturing his own feelings about Yanks.

Yasuo Kayo is now an editor of the Naha *San Kei (Industrial Economic),* a weekly Japanese language newspaper. Native to Tomari Port, he was drafted into the Japanese Army in Okinawa in October 1944, shortly after the softening-up bombings began. Normally such recruits were sent to Japan for basic training, but due to the deteriorating local situation he was given his basic training on Okinawa and sent to Yontan airstrip for further training. He had hoped to go to officer candidate's school, but the Allied landings altered this plan. He was wounded in the left leg by a howitzer shell on May 10 and put into a Japanese field hospital where he was captured on surrender day. According to Kayo he was taken to a Hawaiian prison camp for eighteen months. (Why Okinawan PWs were sent to Hawaii is not known, but Yochu Ishigaki, M.D., now mayor of the village of Ishigaki, was also taken there during this transference.)

Kayo still remembers what he refers to as "the U.S.'s antihumanism." He told me that while traveling in the prison ship to Hawaii, PWs were put into the steerage where they all became seasick. They had poor sanitary facilities, and were issued no eating utensils—they were given their daily rations of food in their cupped hands. Kayo claims that they were taken up on deck for a short time only once a day. He admits that he was treated better in Hawaii. Still bitter toward the United States, he does not believe any stories of Japanese maltreatment of American combat prisoners (from Bataan, for instance). After a year and a half in Hawaii, Kayo was returned to Tokyo and then to Okinawa in December 1946, where he spent some time looking for his family. Kayo told me about receiving aid from the U.S. MG, and about his family's being given "K" rations, milk powder, and clothing. He got a job and then taught school. Although he admits that Americans on the island did render aid, he is still bitter about the treatment he personally received as a PW.

On the other hand, Gisho Funakoshi, now a writer for the Public Affairs Division of the Government of the Ryukyus, wrote in an exclusive article in *Konnichi-No-Ryukyu (Ryukyus Today):*

"The June sun was scorching like fire. I lay on a truck without any cover for my head. I wondered where I and the other wounded being loaded on many trucks were being carried. With a feeling of fear, I tried with all my strength to raise my head. . . . Then it occurred to me that the line of trucks with many wounded was crossing Meiji Bridge: across the bridge, it was dear Naha where I was born.

"I could no longer raise my head because some fragments of shell penetrated the flesh of my body.

"I escaped from the fierce battlefield of southern Okinawa with great difficulty. A boy continuously sobbed beside me, but he stopped sobbing . . . Turning my eyes upon him, I saw he was dead. His emaciated hands were thick with dirt. Strange to say, I had no emotion in observing the dead and closed my eyes, while feeling maggots wriggling on my wounds. I asked myself, 'Where am I being carried?' I had no anxiety toward my future on that occasion. I wished that the sun would go behind clouds, but there was not a speck of clouds in the sky in this southern island in June.

"The row of trucks continued to roll all day long. The trucks sometimes stopped for a while and soldiers gave us a cup of water and a piece of chocolate. . . . I often became unconscious.

"On the evening, I was taken down from the truck . . . Afterwards I found that I was carried into the C-13 hospital of the U.S. Navy.

"On the following morning, I had an operation. . . .

"Coming out of the chloroform, I was aware that an American soldier with hairy arms examined my pulse. When I opened my eyes, he smiled with his white teeth showing. It seemed to me that he said, 'My name is Day. I am in charge of this tent.'

"One day a boy picked up a discarded cigaret butt. Day glanced fiercely at him. The patients in the tent hospital said to each other in a subdued tone that he was a hardhearted American. . . .

" 'Isn't it awful that he picked up something thrown away?' he said to me to get my agreement. I said nothing.

" 'Why didn't he ask me if he wanted it?' His words penetrated my heart, but soothed me in the warm spring day. I thought, 'Day does not dislike the boy or any of us. He regards us all as equals, so he was angry with the boy.'

"On August 15 we were informed of the surrender of Japan to the United States. There was an atmosphere of gloom in the tent. Some sobbed, covering their heads with blankets. At a glance of their grieving for the defeat, Day looked gloomy. Some medical orderlies were angry with those who sank into grief. Day said to me, 'The horrible slaughter among men is over. You understand *this* joy of the end of the war.' In view of the dreadful contrast between the joy of conquest and the misery of the defeat, I think that war will not break out again. If there is no war, there will be no defeat.

"I had lain in bed for three months. . . . I forgot his face, but I will never forget his kindness. . . . His humanity shone from the bottom of his heart as a human being."

Some of the human stories have been immortalized with real shrines. Not too far from General Buckner's memorial, there are two additional memorials. One is the Virgins' Cave (also called the Lily Tower or the Himeyuri-No-To shrine), which is dedicated to nearly 125 young women students of Okinawa's First Girls' High School and the Women Teachers' Training School, nurses, and aides in the Japanese Army. They were all killed at a location south of Itoman.

The "official" version of their demise is that first a U.S. Nisei soldier heard voices in a cave. Not knowing what the cave was used for (it had once been a hospital), or who was in it, he called in Japanese several times for the people to come out and surrender. The young ladies did not come out after several warnings because they had been told earlier by their Japanese commanders that the Americans would rape, then draw and quarter them. The cave was finally demolished by bombs and flame throwers. According to the Okinawan version (which also claims there were two survivors), the girls were herded into this cave by the Japanese, told what monsters the Americans were, and ordered under no circumstances to leave. An armed guard was posted in the cave to enforce the order, and he turned upon them to prevent their surrendering.

Not far from there is the Shiraune-No-To shrine dedicated to young school girls from the Okinawan Second Girls' High School, who were alleged to have been killed under circumstances similar to those in the Virgins' Cave.

And these are not the only instances where various versions of a tale would differ. Perhaps the most noted example is the story of Shimabuku village. One account was published in *Together* (by the Methodist Publishing House, Chicago) in October 1960, and condensed in the *Reader's Digest* for November 1960. Another account of the same story, published in Japanese in *The Okinawa Times,* Saturday, June 2, 1963, differs widely on several basic points.

The *Together-Digest* telling has a U.S. patrol in April 1945 approaching a village, population one thousand. There was a reception committee of two "little old men," Kina Shosei, the local schoolmaster, and Nakemura Mojun, the village mayor. A U.S. Nisei soldier-interpreter says: "I don't get it. Seems we're being welcomed—as 'fellow Christians.' . . . they seem to be asking for just one thing: A picture of Jesus." Back in 1914 an American missionary had stopped in only at that "remote village" and made Christians of them all.

The story relates how the villagers were relocated to the north end so that the U.S. Army could bulldoze their homes "out of existence" to build a "staging area." Eight months later the Shimabukuans returned from the north to the site of their rubble, and with faith and American aid rebuilt their village. Years later it was still a paragon of faith despite its proximity to the big bawdy GI. recreation area of Koza.

By contrast, *The Okinawa Times* story has the village of thirteen hundred in long debate about evacuation before the Americans invaded, and only Kina was for remaining. The mayor's name was Higa. Nakemura was listed here as ward leader. Kina did manage by determined persuasion to keep the uneasy villagers from leaving. Therefore he had to go (with only Nakemura's assistance) to receive the American troops. In halting English he said, "You American gentlemen! Me Okinawan Christian!" The U.S. Nisei interpreter, Thomas (né Taro) Higa, was once a child in that village, and old Kina had been his elementary schoolmaster. Soon the old friendship between them revived when Kina remembered Higa Taro, and Kina requested only a chaplain for the village. A Captain Hyler subsequently went weekly and the "villagers gathered willingly to hear the sermons."

The villagers were later taken in military trucks to an evacuation camp in Kin-son because their village location was right on the line of march and "threatened by the fierce battle." They were returned a year later and began to rebuild the ruins. "Mr. Kina is now leading a comfortable, peaceful life in Koza city. Being adept at the art of karate and other ancient Ryukyuan military arts . . ."

For some reason the American version missed the point of the Nisei-schoolteacher relationship, or the real reason for, and timing of, the evacuation, or how the Okinawan story did not play-up Christian life in an oriental village.

In any event, after the Americans had been there for a while, the Okinawans came to know, for the most part, that they were reasonably generous with the natives in their day-to-day, off-the-record dealings—"off-the-record" because fraternization was strictly prohibited to the Americans by military regulation and to the natives by MG edict. And since the MG was set up in all its channels, departments, liaisons, etc., to deal with the Ryukyuans, there was no reason for any personal contact between individuals, whether indigenous or occupational. However there was a great interchange of cigarettes, candy, "C" and "K" rations, etc., for sea shells, straw handicraft, live seafood, laundry, and other personal favors. Considerable good feeling developed even without a common language. Still the Island Command actively tried to keep relations to a minimum.

The night of our arrival, I remember sitting in the Camp Boone chapel with others from the ship to hear an orientation briefing session by our commanding officer, Colonel Lee B. Washbourne. The colonel, who had been on Okinawa a long time, advised us what we were to find in almost any area, geographical, military, or administrative. Finally he discussed in detail the nonfraternization regulations, concluding with the statement, "There is nothing these people have that you want—and nothing you want to buy." Colonel Washbourne was right about many things, I learned in the little over a year I served under him. But I think in this case he could very accurately have stopped with: "There is nothing these people have." Indeed, the poor creatures had nothing, and all they really wanted was subsistence and friendship.

The surrender was not truly the end of the Japanese era on Okinawa. Due to General Ushijima's final formal order for his men to infiltrate the American lines, work their way north, and continue the fighting on a guerrilla basis, the Americans until the early 1950s faced many dangers. The upper end of the island (always considered marines' country) from about Cross Highway 108 northward was closed to all traffic. The "boundary" line varied, but ran roughly between the town of Kyoda on the west coast and Matsuda on the east. The north end of the island was well suited to those guerrilla activities due to the sparsity of population, infrequency of American military travel, and the rugged, overgrown terrain. South of this line, all was considered reasonably safe from both wild boars and Japanese guerrillas.

The Japanese held out because they would not believe that the imperial household had surrendered. They hoped that eventually the Japanese Army would reinvade and "liberate" Okinawa. They then would be considered heroes. As time passed, word got through to them. Little by little they either surrendered or got rid of their uniforms, firearms, and all other Japanese identification, moved in with villages, and became integrated with the native populace. Some of them even married Okinawan women, had children, and made no further attempts to go home. However, there were some isolated incidents in the south end of Okinawa.

One spring day I was out on an assignment looking for cool damp caves to be used for large commodity storage. Cave mouths facing north were preferable because they had little light. Inspecting all possibilities, I reconnoitered an area just north of where the old road went east up to Island Command Headquarters (and which by the early 1960s had been bulldozed massively over an extensive area to become the colossal U.S. Sukiran Military Reservation). While spotting two caves whose openings did not look quite satisfactory for the movement of fork-lifts, I saw another which, oddly enough, did not appear on the chart. The cave had a rather large mouth facing west and looked good, as caves go, even if it had never been recorded. Folding away the map, I went up to investigate. I had some equipment with me which an engineer might carry into the field: twenty feet of woven cordline wound up tightly; a bayonet which I used mainly for cutting brush; a compass and an Abney level; and a few other useful items.

As I entered the cave, it took my eyes a while to accommodate to its darkness after the bright post-noon sunlight. Suddenly I heard a fast slapping sound as if flat bare feet were running toward me. I must have been easily visible silhouetted against that bright backdrop of the outside. Instantly I caught sight of a flash of reflected sunlight which looked like the blade of a samurai sword. I had been an amateur collegiate boxer, and from life on Okinawa I was down to 137 lean pounds. Almost hair-triggered, I spun over to my left as if to slip a boxer's left jab lead. My right ear almost felt the blade as that samurai sword came slashing down past my head. Instinctively, with one continuous single motion, I pulled my bayonet from its scabbard at my right hip and, while falling away, backhanded him across his right shoulder. I hit his upper arm with the sharp edge. He screamed and dropped his sword. Completing my spin to the left, I hit him forehand once across his big belly. He tumbled to the ground.

I saw that he was a Japanese about the size of a sumotori (wrestler). While he squirmed on the ground, a stuck pig writhing in pain, apparently in state of shock at feeling his own hot, sticky blood, I managed to get my tie line loose to bind him up and dragged him down the hill to the road. He was soon picked up by a passing MP jeep and sent to a PW hospital. Pulling myself together, and armed with a flashlight borrowed from the MPs, I went back into the cave, a little more cautiously this time. With pipe-stem arms held high, another Japanese slowly came over to me. He spoke a fair "pidgin English" for one not having been educated at U.C.L.A., excused himself for the untoward conduct of his comrade, and proceeded to light a stolen Coleman lantern as he showed me through the cave, which they had fairly well set up as a bivouac for themselves.

For more than a year after the campaign was over, they had been holding out, not wishing to believe that either the campaign or the war was over. Apparently they became more bent on survival than on waging any aggressive warfare. Though they had several weapons, none had been fired or cleaned for quite some time. By coming down from the cave at night to steal from American installations, they had amassed many items. Among them were some twelve-inch "V-Discs" including my own favorite, "I'll Remember April," and an old green, cloth-covered, wooden portable phonograph, that familiar USO item which played ten- and twelve-inch 78 rpms when wound by a hand crank.

After showing me through the entire cavern, the little man told me he was a corporal from Nagasaki. (He did not know, nor did I wish to tell him, the fate of his home town.) He and my attacker, who was his sergeant, became isolated from their group during the fighting for Shuri Castle. They drifted up to the cave where they had been safe ever since, coming out only after dark to steal provisions. As with all the other isolated soldiers, they intended some day to join a Japanese force fighting its way back. When I questioned his eagerness to surrender and to talk at length, he said that he had been so completely dominated by the sergeant, he was happy it was all over. He had no useful information about the war or his recent "captivity." He referred to it as captivity because the sergeant had been misusing him. We stacked what was valuable of their loot for later pickup, and I made bearings of the cave location on my chart.

This was only one of several hundred isolated incidents of holdouts which occurred sporadically to harass the American Army's attempt to alter conditions for the war-worn Ryukyuans.

Since the beginning, Asian and Western rulers have taken fullest advantage of the people's inability to help themselves. In 1945, the United States established a MG of the Ryukyus to fill the vacuum left by the defunct Japanese military controlled civil government. MG did not govern the military. The occupying armed forces operated under army and navy regulations and the Articles of War. MG was a government for the local civilians of an occupied land, operated by a branch of the armed forces, allegedly specifically trained for the task. Sometimes these men were excellent at their jobs, while others were abysmal; on an average though, more performed well.

*The Teahouse of the August Moon* concerns American efforts to impose Western ways on the simple village life of the Okinawans at the end of World War II. Although the story appears to lampoon the MG specifically and the officer class in general, it is reasonably well based on fact. The author, Vern J. Sneider, served with the Army in MG on Okinawa during the epoch of which he wrote.

The answers for any reasonable successes this entire MG venture had were the energetic, serious efforts of the Stilwell era, American determination, and the Ryukyuan desire for relief and survival.

A MG, in attempting to be responsible for the health and welfare of an alien-occupied people, must be autocratic, yet sympathetic, while appearing to be democratic.

Enough good was accomplished for Ryukyuans by Americans in the first five postwar years to make the Okinawans at one point really want to stay with the United States permanently. MG in the Ryukyus began on paper on March 26, 1945. Seven days prior to the Okinawan invasion, Vice Admiral R. Kelley Turner, Commander, Joint Expeditionary Force, was named military governor. That day the first MG was established in the Kerama Retto by the 77th Division. Admiral Nimitz's proclamations were dated and posted. As joint Army-Navy-MG spread over the islands, proclamations were dated and posted in each area. Joint Army-Navy operations ceased on September 21, 1945.

Though at the outset a most important event transpired, in the years to come it was steadily undone by the United States. On April 1, 1945, U.S. MG Proclamation No. 7, issued by Fleet Admiral Chester Nimitz, established a custodian of property and provided for taking into custody all abandoned properties; all state property; and all private property which, under international law, is subject to seizure *without compensation.* There is also no provision here for the property's return to Japan when it was "all over."

On Okinawa, April 3, 1945, General Buckner was named military governor, but by April 13 a separate MG headquarters started to function one mile north of Hiza under the Tenth Army, thus enabling Okinawans living behind Allied lines to be cared for almost immediately by a different military organization from that which pursued the fighting campaign. From then until July 1, 1946, there were twenty-six separate changes in structure, designation, scope, and personnel of MG. These were mainly fluctuations from Army to Navy and back. Finally on July 1, 1946 it all became officially Army via General W. Styer's Extraordinary Proclamation No. 1 (Appendix), which looked most foreboding. Yet a form of MG had been functioning, changes and all, for just over a year by then. And under the MG aegis, a civil government structure completely peopled by Okinawans had been started and was already taking shape.

Samuel C. Oglesby, originally with MG and later with the U. S. Civil Administration of the Ryukyu Islands, suggests that the only basic objectives of the MG in the period from 1945 to 1949 were the re-establishment of home and family life and sustaining these while rebuilding a basic social structure. In the difficult days between the surrender and 1947, and the somewhat easier ones until the early 1950s policy switch, many types of people held posts in the MG and the Okinawan civil government.

At the upper end of the scale though, two exceptional contributors were Koshin Shikiya and Colonel D. C. Wilson. I met them both in one day late in June 1946. Shikiya had by then been the head of an Okinawan civil government for nearly a year. On August 20, 1945, fifteen members of the Okinawa Advisory Council, including Koshin Shikiya, were elected by representatives. Later, on September 27, 1945, a meeting in Ishikawa gave him room to shine. It became obvious to many Okinawans that Shikiya was the man to lead their government. He worked well with General Stilwell and his military successors.

When Shikiya was appointed first chief executive of the Central Okinawan Administration (COA), many vital things happened: hourly wage rates for local labor were set; an Okinawan Civil Labor Department was established; and May 1, 1946, saw the first money payment of wages. Finally on June 1, 1946 the Central Bank of Okinawa (Okinawan Civilian Administration Monetary Depository) was established. Therefore, by the time of the Styer Extraordinary Proclamation and the concurrent establishment of MG under the Army, much organized progress on the local level had already been attained under the Koshin Shikiya leadership.

At the new University of the Ryukyus in 1966, I observed the dedication plaque at the library entrance. It said that the building had been dedicated to the memory of Dr. Koshin Shikiya who, after retiring as chief of Okinawan Civil Government, became the first president of the new University of the Ryukyus. This fine old man ended as he began his professional career, as a teacher of his people.

# CHAPTER 4

# Interim Construction

Donald Clark Wilson, Lieutenant Colonel, Infantry, a former San Francisco banker, became a citizen-soldier in World War II, and remained to retire a Regular Army career man in 1965. He served under General Stilwell in South China where he went for some twenty-seven months without ever being out of the sound of small arms fire. Wilson, who was an "Asia-hand," a banker, a proven leader, and an understanding person, became Chief of Economics Section to the July 1, 1946 newly constituted Army MG.

Between July 1946 and May 1948 as director of economics, Colonel Wilson was faced with such problems as: managing rural farming with the oversized mechanized equipment furnished by America; getting the fishing industry restarted with Japanese one-cylinder diesel engines sent by the Supreme Commander Allied Powers; the food problem; the black market money problem (large sums of money were circulated widely by the U.S. nonmilitary interim construction workers. This hampered rehabilitation efforts and had to be stopped without harming anyone). Later, Colonel Wilson rekindled the ceramic ovens in a new location near Ishikawa, thereby creating another industrial opportunity for the locals; and with help conceived a sound Ryukyus disposition plan.

Many Okinawans with whom Wilson was concerned were those who met with misfortune by remaining on Okinawa through the battle, and those who found it impossible to withstand the steady aerial bombardments which began in October 1944 and continued daily for six months until the invasion. They bought passage to Japan, which they believed to be safe from Allied bombing, then met with that misfortune there. The hard times in Japan immediately preceding and following the surrender were difficult enough to bear without

Okinawan emigrants. For an Okinawan, remaining in Japan after the war was miserable, but upon returning to the Ryukyus, refugees found only more misery plus much resentment from those who had remained and then were obliged to share crumbs with the returnees. One typical tale of returning woe is told by Kozen Arasaki:

"The poor people who lost their husbands, fathers, sons, or brothers were very sad, and the more the happy families showed gladness, the more their minds were filled with grief. To them the light of peace was equal to the candles offered before the tablet of the deceased.

"Unfortunately I was a member of such a poor family. Right after the first air raid of the tenth of October in 1944, my family—my parents, the wife of my eldest brother, her son and daughter, and I—left the port of Naha for Japan to escape the suffering of raids, leaving the eldest and second eldest brothers behind. After we landed on Japan, we had been fighting a difficult situation, believing in the final victory of Japan. From place to place my family wandered seeking for a safer place. No smiling days elapsed. And at last we reached the day of surrender.

"Well, what was waiting for my family this time? Nothing but more hardship than before. The economic panic of inflation was giving a vital shock to the poor, not to the rich; and a number of people died because of undernourishment. Especially in the cities such suffering was severe. My family was near the so-called starvation line, and was panting in the awful whirlpool.

"Father was too old to make money. I was so young that I would not think over the serious condition of my family. I was dreaming of a wonderful college life coming soon. The money we brought from Okinawa had been almost spent. There was no job, no money, and no information about my brothers. Day after day passed in grief. What a distressful situation it was! 'There can't be a God,' I said to myself. I began to get tired of society's impartiality.

"Father and Mother were losing their energy for life and became thinner and thinner day by day. They used to keep talking about their dearly loved sons, money, jobs, and the return to their home country, Okinawa, where the sons might have been waiting for them."

But not everyone who left Okinawa for Japan went to escape. Kotaro Kokuba, the island's foremost construction contractor, owner of Kokuba Gumi, which was engaged in building air bases, roads, and barracks for the Japanese Army, went to Tokyo on a business trip March 22, 1945 and was unable to return once the battle began ten days later. After the Japanese surrender he organized a group of thirty-seven Ryukyuans who wanted to return home to help rebuild the wreckage. He requested a "proper ship" to take them home. However Kokuba says he was refused at every turn (even by General MacArthur). He then took his group to a point in Kagoshima, the southernmost prefecture of Japan. In July 1946 on the pretext of a fishing venture he was able to get all thirty-eight aboard a "fifteen-ton" fishing vessel and make the trip home.

"Illegally" landing in the north of Okinawa, he hid out with his followers until he could, through intermediaries, convince MG General Hayden that he was the only one who could assume charge and completely rebuild the harbor facilities. Later in 1946 Kokuba became port manager, and, with U.S. aid, rebuilt all ports in three years. During this time he was mayor of the port village, yet received only six hundred "B" yen monthly for his total effort. By 1949 Kokuba was finished with both jobs and in 1950 had re-established his present construction contracting company of Kokuba Gumi. About a week before General Styer's Proclamation No. 1, I wrote in my notebook:

"Naha, once the heavily populated Okinawan capital, was all but leveled by the bombings and force of battle which engulfed it. Consequently only one building remains completely intact, standing on the north side of town. [Later, in March of 1947, the MG started the first new Okinawan store in it.] The theater still stood—but with a huge hole backstage, and another in the ceiling. The balcony nearly collapsed after shells and mortar fire took their toll. The Police Academy, standing a bit out of town toward the north, fortunately shows just a small vestige of damage which might easily be restored. The town in general is a mass of debris.

"Some buildings near the port are to be reused by the Transportation Corps for port facilities. Most of the original buildings were either Japanese paper-wood style or of reinforced concrete. The wood-paper buildings vanished without leaving an ash. The concrete structures left a mass of rubble.

"There is no population in Naha—all were evacuated at battle time. They are living elsewhere in compounds for displaced persons, or may have dispersed themselves with old friends or relatives in the various villages of the north or south ends of the island.

"Naha streets are unusable. The Corps of Engineers laid some coral roads across lots which are used for general traffic.

"Shuri Castle and village, the seat of the ancient royal capital, were completely demolished. I doubt if the castle or the surrounding village shall ever really be rebuilt."

Although nearly everything in the southern part of Okinawa, including grown crops, was completely destroyed, Okinawa's trouble began long before the American 1944 bombings. The published postwar record of the U.S. Civil Administration of the Ryukyus (USCAR) reveals that attrition, debilitation, and dislocation within the Ryukyuan community began several years before the battle. Repair, maintenance, and development of facilities, resources, and all other phases of civilian life were neglected in favor of the Japanese war effort. Population movements within the islands and to other areas of the empire were extensive. During the last year of the war, many Japanese who occupied responsible positions in government, the school system, and private enterprise departed for home from the Ryukyus. And several thousands of Ryukyuans were sent or went to Japan, Formosa, and other parts of the empire. Immediately prior to and during the battle, nearly all the inhabitants of the densely populated southern half of Okinawa were evacuated to the narrow and mountainous northern part. Ninety per cent of the survivors of the battle were in the north. They were confined to this sector until early 1946. Even at that date, there was little incentive for the residents of the lower part of the island to return to the skeletal sites of their former homes.

The United States had designated Okinawa as the staging area for the invasion of Japan, consequently during the early postwar era practically the entire central section of the island was occupied by military installations and massive matériel storage. Nearly forty-two thousand acres of land were included in the vast military reservation. Until late 1949, the local inhabitants were restricted, for reasons of military security and health, from erecting buildings within one mile of any U.S. billeting area. Native farmers were permitted to use portions of land within military reservations, but they were reluctant to cultivate crops because of the uncertainty of their land tenure in such areas.

When MG operations began with the invasion, small mobile MG teams were attached to fighting divisions and moved up with them, operating in the forward areas. These small units had the single mission of clearing the division's forward firing area of civilians, and immediately evacuating them to the rear. Since over half the civilians contacted in the forward battle areas were wounded or sick, these divisional MG units were obliged to carry some medical supplies and drinking water. All civilian refugees were evacuated rearward and concentrated through intermediate MG echelons until they reached fixed compounds, located well behind the lines. The physically fit among the refugees were permitted to serve on noncombative work details for military units. As soon as the tactical situation would allow, they were encouraged to start taking care of themselves. But, for a long time, it was necessary to provide the principal part of their logistical support from military sources.

Even in those refugee camps, a semblance of normal society was established. "Mayors" were appointed and provided with councils whose members were charged with the supervision of such activities as camp sanitation, labor, land cultivation, and rationing. As a further step in creating an atmosphere of normal life, every effort was made to house the people in makeshift private shelters or in the home of relatives or friends, rather than in barracks-like compounds. Seeds, simple agricultural tools, military surplus, including one hundred obsolete landing craft to be used for fishing, were furnished the people so that they could become self-sufficient in providing the simple everyday necessities of life and in establishing minimum facilities required by a community. For the first eighteen months after the battle, until a welfare program began, the populace subsisted primarily on food, clothing, medical supplies, and other items given from military sources as free rations or as compensation for labor.

The critical problems existing in the immediate postwar period were aggravated by the repatriation of some two hundred thousand Ryukyuans from abroad. Moreover, the complete severance of ties with Japan resulted in the almost total lack of native leaders trained in government, public health, and economic affairs. It all added to the uncertain political future of the Ryukyus. Nevertheless, starvation was prevented and disease and unrest were held to a minimum. I also noted earlier that efforts to re-establish native self-government institutions on Okinawa began shortly before the battle. A fifteen-member informal advisory council was formed in August 1945 as link between MG Headquarters and the civil population. It gradually evolved into executive offices eventually functioning on an island wide basis. The Department of Education, and the Board of Health were created in January 1946. Yet it was many months and in some instances years before these agencies could assume complete responsibility for the basic operations which they were designated to perform in the community.

And there were some personal tragedies for which the MG could do nothing. Yet, life went on. In September 1945, elections of the most primitive sort were held for mayor and councilmen in each of the eleven MG districts on Okinawa. Such district "governments" were only temporary and eventually were replaced by the prewar Japanese city, town, and village (shi, cho, and son) structure as rapidly as the inhabitants were returned to their communities or resettled in other localities. Prewar municipal mayors and councilmen were permitted to resume office, and vacancies were filled by appointment until a general municipal election could be held. At that time COA, headed by an appointed chiji (governor), absorbed the informal advisory council and the executive offices which had developed from its committees. This organization, subsequently designated Okinawa Civilian Administration, included the chiji, thirteen executive and administrative departments, a court system, and an advisory assembly. The chiji was directly responsible to the deputy commander, MG, for proper performance of all government functions in Okinawa. Civil affairs in Okinawa Gunto were administered through this organization until late 1950, when elections were held for governor and assemblymen in all four island subgroups.

Miyako and Yaeyama guntos, the islands south of Okinawa, had not been ravaged by war. The prewar municipal government organizations in these areas continued uninterrupted until the Ryukyu-wide municipal elections of early 1948. The prewar Yaeyama and Miyako branch prefectural offices were replaced by provisional government organizations, each headed by an appointed chiji, with functions similar to those of the OCA.

During 1947, laws were drafted for the election of mayors and assemblymen. Realizing the need for retaining essential familiar parts of old Japanese law and for including new procedures to insure democratic elections, MG drafting officials studied prewar Japanese laws, new laws enacted in postwar Japan, and established American laws; the final draft of the Ryukyuan municipal election law emerged as a workable combination of these three on January 12, 1948. The mayoral election, for an initial trial period of two years, was successfully held on February 1 and that for assemblymen a week later.

The majority of candidates ran as independents. The power of political parties was negligible then. The few party members who were elected were chosen on the basis of their personal strength and not because of their party affiliations. The elections were noted for their orderliness and the enthusiasm of the voters. Women participated fully for the first time, and four women were elected as assembly members. Approximately 85 per cent of those eligible voted.

USCAR further states that the re-establishment of all essential government and community services was seriously hampered by the acute shortage of trained native personnel. In other foreign areas occupied after the end of hostilities, (even those where damage was quite extensive), there were some experienced local individuals to start giving such indispensable services as public health and public safety, and even to resume public education with improvised facilities. All such people on Okinawa were Japanese and had gone.

In the decades before the war, public health services, both with respect to facilities and personnel, were among the most inadequate of all components of the standard of living of the Ryukyuan people. In the years immediately before and during the war, when the nutritional level of the populace was below normal, the quality of these services declined further. Local resources available on Okinawa to care for the thousands of sick and wounded when fighting ceased included no institutions, no medical supplies, and fewer than one hundred native physicians. MG, with the assistance of U.S. armed forces units, was forced to assume complete operational responsibility for the medical care and public health services of the surviving inhabitants. Nearly two-and-one-half years elapsed before the local government could assume a significant share of these responsibilities. During this period, eleven temporary hospitals were established, using equipment, supplies, and, in some instances, prefabricated buildings shipped in as military surplus stock from other areas.

For several months after the end of hostilities, the economy of Okinawa was entirely of a subsistence nature. Supplies from military sources, which constituted the principal support of the people, were distributed as free rations, and as payment to Ryukyuans employed by military units. Except for simple barter transactions among individuals, no commerce existed and no currency circulated. As the people were resettled from refugee camps, they were encouraged to plant crops, engage in coastal fishing, and establish other basic facilities and activities for the production and exchange of goods and services. These were required for even the simplest community life. The re-establishment of a medium of exchange was essential for the achievement of the objective. In prewar days, the Japanese urged the Okinawans to grow sugar cane in preference to other crops. They felt the locals would just eat the other grown crops, but would sell the cane for cash, buy food, and still have some money left. The prewar Okinawans sent all their sugar cane to Japan. In exchange, they received 60 per cent of their total food support. Japan used the cane to produce commercial alcohol for torpedoes and engines—war production. Okinawa was then only 40 per cent self-supporting with sweet potatoes and rice.

The land normally used for these two staple food crops was used for cane, which Japan repaid in rice and rice substitutes.

The persistently peculiar status of the Ryukyu Islands compounded the problems associated with restoration of a currency economy. Effective April 15, 1946, both military type "B" yen and new Japanese yen were made legal tender. A procedure for recalling old Japanese yen, administering blocked accounts, and issuing new currency, similar to that in existence in Japan, was adopted. A "bank," called the Central Bank of Okinawa, was created as the agency for implementing this program. Also, cash wages replaced payments in kind as compensation to workers employed by the U.S. forces. Food and other supplies furnished by the U.S. forces to individuals were distributed through designated stores at fixed prices. Rationing and price controls were extended to nearly all other items, although enforcement of controls over these and other goods was never successfully accomplished. A limited commerce, possible among the various islands, was also subject to regulation.

During the next two years, type "B" yen was withdrawn, and again introduced as a medium of exchange. But as long as the Japanese yen was legal tender, effective financial management by MG was impossible. With a currency common to both areas, the rampant inflation which existed in Japan was transmitted to the Ryukyus. The repatriates who flowed from or through Japan during this period brought in large amounts of inflated new Japanese yen. With the same currency in circulation, smuggling between the two areas was facilitated; it was obvious that the seas were wide open to all sub-rosa traffic.

This chaotic monetary condition confused the people and caused them to lose confidence in the currency. Military units were compelled to supplement cash wages with subsistence or other payments in kind to maintain a native labor force adequate for their essential needs. The people's incentive and efforts were directed toward the acquisition of goods. Nearly every item, regardless of type or condition, which was of some use in the local economy could be sold profitably in the smuggling trade. But for honest, unlocated people without village or registration, finding a job, or even daily sustenance, became a battle for survival. For instance, my friend Maven and I used to go hiking across the countryside on Sundays. One time we heard shouts. As I looked around to my left I saw coming toward us an Okinawan about five feet tall, with a bushy mustache. He wore an old Japanese winter field hat with the earlaps flapping in the breeze, shabby clothing, and a pair of oversize GI shoes. He spoke in perfect Castilian Spanish, which I understood. When he was a boy of nine, living with his family in Shuri village, he was sent to Tokyo to apprentice in the Imperial Palace kitchen as a scullery boy—a great honor for an Okinawan family, though the kitchens were separated from the palace itself. He worked diligently and ingratiated himself with many of the cooks and chefs. Two or three years after becoming friends with one of the middle echelon cooks, the cook, through an army relative, was taken from the palace staff and sent to Lima to run the kitchen of the Japanese Embassy to the Peruvian capital. The boy went along to run the scullery. During the ensuing twenty-two years in Peru, through patience and hard work, the scullery lad himself became chef of the Japanese Embassy in Lima.

When the war broke, all the Latin-American nations, in a formality, followed suit with the United States and declared war on Japan. Consequently, all the Japanese diplomatic corps with their entourages in the Latin-American countries were assembled in Buenaventura, Colombia, where the Swedish ship *Gripsholm* picked them up and transported them safely back to Tokyo. There they stayed and worked at various jobs through the course of the war, until the time of the American occupation of Japan.

One of the first things the Americans did was repatriate all the "displaced" persons whom the Japanese had brought into Japan from such conquered areas as Guam, Tinian, New Guinea, the Bonin, and Philippine islands, etc. Our man was sent back to Okinawa under protest. He didn't want to return because he had not been there since he was a child and he had no ties. But U.S. rules were final, so off they packed him to Okinawa, and turned him loose. He walked back to Shuri village where his family long ago had lived. The battle had demolished all. He knew no one, and since he was not an "Okinawan-Okinawan," he was not registered with MG. He was actually forced to live off the countryside. When he spotted me that Sunday, he thought, with my dark hair and mustache, I was Latin.

I was able to work out an arrangement with MG to have him registered and assigned to me. I employed him as a "straw-boss" over a group of Okinawan construction workers, enabling me to get an amazing amount of work done by them accurately, because I could give the instructions to this man in Spanish and he would in turn translate to Japanese "Okinawan" for them. A short time later I was taken off construction, relegated to real estate, and I lost track of him.

Jobs at translation were much easier to come by toward 1950, and the arrangement for them, though far more formalized, was a good deal simpler than in '46. Moreover, the characteristics of the applicants had also changed appreciably. For those boys who survived the war and adjusted to its aftermath, times and conditions offered a whole new universe to them. Hidetaro Kanashiro tells his story:

"After a few minutes' inspection at the gate box, I was allowed to get into the area of X Intelligence Corps Detachment. As I walked up a zigzag way through army Quonsets scattered around the area, I was caught up by the sweet memory of my school days to which I had said good-by a couple of weeks ago—the images of the cheerleaders in the athletic meetings, those of my friends chattering and singing around the bonfire on some winter night, their sorrowful faces on the morning of graduation and the plaintive strain of farewell song.

"Things that happened in my school days came to my eyes and mind now and then, and I was a little confused as to whether I was still a carefree student or a man seeking a job.

"Guided by a friend of mine who was working there, I was led to one of the rooms of headquarters. A minute later, I found myself before a bareheaded army officer typing up something in an extremely busy manner. I knew, by my friend's introduction, that he was Captain Wallace and in charge of the translation section of the detachment. I shook hands with him and told him why I had come. He smiled at me faintly and kept on with his work as if he had ignored my existence.

"Several minutes later he brought me a sheet of Okinawan newspaper and said, 'Boy, we customarily give a short test before we employ a translator. I know you can make out well.' So saying he pointed out some articles in the newspaper with his pencil and asked me to read the articles in English without changing the original meaning.

"The articles were in no way incomprehensible, but I got extremely excited. My lips were a little shivery and I could not speak out anything of what I had translated in my mind. I lost my usual state of mind and did not know what to do.

"The captain, judging me in trouble, gave me a sheet of paper and asked me to write down what I had translated in my mind. Rendering word by word, sentence by sentence, I finally translated it all. I took almost more than an hour to finish. The captain, comparing my translation with another paper which some translator of this detachment had translated, said smilingly, 'You have done well, boy. You report here tomorrow morning and start your work, you understand?'

"I was so glad that I did not know what I should say. I just smiled back at him."

While the Okinawans vied for jobs, the hundred and eighty thousand-odd enlisted troops stationed in occupational isolation had much leisure time. However, in the Ryukyus there was just no place to go. Some fortunate officer-class individuals were able to wangle off-the-record transportation to Manila, Philippines, or Tokyo, but in general free time had to be spent on Okinawa and in the surrounding small islands. For some, the islands themselves had more than enough to offer—sights, natural and historic, hiking, beaches, fishing, and, when one could get away with it, time with the people, learning their interests, habits, and customs. A lucky few were invited to use the tennis courts at the Ninth Station Hospital, and some people just sunned, read, or wrote.

For the enlisted troops in general, there was choose-up softball for all in every unit, and interunit "league" baseball, in which teams registered with Army Special Services. These games were usually played Wednesday or Saturday afternoons. Lautzenheiser Field near Kadena airfield was the best ball park on the island. Evenings there were endless crap games in both the enlisted barracks and the smoke-filled backrooms of the Officers' Clubs, where fifteen-cent drinks and green beer were served. The evening was also time for outdoor movies (war thrillers gratis from Hollywood), occasional traveling USO shows with only fair, but nonetheless live, talent. On other occasions, the big Rykom outdoor cinema would become an arena for boxing tournaments. The bouts were better than average, since the boys were in fine physical condition, it was a chance to work off frustrations, and there was weather and room for outdoor training. The few times I had the chance to judge these contests, I never saw a bad bout.

In the fall of 1946, Army Special Services under Colonel Arpad A. Kopesak, a 1937 West Point behemoth, was able to organize and equip a regulation football league of ten teams, five each in a northern and a southern conference. The 1st Air Division won the northern and MG the southern military championships that first year. Football has since become a regular pastime on Okinawa. Not being too far removed from my three years on the Cornell squad, I officiated at some of the games. The Okinawans would stand at the ends of the field, amazed at what they thought was mass brutality, while they saw nothing untoward about kendo, the traditional Japanese head-bashing game.

Naturally sports and movies were not enough. Regardless of regulations or consequences, the men had to find women. Nurses and civilian women were quartered in guarded compounds, and had to be escorted by armed males on their evenings out. Later, dependent wives and daughters lived in special communities and were put under the same regulations. Male escorts were generally officer-type personnel. Very few "noncoms" ever went out with these girls, therefore the natural attention of the vast majority of enlisted men was turned upon the Ryukyuan girls. The idea that all female Okinawans were fair game for the conquering heroes was soon dispelled by military authorities reluctantly paying heed to the outraged protests from local leaders. Nevertheless there were always isolated incidents of violence. One, for instance, involved an Itoman girl snatched into the back of a moving truck, criminally assaulted by twenty soldiers, and cast out without the truck's ever stopping. Fortunately for MG, the entire band was quickly apprehended and punished.

However, there were local girls in sufficient numbers who were willing, for a consideration, to entertain the soldiers' wants. Naturally any such traffic could not be organized officially. But for the common good, some wiser, saner heads worked out an off-the-record arrangement whereby all interested girls were assembled in a single area in which drinking, money, medical examinations, and an orderly movement of actually thousands all were controlled closely without creating any disturbance from the outside. After duty hours, military buses from several areas unofficially would take and return the troops. For a while this appeared to be a satisfactory solution. Then some chaplains and others had the bus service prohibited from *stopping* at the area in question. The buses continued to run, and slowed down to a low-gear crawl, so that all would be able to leave and enter without mishap. But this was only a beginning. Eventually the crusaders succeeded in wrecking this project.

The girls were dispersed so that no medical vigilance upon them was possible. Immediately, the island-wide venereal disease rate skyrocketed. With no controls, the fees jumped; black marketing, drunkenness, disorderliness, and violence again became a serious Military Police problem. With no bus service to a central focus, vehicles were stolen, and often men were absent without official leave. Once again innocent Okinawan girls, instead of their more willing sisters, fell victims to the inevitable violent prurience. The disturbance of a controlled solution harmed American-Ryukyuan relations more than condoning the activity ever would have.

Another big problem the commander officer of the Ryukyus had was the perpetual, sophomoric in-service rivalries. As soon as the shooting war against the Japanese stopped, the in-service rivalry between the Army and Navy, between flyboy and doughfoot, between officers and enlisted men, etc., began. The island itself was roughly divided into several sectors. The north end was roughly the domain of the Marine Corps, much as it is still today. The Navy occupied the east coast from the Marine line at Kin all the way down to the south and nearly to Suicide Cliff. This left to the Army the southwestern chunk of Okinawa from Motobu Peninsula to the south end, from a rough line through the middle of the island west to the China Sea coast. The Army also had the offshore islands, including Ie Shima. The Air Force (the Army Air Corps then) occupied all the airfields, and all other army installations took up where they were assigned. Each branch respected the other's boundaries, and seldom did one ever go into the other service's "country." Further subdivisions eventually developed. There was some co-operation with regard to the acquisition of the luxuries. The Navy, for instance, had white tablecloths and real silverware at their Officers' (Ward Room) Mess. Scotch went for ten-cent chits; food on the table was handled by Filipino stewards serving to the left and taking away from the right. There were milk, fresh green lettuce, and other goodies, because the Navy was being supplied continuously by ship.

The Army lived as best it could within the prescribed methods and rations issued. The quartermaster had control of the liquor supply and several other things which became tradable commodities. For these, say, the Ordnance Corps would be able to make available brass shell casings and craft materials which made for other types of "better living." The Corps of Engineers had the construction materials much demanded. Consequently the outfits exchanged luxuries. Whatever couldn't be traded was "scrounged." But under this guise of co-operation lay the deep-seated rivalry which mainly ran between the Army and Navy, and then within each service and within each unit. This fol-de-rol never helped the American image, the occupation, or the service.

I learned of this firsthand at the Tengan Naval Operations Base, Katchin Hanto, because my college roommate, the late Ensign George E. R. Williams was with the 34th Naval Construction Battalion. He had been on Okinawa through most of the campaign and was still there in occupation long after I had arrived.

Attitude had a lot to do with it. One Saturday evening, the Navy Catholic chaplain told me that during the shooting campaign, mass drew innumerable Catholics at all times because they were all aware of the imminence of sudden death. Once the campaign was over and the excitement died down (and the thanks and gratitudes were all said), the chaplain felt at one point that he could hold mass any Sunday in a telephone booth. But the one regular person he had at all times was Williams.

Awase airfield, a small east coast strip, was given over by the Navy to the Army for further developing. One Navy aircraft, a single-engine pursuit plane, remained at the edge of the strip because the pilot was in the naval hospital. The Army requested the Navy to remove the aircraft from the strip because it posed a safety hazard to the Army's operations. The Navy said that in its tradition no man flies another man's aircraft while he's still alive. The Army was requested to let the craft stay and wait until the pilot could move it himself. The Army could not leave an untended aircraft standing on the strip as a safety hazard. After issuing three notifications to the Navy, the Army just put a bulldozer to it and pushed this quarter-million-dollar aircraft off the cliff to destruction below.

The Navy retaliated by cutting out two five-foot sections of an army water main. They filled each of the remaining two ends with a slug of concrete and proceeded to perforate two additional five-foot sections inboard the ends. At that time, all this destruction might have been called a prank, and probably served mainly to relieve the tedium for the lack of something to do for men who were going home after having been on the island too long.

Factional rivalries tend to break down with person-to-person mingling, but this must be spontaneous. On a really hot summer day, I was up north surveying smaller installations. I stopped in at the PX at Yontan air base for a soda and ran into Lieutenant J. J. Driscoll, Jr., former football manager at Cornell, who later became '44 alumni class president and a close friend. He had just arrived with the 8th Air Force from England. This chance meeting gained me a guest privilege to the flyboys' club, where I met Captain Bill Caudill, an army pilot. Three weeks later, on a Saturday, I was returning to my installation for lunch when I saw a P-47 burst into flames and start to fall. Shortly after, the pilot, who turned out to be Caudill, bailed out. He came down burning in his parachute because he tried too long to save the craft or head it away from populated areas. I sped south toward the Hacksaw Ridge zone, where he appeared headed. Fortunately others spotted him also, and I heard the scream of sirens not too far behind me. Almost immediately after I reached him, help was with us to put out his fire. An ambulance rushed him to the Ninth Station Hospital, where I visited him often on his slow road to recovery. He could just have bailed out and saved himself, but he thought of others first.

Fire made other heroes on Okinawa after the shooting stopped. At the Ninth Station Hospital, the medical administrative officer, a young lieutenant, Mike Filosa, was an extremely affable man who took his job seriously. Late afternoon of Columbus Day 1946, there was a fire at the Ninth Station Hospital. In the Army, the Corps of Engineers is automatically the fire department. We were in the next unit south of the hospital. The fire call came and we immediately answered with our pumper and other equipment. Army hospitals in the field were generally built of Quonset huts. It was required that each be connected to the next by a closed passageway through which stretchers and wheelchairs might pass without having to go outdoors. This was good for patient movement but not good for trying to put out a fire. One unscathed Quonset-ward adjacent to another in which we were battling the fire was about to catch on via the plywood structure of the closed passage between the two. Flames started to lick at it; it would be just a matter of moments before they would consume the passageway and then the next Quonset-ward. Frantically we started chopping away at the plywood passage when Lieutenant Filosa pulled a Filipino Scout out from behind the wheel of an idling 6 x 6 truck. Mike threw the truck into low gear and before anyone could try to stop him, he crashed the truck right through the passage structure, demolishing it. The fire didn't pass; he saved the ward. But while Mike drove the truck through the prefab passageway, a two-by-four building stud speared itself through the windshield and through his sternum, impaling him to the seat back. Lieutenant Mike Filosa died of a collapsed chest while saving part of the army hospital he was assigned to operate.

Although there were two army hospitals on Okinawa during the early occupation, the Ninth Station Hospital was the surviving unit. The other, a much smaller installation, was deactivated early in 1947. The naval hospital at the Tengan Operations Base was superior with its well-equipped surgery in a Butler Building. There was a short period in 1946 and 1947 when bored army men with a bit of "sick time coming" and some "influence" would go over to the navy hospital and spend a week in comparative luxury having their appendix or tonsils out or being circumcized. But once the word got out it all stopped.

Life at the Ninth Station Hospital for the officers and men was hardly different from another camp except for a better mess. For the nurses, though, it was different, and either difficult or fun depending upon the nurse. Because they were female (the island had one woman per thousand men), they had to live inside a stockade, surrounded by a high barbed-wire fence, with a sentry at the only entrance-exit. They could come and go freely from this convent-like sanctuary to go to work in the wards, or recreation within the confines of the hospital grounds. But to leave the station to go to a PX, or movie, or sight-seeing they had to go in groups of three in a vehicle, and in daylight hours only. At night there had to be an armed male escort, and curfew was midnight with no exceptions.

The first design and layout of the nurses' compound was unimaginative and dreary. Some girls tried to improve things. In order to make living conditions more tolerable, one had to scrounge or barter. Hardly anything but bare necessities ever came through channels. The negotiable items the nurses at the hospital had were milk for many, and favors for some. They wanted things to make improvements on their club, or their Quonset "homes" in the compounds. Generally the army mess had no milk at all, but milk was flown in prefrozen from the Philippines in wax-cardboard quart containers. Milk was for special patients, but the supply was never completely consumed, nor could it keep. The nurses freely dispensed it in return for things like spar varnish for their dance floors, or mirrors, lamps, light boxes, or other items, while a "select minority" had lots of fun acquiring their goods. Occasionally the nurses could accomplish something by going through channels. On the other hand, going through military channels on Okinawa had its own frustrating course.

One afternoon the U.S. Hospital Ship *Hope* came into Naha harbor, and tied up overnight to take on supplies and refuel from the Naha bunkers. When the word got around, thousands of eligible young men started to look for weapons, jeeps, et al. All descended on Port Naha in order to get near the *Hope* and find a girl. I found out later that the overabundance of nurses aboard the *Hope* were all looking for some "land duty" with some able and ambulatory men. I too, hied myself over to the quartermaster to check out a pistol. They said they'd certainly give me a pistol if I showed them my permit! So I went next door to the Provost Marshal's Office to get a permit. They said they'd gladly give me a permit—where was my pistol? From this little lesson, I learned that situations which appear to be insurmountable always have a hook somewhere to be found.

Those girls were the pioneers. But 1946 brought women to Ryukyuan shores in abundance, and Okinawa was then like anywhere else. The first civilian women employees to arrive were from Australia because the travel distance was shorter. Then came American women, followed soon by "dependent" wives and daughters of the occupation forces people. And then came Filipino girls.

For those men faithful to a girl back home, the local Armed Forces Radio Service station ran a nightly feature after the eleventh hour news. AFRS Okinawa would play a well-worn 78-rpm. recording of Jo Stafford singing, "I Promise You I'll Be There." They would play it once completely, then diminish it to "noncompet" background music while an announcer would read a sad letter from a sweetheart or wife running off with a local chap.

Yet Armed Forces Radio Service did make life far more tolerable. AFRS in the Ryukyus meant something to everyone. Even in those pretransistor days, there were radios all over the islands, and AFRS's broadcast from Island Command Headquarters was receivable all throughout the command. On Saturday afternoons from 1:00 to 5:00 we heard beautiful serious music to go with our free time sunning by the inlet. Machinato is an Americanization of the true name Machiminato, which in Ryukyuan means "waiting port." I shared a corner of a Quonset hut on Machinato Inlet with Basile Nicholiavitch Ouspensky from Odessa, Paris, and Jackson Heights.

The nonenlisted occupational jobs lasted until 1947, when civilian contractors began to arrive in large numbers as did dependent families, general civilian white-collar forces, merchants, tradesmen, and others on private economy. By late 1947, the American Ryukyuan atmosphere changed from a conquered battle zone to a twentieth-century version of an Oklahoma frontier community. Along with the change of character of the American population and the concurrently independent, progressive change of the Ryukyuan natives, the duties and operations of the armed forces changed, as did some physical aspects of the island itself.

Back in 1946, while the operational forces continued their military drill and MG performed its functions, the Corps of Engineers of the U. S. Army was given a fourfold charge. First it was to consolidate and operate all utilities; next, through an interim construction program, to create living facilities for large numbers of dependents soon to be brought to the island. Simultaneously the corps had to build better living facilities for the occupation Army, later to be followed by a builders' camp and full construction field facility for a civilian construction contractor to set up on the island and erect a permanent base. It was then established that at least for the following five to ten years, Okinawa was to be the site (and the Okinawans were to be the "hosts") of a vast permanent American military installation on that island.

# PART III

# The Tortuous Trek

# CHAPTER 5

# Permbase Is Not a Game

Private outside construction help was employed on Okinawa. The repatriation of Japanese PWs and the slow unskilled, untrained, native labor force working under a great language barrier would have made it too formidable an undertaking for the Corps of Engineers (C of E) to accomplish its mission. But as a supervising agency over skilled and adroit American professionals and mercenaries, the corps hoped to be able to complete its task with economical efficiency.

Rarely would any unit ever have a completely good staff. But the C of E on Okinawa had a marvelous top echelon. The commanding officer was Colonel Lee B. Washbourne. (Some years later he became General Washbourne, Chief of Engineers for the newly constituted U. S. Air Force.) He did a good job while on Okinawa, and grew considerably in stature as time went on. His decisions were based on experienced judgment factors rather than a hope for popularity. Colonel Washbourne's executive officer, Lieutenant Colonel Thomas F. Airis, from Eau Claire, Wisconsin, was an equally competent engineer and leader, both strong and aloof. It seemed to me that whenever or wherever I was on the job, he'd come out of the woods in his combat infantry boots, his small service hat squared over a chiseled but smiling face, just to be sure everything was going right. Under these two able men were many good people carrying out their commands, as well as an equal number who were inept.

In the fall of 1946, a combine of Guy F. Atkinson Construction Company of Los Angeles and the J. A. Jones Company of Atlanta, Georgia, submitted a joint-venture bid to the C of E, Washington, and became the low bidder on the project to build the interim construction and permanent base (Permbase) on Okinawa. The contractor started sending its personnel in late 1946. As 1947 came, more and more of its people populated the island. The job progressed.

Under the terms of the contract, the C of E was to build an interim construction facility for the contractor who was then to build an interim contractor's camp. This was off the location site of any Permbase facility later to be constructed. Temporarily, contractor's employees were billeted with engineer personnel at what was called Camp Boone. We were attempting to get along with each other and reconcile differences, since we were all there to do the job. Much matériel on Okinawa originally from the Army (bulldozers, tractors, cranes, and shovels, etc.) was put to use by the contractor, though the combine chose to bring much new equipment over from the States.

Another civilian organization functioned between the corps and the constructor. This was, by negotiated contract, an architect-engineer, professional people from the Los Angeles consulting firm of Holmes and Narver. Things then operated on three levels and grew to a large Parkinsonian scale. By the spring of 1947, more female contractor personnel began to arrive. They lived in a stockade-like women's compound built at Camp Boone. Married couples were put up in a small housing settlement set just outside the confines of the women's stockade; some forty very tiny prefabricated wood huts. It seemed to be a pretty poor order of living. On the other hand, the Army itself developed far better living conditions.

While Quonset installations which the Army had acquired from the Navy were converted into dependents' housing quarters, they were set up by areas in accordance with the army caste system. This meant separate housing areas for families of field-grade officers, company-grade officers, and warrant officers. There was also one for general-grade officers which included four of the five grades of general. The island's commanding general had a beautiful house built on the summit at Awase.

The in-project housing for the average company grade officer with a wife and, say, two young children, was a converted Quonset hut fifty-eight feet long and twelve feet wide, which might have either a concrete or plywood floor base on concrete footings. It would also have running water and electricity. The electricity was furnished within each installation by a diesel-generator set. The water came from the nearest water point, thus both became cases of local distribution. The home layout was a standard cooky-cutter design pattern approved by the Office of Chief of Engineers. Modular parts were all cut uniformly of plywood. The partitions and plumbing were also uniform.

The coming of the wives and children to the island improved the morale of the officer personnel in occupation considerably, but it also created a new problem. This was the occasional wayward wife. Out of boredom, she might have a casual affair with some male who either had reason to pass from time to time or, on rare occasions, worked in the area. There was a suggestion to establish a rest-resort area on Ie Shima, but the command felt that occupation was a type of military life, not a picnic. (In 1966, I did see such a facility on Ie.)

Between 1946 and 1950, Ie Shima suffered and physically showed more signs of American creeping neglect than Okinawa itself. Although the master plan for Operation Iceberg called for the invasion of Ie Shima to begin L + 30 (which would have made it April 30, 1945), General Buckner began it April 15, about two weeks ahead of schedule. The Army 77th Division undertook this operation-phase by itself and it was a costly though rapid one. By April 21, Ie was secure. However, since considerable numbers of the local population were pressed into service by the Japanese, the Allies deemed that between the days of May 18 and May 30, 1945, the entire population of Ie Shima be transplanted in order to make the fullest use of the island, its airstrips, its military availability, and its place for stores. Especially since its location placed it behind many of the ships anchored in the great bight south of Motobu Peninsula, it was necessary to make the most use of Ie Shima as a base to end the campaign as rapidly as possible.

The mass move was not a popular one. Some Ie women and children took up spears and stones to defend their homes. Earlier, in December 1944 and January 1945, the Japanese had forcibly evacuated three thousand of Ie's eight thousand civilians to make more room for their defense preparations. The Allies uprooted the remaining five thousand. Every Ie inhabitant was moved by ship to Kerama Retto; all three islands of Zamami, Tokashiki, and Kerama became interment camps. In this way, Ie was used for the Allied cause, and before the year was out *all* Ie's natives were returned home. Kerama Retto was selected because those islands were in American hands late on March 29, 1945, prior to the landings on Okinawa proper. After the campaign on Ie Shima, the only building of which a semblance remained was the old government house which, though still standing, was a complete ruin patched with GI Quonset corrugated paneling.

On December 19, 1946, an Army Special Order sent our real estate team to Ie Shima to survey, examine, and evaluate all U. S. Army property there. This included Quonset huts, buildings, roads, improvements, utility lines, etc. There is a section in the report form to the Office of Chief of Engineers for general observations. In my December 22, 1946, report on this trip, I noted that the munitions dumps on Ie Shima were in extremely bad shape. The campaign had been long over by then, munitions which had hastily been stored out in the open, things like napalm or jelly gas (which ordinarily came in fifty-gallon drums for loading into flame-thrower tanks), were lying out in mountainous stacks. The outer skins of these metal drums were eroding from the effects of general weathering (the rain, the salt, the sea air, and blazing sunshine). The jelly gas began to creep out and run down the sides, resembling huge Christmas candles, since the red and white composition of this melting material intermingled as would hot wax running down the sides of fancy Yuletide tapers.

Part of my report, under general observations, was the condition of those munitions dumps. I further suggested that since this live stuff had deteriorated, and since there was no immediate chance of its ever being used, it should be taken out to sea and dumped, before something planned or spontaneous "accidentally" happened. During the summer of 1948, while on a business trip to San Francisco, I picked up a stray copy of a local newspaper. Buried far inside, a short seven-line item read: "TWO SOLDIERS DIE IN OKINAWA BLAST, Tokyo August 8 (1948) (AP)—Air Force headquarters said today two American enlisted men, 11 Filipinos and 'probably 50 or more' natives were killed in the previously reported explosion of ammunition on Ie Shima near Okinawa Friday." This gave me no measure of satisfaction. Yet I could not help wondering if anyone had actually seen the report our team turned in. Of if anyone had, was it ever read and understood? Further, was anything ever done about it? Obviously not! And apparently the reasons for this neglect on Okinawa were mainly the distance from America, the lack of any apparent purpose for our remaining there, the rapid change-over in personnel of the U.S. armed forces in the occupation, and the vast turnover of senior officers in the Pentagon and lesser commands.

One bleak November day in 1946, while driving up Highway 5 along the Pacific, Navy, side, I passed a group of Seabees busy building a side road into a new installation. According to their survey, the road was going off across what had been a Japanese military cemetery in lowland, then destined to become buried more deeply under the road sub-base fill. Japanese do not mark their graves with crosses; they plant a single vertical wood staff carrying the man's data and vital statistics. These grave markers were being pulled out by the road men and thrown into a bonfire solely for vendetta over Japanese conduct during the war. Each cadaver was in effect being made an unknown soldier by this unofficial postwar act of some immature individuals. I managed to pull from the fire a single grave marker which I still preserve today. It was for an Okinawan eighty-three years of age, pressed into Japanese service and killed on June 11, 1945.

Happily there was not too much of this untoward behavior. Nearly all Americans knew who won the war, knew who had established a supremacy of right and reason, not race. There was one place in this overall picture though, where the U.S. made a very basic error in judgment. It was in its determination of policy with regard to the land.

"Real estate" means natural land *in situ,* immovable property. Buildings and appurtenances are a secondary consideration. The fabricated things men put on the land for their comfort, convenience, and utility are not "real property" in the basic sense of the word but are termed "personal property." On Okinawa during World War II and after, everything appertaining to the land belonged to the U. S. Government. And since government is impersonal, the Office of Chief of Engineers, U. S. Army, chose to term it all as "real property." Thus the Real Estate Branch, C of E, was charged with the responsibility of assembling, keeping, and maintaining records of all U. S. Government property put into "improving" the land of the Ryukyus. The job was tallying and inventory, to establish and appraise an in-place depreciated dollar value of it all. But nowhere in any report form was there a place for any information about the land itself, or its value. The basic item of "real estate" thereby became expunged in the rationalization of U. S. Government thinking about its installations. And with this elimination was automatically created the Achilles' heel of the Ryukyuan real estate riddle.

From 1879 to 1945, the Ryukyus had been recognized as being under Japanese sovereignty. It is also true that in a war, all property, state or private, is subject to seizure without compensation, and there is no doubt that the U. S. armed forces actually won Okinawa in battle. Therefore the "government thinking" could be best described by Senator William L. Marcy's words to the U. S. Senate, in January 1832: "They see nothing wrong in the rule that to the victor belong the spoils of the enemy." The little Okinawan farmer whose square yard of land grew the food for his family, or the tract owner whose sugar harvest provided sustenance for the whole village found themselves stripped of their land by a new people purporting at the same time to want to rehabilitate them. They had not incited the Japanese Emperor to war, nor had they requested the Allied invasion and ensuing battle. Naturally they were confused and mistrusting. They wanted their land back, or some compensation for their dislocation and hardship. This the Americans recalcitrantly refused to recognize at any time until 1950.

However, willing or not, many Okinawans did serve in the Army of Japan in fighting off the Allied invasion. Naturally, in the aftermath, the U.S. armed forces had to utilize some land to build defense facilities wherever strategy and tactics best indicated. The safety of U.S. personnel and the security of peace in the Far East transcended the personal desires of the individual Ryukyuan. The Okinawans now claim the problem mainly arose from the *manner* of American action rather than in the acts themselves. The resentment from the natives came out of the visitors' initial and continued ignorance of their existence as people with ancient deep-rooted claims.

I was ordered by Colonel Washbourne to establish and operate a Real Estate branch late in the summer of 1946, and catch up on the reports which were, in theory, initially due as soon as the island was secure. And, it was required that they be maintained periodically thereafter. Among other military and statistical information on each installation regardless of size or tenure, reports were required to show types of buildings, flooring, latrines, and other sanitary facilities, water lines, electric lines, water sources, storage tanks, motor-generator sets, other improvements such as fences, walkways, recreation, and motor pool facilities, etc. The census and purpose of the unit occupying the installation were also required. But the land itself was an item neither considered nor required by the forms, except for its graphic picture. Every unit had to be mapped. In many cases, maps anywhere from crudely paced-off schematics to finely annotated plats of surveys had already been prepared by the commanding officer. Where no charts existed we ran plane-table surveys and checked out reference points with a transit.

When we went to do an evaluation survey, some unit commanders treated us as potentates and offered us gifts. Others resented us and would not co-operate. Some feared we would discover non-GI improvements which were either scrounged or built in by the men. Assuring them we were neither inspector general nor tax collector, we managed, in most instances, to get our survey done and leave on excellent terms with the cadre. Bribery was not a factor, since neither licensing, fees, nor restrictions were involved. From time to time, we did get a bottle of scotch or a carton of sweets or smokes and invitations to clubs.

Starting with nothing, our group had a lot of work to do, and we did it. We were all over the island, and also had a Quonset at Camp Boone for our central office, storage, drafting room, and desk work. We were a small, friendly group who worked well together, although we seldom shared any off-duty hours with one another. Along with me were: the administrative officer, Norman J. Savignac from Milwaukee; surveyor-draftsman, Kenny Lenzeman, St. Louis; draftsman-computer Carlton P. Greene of the Providence Greenes, the Episcopal clergy, and the quartermaster, Ralph Young, who came to us from the Navy Seabees, helped us much, and took my job when I left in '47.

All the work we did on Okinawa, Ie Shima, Amami, Kerama, etc., in no way concerned any native village or facility, thus their existence on their own land—at that time—did not pose a problem for the Americans who threw the Okinawans some crumbs. Locals had to make do with what was not needed in a U.S. military reservation. The difficulty was at the top. From 1945 the U. S. Land Program in the Ryukyus had had a turbulent history. Land records on Okinawa were virtually all destroyed during hostilities. Following their cessation, MG promulgated laws establishing Okinawa land committees and procedures to re-establish native land ownership; and to issue land ownership certificates. Independent surveys needed to establish tract location and boundaries were made by Okinawans using strings, sticks, and other makeshift equipment. For security reasons, such surveys were not permitted within any U.S. reservation. The maps thus developed from these inadequate and incomplete cadastres were, for the most part, still in use in 1960 and accounted for a plethora of problems in relation to the land program as it subsequently developed.

Finally a break came in the American recalcitrance. On December 5, 1950, a directive to USCAR, issued by General Headquarters, FEC, stated that the United States would pay rental retroactive only to July 1, 1950, for land used by U.S. agencies in the Ryukyus. The directive also contained authorization to acquire a title to land and facilities needed permanently by the United States either by negotiated purchase or condemnation. The directive further stated that the services of the U.S. District Engineer would be utilized in connection with appraisals, acquisition of real property, and initiation of condemnation proceedings. Now the Americans had to decide how much the Okinawans were to get. Also they would have to decide who was to be paid and who was not to be paid. All this was left to be resolved by the real estate people of the next era.

The December 5, 1950, recognition of Ryukyuan rights to Ryukyuan lands not only reversed the implacable American policy toward the native claims, but it completely altered both the nature and the job of the Real Estate branch. RE finally and properly became a land office concerned with the Ryukyuan interests in their own territory while simultaneously continuing to carry out its previous functions with respect to assigning and cataloguing U. S. Government civil and military installations. To accomplish all these services, the old branch became a division of the District Engineer, Okinawa, and was expanded in 1951 to a table of organization sufficient to perform its complete task. In the earlier of the fifteen turbulent years of continuous expansion and activity, there were several division chiefs whose work was adequate until David I. Long took firm hold of the office and in six years put it on a going-concern basis, where he kept both factions contented while continuing to get the job done. Long feels his job is to "keep the RE situation going on the back burner," and his mild but forceful manner has accomplished just that: there have been no recent major clashes. The RE division has had as many as sixty-three people, but now has settled down to a staff of forty, the majority of whom are Ryukyuan natives. Most of these have moved up from jobs like drivers, draftsmen, and interpreters. Even the former mayor of Koza city is employed in the position of senior appraiser.

Long has received three important tributes. In September 1964, Okinawan director of legal affairs for the Government of Ryukyu Islands wrote: ". . . you have devoted yourself to attain . . . the solution of the problem of restoration compensation, while you have dared to achieve a considerable betterment of . . . service agreements . . ." ". . . the smoothest and closest contacts . . . we have ever had . . ." ". . . Ryukyuan people are unanimously speaking highly of your actions." A month later, Long received a certificate of achievement from the chief of engineers, Department of the Army, commending his efforts which ". . . resulted in a cost avoidance saving of $68,000 to the U. S. Army Engineer District, Okinawa"; he also received a presidential citation signed by L. B. Johnson.

In order to appreciate why Long got such recognition, one should know that the Okinawans have traditionaly measured land not in terms of acres or hectares but in the unit of a *tsubo.* There are 1224 tsubos in one acre, or one tsubo is equal to thirty-six square feet, (a square 6 feet x 6 feet). Initially, the Americans wanted to pay the Okinawans at the old Japanese prewar rate which later translated to three to four cents per tsubo for rent. This would mean that a family of five owning a small plot of land would get about ten dollars a year for rent for its land.

The U.S. services and agencies currently occupy or hold nearly 75,690 acres of land in the Ryukyu Islands. This total comprises what was formerly 51,635 acres of privately owned Okinawan land, and 24,006 acres of what was formerly Japanese Government and Okinawan prefectural-owned land. To this there are forty-nine acres of U.S. "reclaimed" land which has been "rescued" from the sea by land fill. The former privately owned land consists in about 135,000 tracts with an estimated 38,000 individual owners. The Japanese Government and Okinawan Prefecture were never divested of ownership of their land regardless of what international law may indicate. Custody of this island is held by the Office of the Ryukyuan Property Custodian, USCAR. This land, as required, is allocated to the U. S. Army Engineer District, Okinawa, for its use and distribution via its RE division. No compensation is paid to the Japanese Government or any former Okinawan Prefecture for use of such land. Nor is it intended they shall.

When the RE division was expanded in 1951, one of its main jobs was the establishment of boundaries, the actual mapping, and other preparations necessary to initiate acquisition proceedings. This was accomplished in due time. Although the December 1950 directive authorized the purchase of land, the policy of acquiring twenty-year leases was established. One of the difficult problems facing the District Engineer was the establishment of land values as a basis for arriving at fair rental compensation. The problem was further complicated by the lack of land sales records and the nonavailability of competent Ryukyuan land appraisers. Although these were later developed by RE, at the time they were needed there were none. The Hypothec Bank of Japan had extensive banking interests in Okinawa prior to the war. Therefore this bank had voluminous records of production costs and other general information concerning prewar land values which proved a good basis for determining postwar values. A contract was made between the GRI and the Hypothec Bank to conduct an appraisal to determine the fee value, as of the retroactive July 1, 1950, date, for the different classifications and grades of land in each municipality on Okinawa. Eventually these values were established and rental was computed at 6 per cent of the fee value. This did not please the Okinawans, nor was it the way it was ultimately done.

In the decade between 1950 and 1960, too many ways were tried to preserve the façade of American generosity in using Ryukyuan soil. American devices such as twenty-year basic leases, master leases for which the chief of GRI had to accept lump payments for local distribution, post-treaty reappraisals, mass condemnations, "declarations of taking," creation of U. S. Land Acquisition Commission (USLAC), and "determinable estate" all met with resistance from the locals. No Okinawan enjoyed the privilege of refusing to rent his land.

In 1954 the United States announced its intention to take a single-payment interest in the land required for an unspecified time since by then it was decided that they would remain in the Ryukyus for an indefinite period. Protests by landowners, landowner representatives, and political groups were promptly made. In May of 1955, the chief Executive of GRI and six representatives visited Washington to ask for increased rental and protest the single-payment plan to the House Armed Services Committee. As a result, a subcommittee under Representative Melvin Price (which generally became known as the "Price Committee") visited Okinawa in October 1955 to investigate and report to the Congress the entire land situation. In June of 1956 the Price Committee announced its recommendations, the principal of which was that the United States acquire fee title or maximum interest in land which would be required for an indefinite period of their security needs. Strong objections commenced immediately in Okinawa. Public protest meetings were held continually throughout the Ryukyus and in Japan. A number of major officials of GRI and municipalities threatened mass resignation.

In January 1957, General Lemnitzer, then governor of the Ryukyus, issued a land-policy statement wherein he established the intent of the United States to acquire an indefinite interest in land by a single payment. He also made it clear that the United States would not *take title* to a single tsubo of land in the Ryuku Islands. He was saying that America wanted indefinite tenure but did not wish to take possession. The Okinawans' argument to this was that, in effect, the United States was saying, "We would rather owe it to you all your lives than to cheat you out of it." This only created more trouble.

A Ryukyuan delegation consisting of the chief executive, GRI, and five other members made a second trip to Washington in June 1958 to discuss the land problem with any high-ranking U.S. official. During these discussions, members of the delegation assured Washington officials that if the single-payment program were to be terminated, the land problems could be solved by the development of a mutually agreeable land program. As a result of these discussions, the high commissioner was then authorized to hold joint Ryukyuan-American land conferences. These were held in the latter part of 1958 and the outcome was the establishment of the present program dated retroactive to July of 1958. This program allows the United States two types of leasehold interests: an indefinite leasehold with long-term advance payments, or a five-year minimum lease without any long-term advances. In 1959 the high commissioner replaced the USCAR land court with a U.S. Land Tribunal for the Ryukyus, to handle the haggling, but it was still academic with the condemnation action always in force. Another type of land acquired by lease by the United States is land privately owned, which is used on a temporary basis for training purposes. If the United States Army brings a new unit in preparation for battle training, and it wishes the entire area, it may then, through the co-operation of the local mayor, go in and acquire lands on a short-term basis and pay for them on a percentage of the annual rental.

The real reasons behind all these negotiations were the high land values prevailing in the Ryukyu Islands. These were not brought out immediately through the negotiations with the Hypothec Bank of Japan, but it was definite that Ryukyuan lands were valuable due to the density of population. The vast majority of U.S. land holdings in the Ryukyu Islands are in Okinawa and few on the peripheral out-islands. The island comprises 290,555 acres (some 454 square miles). The census figures show the population of Okinawa approaching the million mark, which means there are close to two thousand persons per square mile. And this population figure is steadily increasing; therefore the land is increasing in value to the natives. Although farming is the principal means by which Okinawans earn their living, there are only eighty thousand acres of arable land on the island. The rest is left wild except for the program of hilltop shaving in the north end. The United States had acquired approximately 17 per cent of this arable land for its military installations. No Okinawan may grow anything on it.

The growing season extends throughout the year, thus tilling the soil provides steady employment for an entire family or group. The children and elderly persons in most cases would not have jobs if they did not work on the family or neighboring farms. Ownership of agricultural land is a status symbol to Ryukyuans. The ownership remains with the head of the household until his death when, traditionally, title passes on to the eldest son by primogeniture. Americans cannot understand why Okinawans believe this heritage should never be sold for money. Land holdings average about one acre per owner, and this will by all means continue to uplift the Okinawan land values. In 1966 I discussed the U.S. land court program with its conceiver and former presiding judge, retired Colonel John A. King. Formerly with Judge Advocate's General section, "Old Judge King" originally came from Alabama and grew up through the civil courts in California. He hold me there was one additional problem the major land program did not cover. That was the full compensation to the Okinawans for land damaged or destroyed by the Americans during the token-payment period of July 1950 through April of 1952.

An agreement was eventually reached and a memorandum of understanding was executed by the district engineer for the U. S. Government and Ryukyuan representatives for the local people. This pact was approved by the High Commissioner, and the DE was directed to proceed with documentation and payments of about 3.8 million dollars to those with bona fide claims. D. I. Long felt this did not resolve completely the RE problem, since there remained smoldering some twenty-two million dollars in claims of the Ryukuans for damage to land and crops between the time of cessation of hostilities and the time of the treaty of peace with Japan in 1952. This matter still has not been settled.

According to the Geneva convention, the United States is not liable for war damage, but the Japanese cannot pay the sums. Even if they could, the United States would not want Japanese appraisers to come to the island and scrutinize installations in order to make their evaluations. At the same time, the Japanese do not wish to admit any responsibility. America does not wish to accept the responsibility either; however, she finds it easier to pay the twenty-two-million-dollar collective claim than to harangue with the Japanese. The U.S. Congress passed a bill in June of 1965 to make this twenty-two-million-dollar payment to the Okinawans. The RE division is set up to handle this in accordance with a formula, but as yet no appropriations have been made for it. This still poses one of the unresolved difficulties between Okinawans and Americans, but it is nonetheless provided for, and should eventually be resolved.

As its needs arise, the United States wants new land for additional installations. First it must canvass the general area to find out if American-held land is available to suit the needs. Then the facility intended to occupy the land must be good for more than a five-year tenancy. Finally, approval must come from Washington. For areas up to five acres adjoining fixed U.S. installations, Washington approval is not necessary and additional coverage may simply be embraced into the original lease without any prior approval. Through negotiation and advance payment, the U. S. Government then requires title to the new land desired for the installation, and if this cannot be done, acquisition is made by condemnation. At the end of five or more years, either a renewal is negotiated or the land is returned to its original Okinawan owner; but the United States must restore the land to the same or better condition than when it was acquired. This is still acquisition by right of eminent domain with the exception that Okinawans are being paid according to a fixed formula.

Though Ryukyan RE problems appear to be closer to resolution, the Okinawan industrial problems, which in 1946 seemed almost impossible, show a fine healthy condition in the 1960s. This was not easily accomplished. After the war, the vast quantities of military supplies on Okinawa, which could not successfully be safeguarded with the reduced number of military personnel, presented much temptation to the locals. This opportunity for theft and black marketing was fully exploited by some. Since in many instances the same item of military supply had been distributed legitimately within the local economy, illegal operators were afforded an effective cover for their transactions. For others, the condition of inflation and scarcity encouraged or even compelled the people to grow foodstuffs and improve crude facilities for the production of agricultural tools and household items from war scrap. Few of these cottage industries were fundamentally sound ventures. Most of them disappeared as better-quality and lower-priced items were later imported from Japan.

In mid-1948 an American-type banking institution, the Bank of the Ryukyus, was established in place of the Central Bank of Okinawa, and type "B" yen was made the sole legal tender in the Ryukyus. These essential provisions were the first effective steps toward economic stability. Though full purchasing power of the currency was still not achieved, nor was inflation eliminated at the time, confusion about the currency disappeared and inflation was contained effectively. This was evident in the decline of prices on essential commodities during the latter part of 1948. Smuggling continued until private foreign trade was established effectively. Nevertheless, smuggling became more difficult, as it had to be carried out through different currencies or on a barter basis. Most important of all, MG was able to regain control of the money supply.

Following these actions, ration and price controls were removed from all items except welfare and military supplies. Restrictions on domestic commerce within and among the islands were relaxed. Exports were allowed on a government-to-government basis with Japan. Even though private imports of merchandise was not permitted, the variety and quantity of consumer goods brought in under the welfare program increased. As a means of encouraging the development of private enterprise, welfare items for personal consumption, other than staple foods, were sold to legal wholesalers for resale at fixed prices, and military surplus materials were turned over to fisheries, agricultural, and industrial associations and other production and service enterpries at prices well below the original costs of these items. It was not expected that a stable, free-enterprise economy would be approached even as a result of these limited measures. However, a greater flow and exchange of goods was achieved and private commercial organizations increased in size and number. Within one month after controls were removed, the price index of five major commodities declined 9 per cent. Many farmers who had grown only food crops during the inflation period began to direct their efforts to sugar cane, the traditional cash crop of the Ryukyus. Others joined the gradually increasing military labor force, or devoted more of their time to fishing, charcoal production, and other secondary prewar occupations.

In just four years, the island which cost the U. S. so much in all ways had outlived its usefulness. Ryukyuan matters were of scant concern to Pentagon powers. The man in the market had forgotten, and even the press all but stopped mentioning Okinawa. One summer day in 1949 I offhandedly asked a colleague, "Where are the Ryukyus?" His answer was, "How should I know? If you'd organize, you'd know where you left your things." The centers of occupational and tourist attention had become Tokyo and Berlin. The duties of the occupation soldiers began to be concerned with protecting those poor people and their outlying neighbors from Communism.

The American citizen-soldier who had actually won the war was replaced by the callow youth who grew up through wartime austerity and was now demanding his creature comforts from the armed services. The dilution in the

U.S. forces overseas became evident in their field performance. And from these only the worst were sent to "The Rock" to augument the Filipino Scouts. But the Philippines became a sovereign nation and their soldiers were returning to their homes, leaving the Ryukyuan occupation to the American hindmost. Anywhere in the Pacific, unruly troops were kept in check with the threats that "goof-ups get shipped to Okinawa."

Even as late as 1946 Okinawa was a reasonably beautiful island, only the unrepaired, unrestored wakes of natural typhoon damage and the approaching poverty-stricken hopelessness of much of the native population combined to make a physical and emotional shambles of the Ryukyus. One American news-photo magazine ran a searing article in December 1949 calling it "The Okinawa Junk Heap," accusing the commanding general of refusing even "to let the American correspondents see the damage." Even the atmosphere was bad. Americans donated surplus rubber tires in order to help fuelless native salt plants operate. Tires were burned at the rate of eight stinking tons per day. Other surplus articles of war not already taken by the Chinese purchasing mission were scrounged by the locals, allowed to rust and rot, heaped in ruinous stretches which daily became more desolate. Boredom set in. When outdoor movies or occasional USO shows ceased to augment underground drinking, dice, and doxies, the troops again went after the Okinawans. In the first six months of 1949, American soldiers robbed and/or assaulted forty-nine, raped eighteen, and murdered twenty-nine innocent Ryukyuans.

Then there was talk about a complete deactivation of the bases and possible "abandonment" of the island, if only a way could be worked out to continue operations from and maintenance of nine active airfields which the Air Force needed for its tactical jets. (This idea still rears its ugly form in 1968!) Unwilling to believe accounts of the conditions, in 1949, Tracy Voorhees, Assistant Secretary of the Army, made a personal and unannounced tour of inspection of Okinawa. He was flabbergasted with what he saw. At this point, the course of events in the Ryukyus was profoundly affected by serious developments on the international scene, and a natural disaster. The importance of Okinawa as a vital link in the security of the free world and in particular as a bastion for the protection of Japan and other areas of the Far East was recognized. Army Major General Josef R. Sheetz and Air Force Major General Alvin Kincaid, two able and understanding men, were sent to assume the Ryukyuan command. They were firmly ordered to eliminate the load of four years of neglect. Congress appropriated 58 million dollars toward a thorough, organized cleanup. But there was still serious talk in some quarters about pull-out "before we are forced to feed seven hundred thousand Ryukyuans."

During 1948 and 1949, the Ryukyus were devastated by five severe typhoons. Typhoon Gloria of July 22–23, 1949, with winds of 175 mph, was the most destructive in the history of the islands. Since virtually no "permanent-type" structures existed on Okinawa, destruction of both military and civilian facilities and supplies was vast. Total damage was estimated at eighty million dollars. This created an emergency situation almost as severe as that which existed in the early postwar period, but now there existed in the Ryukyus a fundamental institutional framework in MG, and a more organized society, which made it possible to cope with this emergency more effectively and expeditiously.

Following this disaster, a selected group of American engineers went to Okinawa and made a thorough study of military requirements for permanent-type construction, with emphasis upon facilities such as harbors, roads, electric power plants, and transmission lines, which possibly could be of joint benefit to the U.S. forces and the resident Ryukyuan community. The government-assistance programs for fiscal years 1950 and 1951, which totaled eighty-six million dollars, provided approximately thirty-one million dollars for construction of such facilities, as well as increased amounts for the rehabilitation of other community services and basic natural resources. An additional 2.8 million dollars was also appropriated in fiscal year 1952 for the completion of these construction projects.

Security considerations required that the United States retain control of the Ryukyus until tensions in the Far East subsided. For this strategic importance of Okinawa to be achieved, it was believed necessary to proceed with the immediate construction of an extensive permanent military-base complex. Long-range programs for more fundamental rehabilitation and development of the Ryukyus were both necessary and practicable of achievement as a result of this enlarged strategic mission and prolonged occupation of these islands.

Outside situations brought about internal changes. Korea again became a battleground. The United States again needed a nearby staging area and Okinawa was automatically it.

# CHAPTER 6

# Scapegoat Scouts

To accomplish any special mission, one best assigns it to an expert in that specialty. And that was the way it was with jungle fighting against the Japanese. Those with the greatest protracted, organized experience in this specialty were the Filipinos. Philippine Scouts in the Army of the United States (under Philippine or American officers) were widely used to great advantage in the Okinawan campaign, especially in the rugged north.

These people were superb at ferreting out Japanese ambushes, booby traps, and snipers. One day early in September 1946 I was headed north a bit beyond Genka. The road runs along the west shore about ten feet above the sea. Landward the wooded hills rise sharply along the line of plain coast. As I was thinking of the job at hand and what I was going to do later that evening, I was jarred back to reality by a sudden large hole in the windshield, followed by the whistling of a bullet out over the ocean. A second one slammed through the jeep floor and skipped along the road into the water. Unfortunately I did not take off at high speed to get out of the neighborhood. Instead I stalled out the jeep and dived into the roadside ditch. One or two more shots fell not far from me.

I don't know how long I lay in the ditch. Soon, from the north, a 6 x 6 truck came with some Filipino Scouts. A lieutenant stopped the truck and stepped out to investigate. When I told him what had happened, he sat on a rock beside me after giving quick instructions in Tagalog (the Philippine national tongue) to two of his Scouts. The two disappeared quickly and soon returned as silently as they had vanished. One of them held a prized samurai sword and a Japanese battle flag; the other had a very beautiful Mitsubishi rifle complete with telescopic sights and dust covers. Both saluted the lieutenant and this time addressed him in good English, one saying, "I am sorry, sir, we find no one there." Again they saluted and, with their loot, got back into the waiting truck. The lieutenant snuffed out his cigarette and boarded, saying, "I think you'll find it safe now to resume your journey." We shook hands before he went on his way and I continued on mine.

Philippine Scouts were brought to Okinawa in organized units for a specific task. They carried out their mission with courage, dispatch, and élan. As a whole, they showed little or no interest in remaining in the Ryukyus past the duration of their assignment, because they had a nearby homeland which had just been liberated from four years of Japanese occupation. It had also just become a new republic, and President Roxas needed every available man to rebuild the nation. The repatriation of Filipino units began in 1947; then the U.S. military hierarchy felt perhaps it might be better to "let *them* man the occupation" and send the U.S. personnel "stateside." To accompany the Scouts, hundreds of Filipinos from all walks of life, male and female, were brought in to help train and guide the Okinawans.

Ryukyuans and Filipinos got on well together. They enjoyed a sort of ethnic empathy without the taint of any previous Chinese or Japanese association. Thus some progress was made in Ryukyuan rehabilitation. The Philippine Scouts not only participated in the battle for Okinawa, but they were retained afterward to help American troops and the Okinawan people understand each other.

The first U.S. policy regarding Filipinos shortly after the campaign—to send them back to assist their homeland—was then countermanded due to the realization that these people could be used to a great common good for assistance with development of the Okinawans. Also for ease in dealing with the Okinawans on behalf of the Americans, it offered the Filipinos a chance to do something for themselves in a pioneering way if they did not wish to go back and refurbish their own homeland.

A good many Filipinos were kept to fill both the military posts and the civilian positions. Many Filipino girls came to be companions for the Filipino men, and also to fill some supervisory positions. It must be understood that they came at the request of the United States—and voluntarily.

The American attitude that America fought and won the island of Okinawa and therefore should be its lord and master can be extrapolated to include the Filipinos, because the Filipinos were among those who fought the Japanese and won the island for the Allied cause.

In the fall of 1963 a ten-year-old general ruling was enforced for all Filipinos. Regardless of position, they were to be returned home to the Republic of the Philippines. There was much American objection. Feeling was strong that after so many years of residence the majority of the Filipinos were conveniently to be sent home because they were no longer "needed." However, those Filipinos who held key positions had to be retained since no qualified Okinawan replacements were available. It was advantageous to the Americans to keep them, since the cost in salaries of replacing them by Americans would be exorbitant and it was impossible to replace them with Okinawans. This plan met with a great deal of disfavor, since Americans were again accused of duplicity.

Filipinos who were on Okinawa had been there for some ten to fifteen years and they had adapted admirably. They got on well with all people and created absolutely no problems whatever. Suddenly enforcing a ten-year-old policy was somewhat arbitrary and shortsighted. Originally it had been anticipated that within a decade from 1953 enough Okinawans would have been trained to replace the Filipinos. But this was not the case and in 1963, apparently just because the policy was there, they felt obligated to follow it.

This was an injustice to the Filipinos. Hadn't they been in the Ryukyus for a decade, some for a decade and a half, and hadn't many of them given up contact with their homeland, even though it was so close? In addition, the majority adjusted well to their new life on Okinawa and they may very well have felt like foreigners upon return to their own country.

The attitude of those Filipinos who were left with the burden of rebuilding the Philippines while the others went off, apparently to seek their fortune elsewhere, was not considered. Their resentment toward the repatriates is only natural. Moreover, unlike the Americans on Okinawa and surrounding islands, the Filipinos took an active part in Ryukyuan life. Though they always remained a foreign community, they never isolated themselves from the Okinawans.

The general resentment over U.S. Civil Service on Okinawa employing people of Japanese and Chinese origin or extraction made it appear as if the Filipinos were being discriminated against. They had been fine citizens in the Ryukyus, and the local people felt very reluctant to see them go. Eventually, though the policy was never rescinded, it was never in truth enforced. Gradually the Filipinos in small numbers went home on their own, until just a few remained in the Ryukyus to keep their supervisory positions. This was the way one "problem" resolved itself to spare the United States further embarrassment in the oriental community.

# CHAPTER 7

# Where *Do* We Stand?

Amorphous is the only word to describe the U.S. position with regard to the Ryukyus. The American posture on Okinawa appears to those at home as "for the duration" of the Far Eastern tensions; to the Japanese it is residual sovereignty soon; to the Okinawans it is reversion eventually; to the rest of the area it is for the life of SEATO. Hopefully, America will come to realize that one cannot be all things to all people.

Unfortunately, the United States hastily passed up the Ryukyuan suggestion for annexation and now must try to live with an alien people who have adopted some poor examples of Americans on their return road to Japanization. Nippon too (without losing its own ethnic identity), has taken to its heart neon signs, pizza stands, rock-and-roll, "B"-girls, mini skirts, and bargain basements. In meeting its obligation to Far Eastern security, the United States owns billions of dollars worth of tangible goods irretrievably implanted in Ryukyuan soil. The American presence is the basis for the local economy and industry. And the people seem to want to live in a perpetual present, forgetting the past and eschewing the future.

In today's Okinawa, the U.S. military personnel, living on miliary reservations under military regulations, is attended by American civilians. Some of the latter are employed by the forces, and are themselves subject to military regulation. The rest are under Civil Administration law, and are disdainfully regarded, along with other American nongovernment people, as "commercial entrants." Nearly a million Ryukyuans live under a law code set up and enforced by themselves.

There is utter chaos when a triple motor collision involves vehicles owned and driven by an Okinawan, an American merchant, and a military man; or when a person from one group wishes to take a man from another into litigation. Fortunately, life is more peaceful than would be reasonably expected, due mainly to the placid nature of the Ryukyuans and the deep regard by all for the serious reasons behind the continuing American presence there. But this presence means different things to the various peoples concerned.

For the United States it means a great responsibility as well as much pride in accomplishment which it must not exhibit. For the Japanese (without the strangling burden of a military budget) the American armed presence in the Ryukyus means their national security on a nearly gratis basis. But it also puts off indefinitely the day of Ryukyuan "reversion" to them. For the Ryukyuans, U.S. bases means jobs, money, security, and the second highest living standard in Asia. Possibly it is chauvinism which forces the natives to clamor for an end of the "occupation." And occupation it *is,* according to the Department of Defense, which classifies Okinawa along with West Berlin as the only two occupied areas residual from World War II. In eighty-two gory spring days of 1945, the U.S. armed strength won from Japan the indisputable right to possession of the Ryukyu Islands. For this force-of-arms triumph over the Japanese, the U.S. lost ten thousand young men, who, with their predecessors, died to finish a desperate four-year conflict America neither started nor wanted.

The term "gook," an epithet equal in opprobrium to "nigger," "kike," or "wop," and having none of the semi-affection of "harp," "bohunk," or "limey," has been completely unheard in the area since the late 1950s. It was once the only way the postwar occupation soldiers addressed the natives. Though it grew to be a term of disdain, it did not begin that way. Americans landing on Saipan and other Japanese-held Pacific Islands were greeted by non-combatant natives with the Japanese term for foreigner, "outside countrymen" or Gai-koku-jin. In the exchange of "me no Gaikokuwhat, you Gai-ko," the transition to "gook" followed a quick, unhealthy downhill evolution, the complete reverse of how Americans acquired the name "Yankee" from the British in the Revolution.

Although the objectives and character of the American fighting man today are vastly different from those of the men who achieved the 1945 Okinawa victory and thereby ended World War II, Okinawa-based military personnel of the present are unanimous—and the few aging veterans of the campaign concur—in the opinion that the United States must remain to man the garrisons and ramparts of Okinawa. The Ryukyus, not the Asian mainland, form our security frontier. They must remain, these men agree, as the first line of America's defenses, as long as even the slightest hint of nonsecurity exists in that part of the world.

In deferring to this need for security, my initial request to the Department of Defense when I began this book was for ". . . access to all *un*classified locations," and the military questions in my 1966 interviews with the High Commissioner involved unclassified information relatable for public consumption. In effect, all Okinawa is one tremendous American base. U.S. installations of all the armed services cover so much territory on and under Ryukyuan ground that isolation of the bases is virtually impossible. There are nearly two hundred thousand Americans in the Ryukyus; about half are in uniform, and nearly an equal number comprise dependent families, civilian employees (some with kin), and Americans on private economy, doing nonmilitary business. There are virtually no non-American "foreigners." The bulk of U.S. citizenry in the Ryukyus forms army, air force, and navy installations. The Army includes the U. S. Army Engineer District, and the Navy includes the Marine Corps. In order to get a general idea of their structure and purpose, I offer a cursory look at each of these services.

While standing as the bulwark of the first line of Pacific defense, the U. S. Army in the Ryukyu Islands, headed by the High Commissioner in his other role as commanding general of USARYIS and IX Corps, has three principal tasks on Okinawa. First, the Army's day-to-day logistical operation on Okinawa involves all those things which stem from supporting an American population comparable to any large Stateside city: providing electrical power, operating a basic military system, running a wholesale grocery business, maintaining the island's highway system, operating the American school system, and running a major military (and commercial) seaport. The second logistical mission supports military operations in the Far East. Centrally and strategically located on the forward edge of the free world, Okinawa is the most important base in the Pacific. In any emergency it serves as a forward staging area and a logistical supply base. The Army is also prepared to expand its logistical base for defense against attack. The 30th Artillery Brigade (Air Defense), with its missile units, will assist the Air Force in air defense.

Operationally, IX Corps commands the deployable army units on Okinawa, the real *force* units ready to move on short notice to any trouble spot in the Far East. These units include an Airborne Infantry Brigade, a Special Forces Group, a Logistical Command, a Broadcasting and Visual Activities unit, a Utility Tactical Transport Helicopter Company (in 1965 deployed to South Vietnam), and the 999th Airborne Brigade (separate) of some three thousand paratroopers capable of moving quickly to any area in the western Pacific under actual or potential invasion. The Special Forces Group (Green Berets) develops, organizes, and controls guerrilla forces in support of military operations. In the cold war it advises and assists our allies in combating terrorist activities. The 9th Logistical Command is a deployable field unit providing logistical support to combat units in the western Pacific area. Subordinate units representing each major technical service are Engineer, Signal, Quartermaster, Transportation, Chemical, and Ordnance. In any combat situation, these units will move rapidly from Okinawa in co-ordination with air force, naval and marine forces; or the forces of our SEATO allies.

Since U.S. Army Engineer District, Okinawa (USAEDO) first came into being, under Colonel L. B. Washbourne, February 18, 1946, a vast variety of construction projects have been undertaken. These range from civil projects like the new million-dollar Bank of the Ryukyus building in downtown Naha to the missile silo facilities and troop camps recently built to back up the U.S. Vietnam effort. All these projects have had, in common, the technical skill and supervision of USAEDO personnel during all stages of design, planning, preparation, and construction. Millions of dollars have been, and more are being, spent on projects from which both the civilian and military population of Okinawa will derive benefits. In support of USCAR and GRI, USAEDO has been responsible for construction of all essential utilities, highways, port facilities, and other miscellaneous structures needed for the defense facilities and the civilian populace. Inspectors and other technical personnel from USAEDO are always present at all construction projects to insure compliance with contract specifications and army regulations.

Basically their job, which they have done well, is to try to see that the United States gets what it pays for. It is, in effect what the public works department of an equivalent civic organization would be. It has no money of its own, but carefully spends the funds of the "owning agency," whether it be the Bank of the Ryukyus' million dollars, for a new building, or the Army's endless funds in maintaining or operating Army utility—responsibility projects.

A most significant island-wide project of the district engineer (DE) is the Kin power plant located near Kin village about thirty miles north of Naha on the Pacific Coast. This power plant, producing 88,000 kw, instead of becoming a supplement to the island power system, has become the main source of power. Kin plant consists in a large reinforced concrete building to house the four turbo-generators, and all ancillary structures necessary for its flawless continuous operation. Under contract with Gilbert Pacific Company, the Army is responsible for the electric power systems on Okinawa, operating the integrated power system which ties into the local distribution net. The Army has three other major plants for generating power: the Machinato steam plant, the Impedance power barge at Naha port, and the Jacona power barge in Sukiran Basin. Including diesel power plants totaling nearly 40,000 kw—and the Kin power was added to the sources—there is an Okinawa-connected capacity of 169,000 kw.

The water system is presently being expanded by some 25 per cent to make additional water available from the integrated system for use of the local population through the Ryukyuan Domestic Water Corporation (RDWC), and further expansion is under study now. The Army operates the island water system and delivers about twenty-four to twenty-six million gallons per day to all users. Okinawa's paved highway system is Army constructed and maintained. The Army pays the GRI rental for the land under the roads: twenty miles of four-lane black-top highway (Naha to Kadena), and 112 miles of two-lane black-top highway (from Camp Schwab in the north to Chinen Peninsula in the south), are maintained by the Army. The Army operates the connecting lines of the island military telephone system. Each military service operates its own on-base telephone exchange. The Army also operates Okinawa terminals of a global communications system. Army's StarCom receiver and transmitter serve all military agencies on Okinawa except the Air Force, which has its own global communications system.

The Okinawa military petroleum, oil, and lubricant (POL) system is Army operated. Off-loading docks are at Chimu-Wan, White Beach, and Naha with various petroleum tank farms scattered throughout the Island. The Army provides about a half million gallons of POL per day to all U.S. forces. For emergency cases, this ties in with the civilian American and native POL systems, although the two are independent of each other. The Ryukyu Oil Company, a 100 per cent native-owned organization, has been granted the sole distribution rights for all civilian POL. It, in turn, enfranchises local stations as individual private businesses. Some are American, but nearly all are Okinawan owned. The distributor's source too is a monopoly. In 1960, open tenders for this concession were asked by the United States, and Caltex was the low bidder for a three-year contract. This has been renewed each three years thereafter, and Caltex is now entrenched. Caltex has also acquired the direct sales to air lines for all commercial fuel used at Naha International Airport, as well as some POL products to the military. The domestic automotive fuel price for only the one grade sold at the retail pump is regulated by the High Commissioner at 23¢ per U.S. gallon.

All the airports in the Ryukyus are maintained by the same Corps of Engineers which enlarged some and built others. Most were originally planned or built by the Japanese. At one period straddling the war's end, ten airfields on Okinawa and nine on Ie Shima were operational for tactical aircraft. Eventually these nineteen airstrips were disposed of in a manner which best suited the needs of the time and place. Of the nine strips on Ie Shima, the eastern and westernmost, are reasonably well maintained for occasional aircraft. Ie is serviced by helicopter, and no normal, operational flights are scheduled there. One Ie strip has been incorporated into the perimeter highway system; three are slowly being destroyed by air-force bomb practice runs; and three have been abandoned to the elements. Weathering and the irrepressible penetration of weeds growing up from below the subgrade contribute daily to their demise.

Of the ten on Okinawa, Awase has been converted to the antennae area for the Ryukyus station of the Air Force global communications system; Bolo's northern end is incorporated into the missile firing area, while the southern part is unused; Futema, once reduced to an MG labor pool site, is today a live and busy operational strip for Marine Corps aviation; Kin is now in and under the Marines' Camp Hansen; Machinato presently supports the permanent plant and warehouse structures of the Quartermaster's Machinato Supply Depot; Motobu, dormant and weathering, is unused but stands at Marine disposition; Yonabaru has been returned to the Okinawans to become the decking for a large sugar mill which stands at its middle; Yontan boasts a jump school for paratroops which sublets a small facility to a private flying school; Kadena has been enlarged and developed into gigantic dimensions. It has become the prime base for tactical and strategic air operations in the area. Since the Vietnamese escalation, Kadena has served as a way station for refueling and arming Guam-based B-52s. Finally, Naha airstrip, once the site of an important phase of the 1945 battle, is today the busiest field of its kind in the Orient. It serves as the international port of entry into the Ryukyus.

In 1947, Pan American pioneered a negotiation with the U. S. Government for way-station privileges. Due to its strategic location at the hub of the western Pacific region, Naha affords a natural fueling and rest juncture. Pan American was also interested in carrying the influx of civilians once the island was "opened." Then, within a decade, the dwindling American movements, combined with the longer flight range of the jet aircraft, caused Okinawa to suffer the same bypassed way-station fate as Shannon, Ireland, and Sondre Strom Fjord, Greenland, and Pan American bowed out. Yet by 1960, commercial airlines of Taiwan, the Philippine Republic, Japan, and the United States were making a surprisingly large number of scheduled runs to Naha from Tokyo, Manila, Taipei, Hong Kong, and some southern Japanese cities. Although everyone entering at Naha must go through customs and immigration, Japan regards Okinawa trips as "domestic flights." (I was prohibited from taking any photographs during my official Okinawa helicopter briefing overflight in January 1966. Yet any person, regardless of nationality, is free to take as many pictures as he wishes from the windows of any commercial aircraft flying in and out of Naha.)

Naha airport is also the terminal for the 115th Air Division's three troop carrier squadrons. Military Air Transport Service (MATS) flights are constantly moving in and out, and tactical aircraft also use the strip. The huge commercial terminal building on this busy military air base is a further incongruity associated with Okinawa, yet the field is not as it was at the war's end when the flyers used to sing of it:

*"You can stand at Naha airstrip*
*Any hour of any day—*
*You can see those 46s*
*As they cream into the bay!"*

There is one more small field these days—Hamby Field, close to the first Love-Day landing site, is a helicopter and small aircraft facility for VIP flights and special missions for the High Commissioner. It is not an Air Force installation, but belongs to the Army. Lieutenant Hamby, for whom this vest-pocket vehicle park was named, was a liaison pilot of a Piper Cub observation craft who was killed in action in the early days of the 1945 campaign—a hero in the annals of army aviation, something distinct from the Air Force.

There are no trains on the island. In the prewar days there was an old Japanese steam-driven, narrow-gauge railroad which ran from Naha to Kadena, with a spur from Naha uphill to Shuri. Another steam line connected Naha to Awase. In the long, long ago there was a short horse-drawn line which ran from Naha down to Itoman. This was more like a streetcar, and was sometime later replaced by a small steam line, which in turn, was discontinued. All the Okinawa railroads were destroyed in the battle. Since then, the United States has found no need whatever for restoring them. Mid-island, the only remnant was an old Japanese station building once called the Kuwae station. This old concrete structure was actually a warehouse in the prewar Okinawan prefectural railway, which suffered only slight battle scarring. It remained in its damaged condition until June 1955, when the Army acquired it on official property records. Patching it up, the Army used the building for target storage at Moskala range until December 9, 1965, when the Fort Buckner post engineer razed the building.

No trace of the old railroad now remains other than an old length of track here and there, or a stray railroad car which some Okinawan at the south end will use for a dwelling or a store. Since the right-of-way land of the railroad belonged to the Japanese Prefecture, and was not Okinawan territory per se, it does not fall under any real estate agreement and consequently remains "U. S. Occupied Territory." As such, the old railroad right-of-way is of free use to Americans, and is now utilized for POL pipelines. One may now trace the old railroad through current POL lines or, conversely, by following old railroad maps one can now locate POL lines.

Japan today has a very fine monorail which runs between Tokyo and Haneda airport, furnishing public two-way rapid transportation. Ryukyuans who have visited Japan schemed to copy this idea for Okinawa. It did not meet with American approval, but in order to assuage the feelings of the Okinawans, USCAR invited a top-level team from Japan (the same group which assayed the existing monorail in Tokyo) to evaluate a proposed pilot line from Naha to Shuri. Their conclusion was that under no circumstances could it ever pay its way. Consequently the suggestion was dropped because the Japanese concluded that it was not economical. The Okinawans then suggested that the United States build a monorail between Naha and Kadena for the Marines, which the Okinawans would run as an enterprise. The Marine Corps refused to go along with this, and from then on all ideas for an Okinawa monorail ceased. The only place in the entire Ryukyu chain where any railroad now exists is the off-shore island of Mawami Daito, with a small, narrow-gauge line. It is an island perimeter railroad whose width is about 2½ feet between centers of rails, the total perimeter line length thirteen miles. Its fifty stops are all used, but only for cane pickup during sugar harvesting. This one train was pulled by an old German-made Meiji-style steam locomotive replaced in 1966 by a ten-ton diesel engine at a cost of just $12,000.

Basic responsibility for all these public works rests with the district engineer,

Colonel George A. Austin, Jr., C of E, a Regular Army man. He was on Okinawa briefly in 1948, and in 1965 returned to be the district engineer. He described his mission as one to provide engineering design and construction services to all armed forces in the Ryukyus as well as to other U. S. Government agencies when requested. He acts as agent for the "owning organization," and as contracting officer. Having no funds of his own, the DE spends only the money of the owning agency, whether it be Navy, Air Force, civilian, or Marine. Civil works for the local economy are built from USCAR, not GRI, funds, and include the electric corporation and the water works. Things like the Bank of the Ryukyus building, etc., are built with private funds.

"The construction industry here has matured at a really good pace," Colonel Austin said, "and due to this, now only U.S. and Ryukyuan contractors are eligible for job bids." Japanese contractors were eliminated as soon as the locals were able to mount a responsible competent force. This also eliminated any Japanese property encroachments or claim opportunities.

Projects in the mill include a ten-million-gallon-per-day reservoir and distribution system for the Ryukyuan Water Company at Ishikawa; a pipeline to feed down raw water from the north, and a big storage tank at Naha. To accommodate this, the American Concrete Pipe Company put 1.7 million dollars into a reinforced concrete pressure pipe factory near the Bolo Point missile range. There are also hopes of expanding the land mass by fifteen per cent or about eight square miles in the next fifteen to twenty years, by reclaiming offshore areas, especially coral-based territory in shallow waters. Eldridge Lovelace, an American consultant, has succeeded in adding a section to Tomari port which is now used as a driving school.

The Air Force on Okinawa springs a "scramble" on the duty force every single day. Only the time is a surprise. The command "Scramble" is barked over a red telephone. From the moment of that terse signal until the time a squadron of fully armed jet fighter-bombers is rolling down the runway, nearly three minutes will have elapsed. This activity keeps these fighter pilots tuned up. The ready room is manned around the clock by thoroughly briefed fliers in full flight dress who attempt to relax by reading or playing poker. But each one's ear is at the red telephone, and one eye is on a locked leather briefcase marked "Top Secret," which carries the specific counter-attack plans should that call be real. Once the "scramble" is on, klaxon-called ground crews, who keep the aircraft keyed up as tightly as the pilots, get the F-105 Thunderchiefs ready to roar. In an instant each skipper tumbles aboard and guns his baby out. Not until a hot pilot checks the tower for take-off clearance does he learn if this flight is the "goods" or not. It has to happen once a day.

If the real call ever comes, no one can afford to fumble, and that is why a base alert affects everyone at any base. In pursuit of its assigned task, the U. S. Air Force on Okinawa, Pacific Air Force's 313th Air Division, has two primary missions. It is responsible for aerial defense of the Ryukyus, and for preparing assigned and attached units for combat missions. Two of the top fighter wings provide the deterrent air power of the 313th: the 18th Tactical Fighter Wing at Kadena, and the 51st Fighter Interceptor Wing at Naha; it also has units as weather stations, communication facilities, and firing ranges in outlying islands. Supporting organizations for these primary units include photo reconnaissance, airlift and troop carrier, communication units, medical facilities, air rescue, and many other specialized outfits necessary in maintaining aerospace deterrent power and, hopefully, peace.

At Naha Air Base, three troop carrier squadrons equipped with C-130 Hercules aircraft are assigned to Detachment One of the 315th A.D. The Hercules is a large four-engine personnel and cargo carrier which makes many round trips to Southeast Asian trouble spots. The 31th A.D. is the successor to the Twentieth Air Force of B-29 heavy bombardment fame in the Far East during World War II. It is now a portion of the Fifth Air Force, based at Fuchu Air Station, Japan. The Fifth, in turn, is an element of Pacific Air Force, with headquarters in Hawaii.

Relief from the tension of hair-trigger air force duty on Okinawa is readily had at Okuma Beach and Rest Center located between a forest of Voice of America radio antennae and a hillside of Japanese cherry trees on the northwest coast. This litttle paradise boasts a mild, cool, shallow white sand beach. On- and offshore fishing are superb, water sports unparalleled, and sea food dinners unequalled in New Orleans.

Also abundant in the sea round the Islands is the Navy. U. S. Fleet Activities, Ryukyus, was commissioned in April 1957 as a shore activity assigned to the operating forces of the U. S. Navy in the Pacific Theater, responsible to Commander, U. S. Naval Forces, Japan, and under the management control of the Bureau of Naval Weapons. The mission of FAR is to co-ordinate the provision of logistic support to units of the U. S. Seventh Fleet calling at both Buckner Bay and Naha port; and to maintain liaison with other military services in the islands.

The U. S. Naval Air Facility at Naha Air Base is Command HQ. It operates a Navy Port Services Office at White Beach, on Katchin Hanto Peninsula, Buckner Bay, which assigns anchorages, makes arrangements for pier berths, and co-ordinates delivery of fuel and provisions to fleet units calling in the Ryukyus. The Navy Port Services Office at White Beach also maintains a boat basin to facilitate the movement of liberty and cargo barges to and from the ships at anchor in the bay. The Navy also operates and maintains an Officers' and an Enlisted Open Mess at White Beach, along with one of the outstanding recreational facilities in the Pacific area, including ball fields, basketball and volleyball courts, picnic facilities, a swimming pool, and a bowling alley. These facilities are primarily for the land use of the units of the Seventh Fleet calling at Buckner Bay.

The U. S. Marine Corps is on Okinawa in full strength. The 3rd Marine

Division (Reinforced), Fleet Marine Force, is a war-born unit which came into maturity during World War II campaigns at Guam, Bougainville, and Iwo Jima. Spending almost all its life on foreign soil, the "3rd" was deactivated at the war's end. In the waning days of the Korean conflict, it was called up again. Arriving in bulk in Japan in August 1953, it was moved to Okinawa by 1957. The 3rd Division's mission is "to execute amphibious assault operations as may be directed, supported by Marine aviation and Force Troop units. Movement is the normal order of the day for the 3rd MD. This ready force, with the inherent mobility of the fleet, is prepared to move on short notice anywhere that sea or air transport will take it. Under the operational control of the Commander, Seventh Fleet, it is capable of quick-reaction deployment as the ground element of the Marine air-ground team in the Far East. Each 3rd MD camp on the island is named for a marine who gave his life and was awarded the Medal of Honor posthumously for heroism during the 1945 battle for Okinawa. Camp Schwab, the northernmost, was the first permanent marine camp establishment on the island, completed in October 1959. Ten miles south is Camp Hansen. Camp Hauge, ten miles farther south, is the home of the newly activated Shore Party Battalion. Across the road from Hauge is Camp Kinser, the home of the Mobile Construction Battalion (Seabees). Located within the confines of Camp McTureous are the Headquarters of both the 3rd Service Battalion and Camp Smedley D. Butler. The 12th Marine Artillery and the 3rd Force Service Regiment occupy areas and quarters at Camp Sukiran, and the newest of the typhoon-proof marine camps on Okinawa is Camp Courtney, expanded to full strength since Vietnam. Other marine units on Okinawa are the MC Air Facility, Futema, and Marine Barracks, Naha.

In a land where the people burn incense in their religious pursuits, the Americans' burning of solid rocket fuel in their military pursuits causes a good deal of native concern.

The 1944 maturity of radar (which made it possible to measure the changing distance to any flying object instantaneously) and the electronic computer (which converts distance, speed, and other pertinent data to firing instructions instantaneously), parlayed with the development of rocketry to make the Missile Age a reality for the Defense Department. The first U.S. air defense missile was conceived at Fort Bliss, Texas, late in 1944, and with it the basic plans for an air defense weapon system so sound in principle and flexible in application that it remains in 1968 substantially unchanged from its origin. The 1949 rout of Chiang Kai-shek to Taiwan necessitated the U.S. organization of the Okinawa air defense to constrain any possible Chinese new-found strength erupting from its mainland home out into the western Pacific. Thus the 97th Anti-Aircraft Group was activated with conventional weapons. In 1959, part of it converted to Nike-Hercules missiles. A year later, two HAWK missile battalions were added and so, fully modernized, it was redesignated the 30th Artillery

Brigade, comprised of four battalions, the 1st, 3rd, 61st, and 63rd. The 1st is the U. S. Army's oldest artillery unit. The 3rd, since the War of 1812, has served in Florida, Washington Territory, the Philippine insurrection, China's Boxer Rebellion, and crossed the Rhine at Remagen Bridge in 1944. The 63rd was under General Buckner in his Aleutian rout of the Japanese in 1943. And the 61st, converted on Okinawa in 1959, was the first unit to accomplish on-site firing of the Hercules missile outside the United States. The 30th gets radar technical maintenance support from the 86th Signal Detachment; and the 51st Fighter Interceptor Wing of the 313th Air Division, USAF, co-ordinates with the brigade to insure Okinawa's airtight defense.

Brigadier General James S. Billups, Jr., the commanding officer of the 30th, is a big man with a smile. At firings he is a ubiquitous and busy general who reminded me so much of the late General George Patton, complete with pearl-handled revolver in a custom leather holster, and belt with a gold buckle. He speaks firmly but softly, and knows his business completely. He has no easy command. It is a collection of small installations flung out to the far corners of Okinawa and Tokashiki islands. Yet it is a unified command with alert officers, and men kept in perfect combat condition through constant drill in surface-to-air missiles. On each firing site, the systems of the Hercules and HAWK missiles are subjected to daily checks to insure an instant "go," if ever necessary.

Sham tracking missions in which the 51st Wing aircraft pose as "attacking" elements provide additional live training. But once a year at Annual Service Practice (ASP), the training tells. In all other missile commands, ASP means that a firing crew from each unit travels to Fort Bliss, Texas, for an annual week of intensive exercises, culminating in an actual pair of firings. On Okinawa, however, it is all done at the Bolo Point Nike-Hercules range No. 1. All Nike units use that No. 1 installation. All HAWK units, being portable, bring up their own tactical equipment for firing out over the China Sea. Each of the eight pairs of units gets a week on the range and a Friday firing session from early January through late February. All "Herc" missiles are fired at a mythical target and, being ground controlled, are ground detonated at a calculated kill point. The HAWKs actually seek out and destroy a drone target missile, launched from a "mother" aircraft in flight. All of ASP is scored for proficiency by an expert team of evaluators; and there is a prize for top ASP battery.

Warnings are posted on land and broadcast to sea well in advance of ASP dates to keep ocean traffic away from the firing range limits. It is this loss of fishing time, plus the noise, the fire trails, and the psychological effects that annually cause a furor among the villagers in the entire west-central area. Toward relieving the frenzies of the Okinawans, local mayors, legislators, and other ward dignitaries were invited to a firing session as a public relations gesture, since ASP will not be discontinued.

It was a cold, damp, January day that the VIP stands were filled with Okinawan leaders, U.S. officers of various services, some VIP dependents, and some journalists. It was a long affair with nearly forty-five minutes between firings. At the outset, the time was used in bilingual explanations of the entire procedure, well illustrated with expensive models. The intermission times grew heavy, and there was a biting, chilling wind.

The Okinawans were calling the missiles "udodan" and "dondudan," two Japanese words for rockets ("dan" means "loud"). Complaining about having to beat out brush fires caused by the falling of burning solid fuel, an Okinawan mayor was being assuaged by the 30th's incumbent public relations officer, a cheerful Lieutenant Bernacchi. In another spot, an Okinawan warmly shared his blanket with a shivering GI while neither could understand the other's conversation. The big firecrackers we all went out to see were spectacular and impressive, even though two did not fire that morning. The Nike and the HAWK systems are complementary, although they function differently, while accomplishing the same four tasks: detecting, identifying, tracking, and killing the target.

HAWK means *H*oming *A*ll the *W*ay *K*iller. It is a portable system meant for mobile use by forward ground troops. Designed for transportational mobility in fixed-wing aircraft or helicopter, it is relatively simple and unerringly accurate. Carrying a "modern" explosive charge, HAWK fires off horizontally and is most effective with low-altitude aircraft which fly below the operational level of the Nike (and with a far greater rate of fire). It has destroyed targets as low as 500 feet, yet has hit a drone flying 1500 mph at 30,000 feet. When the medium or the low-altitude radar detects a target, identifies and tracks it, it causes the HAWK to be fired. Once airborne, HAWK's built-in guidance control homes-in on the target.

Only by actually making a ninety-degree turn can the attacking aircraft avoid being hit, but then it has also veered from its objective. Developed in 1957, the HAWK missile is seventeen feet long, a bit over a foot in diameter, has a four-foot wing span, weighs about 2/3 of a ton, and is propelled by solid fuel.

The Nike-Hercules is an intermediate model between the now superseded Nike-Ajax, and the soon-to-be operational Nike-Zeus. It is fired from a fixed system of permanent structures consisting in a control area and a launch area, generally one to three miles apart. A multipurpose weapon, it is good for ground-to-air or ground-to-ground attack. It is fired vertically and has destroyed targets moving faster than 2000 miles per hour at altitudes above 150,000 feet (thirty miles!) at ranges beyond seventy-five miles (the entire length of Okinawa). Since it goes off by ground control, not by contact, it can destroy a single, or a whole formation of, aircraft. Nike-Hercules has intercepted and destroyed other guided missiles in flight. When radar No. 1 acquires a target, radar No. 2 tracks it, reporting its data to a central computer. The Nike is fired, using initial data, and is then tracked by radar No. 3. The computer reconciles the target's movements as reported by radar No. 2 and the missiles from radar No. 3. Then it corrects the missile's course until Nike-Hercules comes down on top of the target, regardless of evasive action. When both vehicles reach the identical location on radars No. 2 and No. 3 (the kill point), the missile's detonator is automatically triggered.

Developed in 1958 by Western Electric, Nike-Hercules missile (with its booster rocket) is thirty-nine feet long (actual missile twenty-seven feet), just under a yard in diameter, has a twelve-foot wingspan, weighs ten tons, and is propelled by solid fuel. The comparable Russian M-2 is twenty-five feet long, a yard in diameter, weighs about the same, and also has a two-stage solid-fuel rocket. On October 13, 1964, the United States signed contracts with the Japanese to have HAWK and Nike-Hercules missiles manufactured in Japan. But these big ones are not made of used tomato juice cans; the costs—a fact which filtered through to a good number of the witnessing Okinawan VIPs—seemed to burn them more than the missile trail brush fires. The HAWK missile costs eighty thousand dollars each. Each target drone costs ten thousand dollars, and complete overhead expense connected with each costs another ten thousand; thus a hundred thousand dollars is spent for each HAWK fired. There were four a day for eight ASP days, or thirty-two HAWKs for 3 million dollars. The Nike-Hercules without the expense of target drones cost about double that amount. The ASP period on Okinawa alone costs the American taxpayer nearly ten million dollars annually, a sum the Okinawan VIPs feel could much better be spent, even in part, on their health and welfare.

Concurrent with the American policy of playing down memorials or monuments to the 1945 victory in the Ryukyus, the Japanese have stepped up their program of memorial shrines to the martyred defenders of the dooryard of the national homeland. These are religious shrines, which bring pilgrims on excursions from Japan. Quite apart and distinct from the Okinawan memorial shrines, Japanese monuments have mushroomed all over the "Suicide Cliff" area of the south end. Mainly massive artistic stone efforts of ultramodern architecture, the memorial nucleus is a big canopied structure immediately above the cave where General Ushijima took his life at the battle's end. Today there is no restriction on the number or size of such shrines which tie the Ryukyus spiritually and emotionally back to Japan.

There is a self-imposed embargo on American memorials. A marker in Stilwell Park at Kadena still notes the spot of the signing of the general's surrender document. And the "impromptu" memorial he dedicated to General Buckner at the point where he died in action is just as it was, an almost shamefully crude pair of boulders surrounded by a peeling white wood fence. On Highway 5 north of Hacksaw Ridge, the Army is hard pressed to maintain against weather and vandalism a simple stone marker to Pfc. Desmond T. Doss, a Seventh-Day Adventist medical aid who, under fire, remained alone atop the escarpment to carry seventy-five men to safety below. I do not recall anything commemorating the point of the initial Love-Day landing, and other than the eloquently plain memorial to Ernie Pyle on Ie Shima, there was an artistically tasteful, reasonably sized, and historically significant monument cut as a stone memorial to the heroic 27th Army Division, but it was neither placed nor dedicated. The action officer on this project, Captain Burleigh M. Cubert, says it is languishing in a storage depot because present political policy precludes its placement. His detail was unable to secure an American area in which to erect it. Captain Cubert is now reported as retired and continuing his efforts to locate the monument to the 27th.

The "monument" or "memorial" title became so taboo that the collected historical archives of the battle had to be called the "Armed Forces Museum," and perhaps it is in truth, a museum. In a permanent building at the Sukiran HQ complex since its dedication in September 1959, it is a living record of the terrible spring of 1945. Incumbent museum director John Palmer, a man with the combined talents of the theatrical and the literary, demonstrated his battle story in lights. The main hall is taken up with seats around a full three-dimensional relief scale model map of Okinawa. In a tape recording he narrates a truncated version of the battle to the accompaniment of flashing and still, colored lights at the appropriate spots on the map. Then the military memorabilia exhibited in the glass cases around the walls take on an added dramatic dimension. John Palmer's incisive comments were most helpful to me in condensing volumes of battle data.

The universal memorial given long ago by Okinawan King Shō Kō is the little International Cemetery in Tomari port. There lie in peace together the Reverend Father Adnet of Paris (d.1848), and the seven sailors who came with Admiral Perry, (d.1854). The earliest stones I was able to find were two cut in crude letters: "WM. HARES ENGLISHMAN 1816"; and "J. J. DOSS BORN 1818 DIED 1843." I still wonder why the English in the empire-building years never pursued the matter of their 1816 Okinawan landing, or did Hares get there on his own? And was J. J. Doss with him, or by himself? Was Doss American or English? What got him so far from home and then did him in? And was he an ancestor of Medal of Honor hero Desmond T. Doss of a century later? There are four fully covered graves marked only "AMERICAN." The oldest person interred was Huang Chu Wen Ying, b. May 4, 1881, d. March 19, 1963. There were far too many young, all babies of American occupation people. Death's child-claims are marked by a six-pointed Star of David for Randi M. Rubin, between crosses for Infant Pontillo and Sue A. Lindemuth, among numerous others. I was saddened to see an old beer-drinking chum, Ray T. Tochman (d. Sept. 3, 1956) in this "living" memorial park once given by an Okinawan king to keep the foreigners out of Okinawan tombs. It is now maintained by American V.F.W. Post 9723. A small tablet declares "This cemetery was rebuilt on 30 June 1955 by the City of Naha with help given by the USCAR as it has been destroyed by the World War II." Obviously, that local administration did not last; another tablet dates the latest reconstruction under V.F.W. at July 17, 1964. Fortunately, its boundaries are walled, since the docking facilities and plant of the Okinawa Cement Company, a thriving local industry, are expanding.

In a scant shingled shed just a few steps from the old Futema shrine, within a barn surrounded by a quiet Japanese rock garden, an "unknown" Okinawan artist, Shinzan Yamada, has dedicated his life to the production of perfection itself. He is sculpting in white stone a serene Buddha of monumental proportions, which he hopes to dedicate as a memorial to all and a plea for peace in the world.

Albert Watson II of Mount Vernon, Illinois, simultaneously wore the polished brass helmet of the commanding general of U. S. Army Ryukyu Islands (which included his being representative of the Commander-in-Chief, Pacific) and the neatly blocked Homburg of the U. S. High Commissioner of the Ryukyu Islands until he left in 1967. As such, he reported both to the Secretary of State and to the Secretary of Defense. In the islands, General Watson was referred to by nearly all as the "Hi Com"; by many as the "Old Man"; and by a unique minority as "that s.o.b." His job, clearly defined and detailed by Section 4 (a) of Executive Order 10713 (see Appendix), was carried out with a great deal of dispatch, aplomb, and personal magnetism. Often accused by the U.S. civilian population of being overtly partial to the military, especially in regard to housing, he also created the greatest atmosphere for common, co-operative growth and development among the military, civilian, and native populations since 1945. His authority, although broad and deep, was subject ultimately to the policy established at his two different superior ministries, thereby placing on his right hand a white kid glove over an armored fist. One interview with this man was not sufficient to plumb the depths of his job and himself; he managed to find time to see me whenever I requested, and each time had something new to offer.

Including the 1967 incumbent General Ferdinand T. Unger, there have been five Hi Coms since the executive order went into effect, and prior to that, there were eleven commanding generals beginning with General Buckner. In the twenty-odd years since April 1945, only fifteen men have presided over America's hard-won Pacific prize. Those who have been popular with the military have not been so with the civilians or the locals. Those who were generous with the Ryukyuans found disfavor with both American elements.

"What the United States is doing now could and will be continued—in providing needed economic and technical assistance both directly and indirectly. This need reflects the fact that Okinawa's standard of living must continue to grow, to meet the requirements of a growing population seeking to advance to the level of comparable areas in Japan. The United States, as the administering power, must help meet these requirements in order to carry out its responsibilities." This was what the Hi Com answered when I asked him what more the United States could do for Okinawa now.

"On the other hand," he continued, "Japan in its fiscal year 1966 provided more than sixteen million dollars in economic assistance to GRI—twice as much as the previous year. In addition, in each of the past two fiscal years, Japanese pensions and donations have amounted to 8.5 million dollars. Besides this, Japan buys all the Ryukyus' sugar production—a total of 53.4 million dollars' worth in the 1964-65 milling season. Japan did this by exempting Ryukyuan sugar from an import tariff of $115 a metric ton—an indirect subsidy—and by exempting Ryukyuan sugar from foreign exchange controls while restricting imports from other countries." I suggested that the sugar business was a two-way street. Japan got all its prewar sugar from Okinawa, and therefore it is merely a restoration of the status quo which saves them the chore of pulling it in from farther away. Actually, with all Cuba's sugar cut off, it might be beneficial to sell Okinawan cane in the United States if the transport economics could be worked out. When I asked if he thought America received any monetary gain whatever from the Ryukyus, he said "No." To my thought of what Okinawa might have been like today had we given it back to Japan at treaty time, he smiled as he said, "That is too hypothetical for me to comment."

The Hi Com is responsible for the largest American armed installation outside the continental national limits; as such he was able to tell me that Okinawa is still a staging area for "the Marines in particular," and of course it serves as a major logistic and supply base for the Army. Kadena AFB is reputed to be the busiest U.S. overseas military airfield in the world in terms of total operations." He proudly reiterated the missile information mentioned earlier, and went on to say that the passage of troops to Vietnam has naturally increased because this is a staging area. Not too many Okinawa-based troops go south, and if they do, "their dependents return to the U.S." There are "approximately forty thousand dependents" living in the Ryukyus because of the military establishment.

While reaffirming that the "established U.S. policy is to remain in these islands as long as conditions of threat and tension persist in this part of the world," the Hi Com evaded my question as to what would happen to U.S. effectiveness if reversion were to happen. "That, again, is a very hypothetical question that depends on many factors impossible to foresee in the future, and some matters that are beyond my competence." I thanked him, but I felt very few matters were beyond the Hi Com's competence.

One great pillar in the Hi Com's arc of confidence is the efficiency of the troops in the various military units. The moral/morale problems of the postwar and interim construction eras have evolved to a condition of normal abnormality. I mean eventually everything sought its own level. When feminine companionship ceased to be a commodity reserved for the select minority, the clamor diminished. The big thing is that the privacy of the individual Ryukyuan maiden is no longer a matter for concern. Nor was the "compromise solution" of the postwar days reinstated. Right now, balance is maintained by a state of free enterprise, but there were some growing pains along the way.

In the mid-fifties, segregated Negro troops went to a shantytown Okinawan saloon district southeast of Naha called Perryville. Cheap booze and questionable girls, both at high prices, perpetually brought about the usual consequences. One night, in response to a call for help because a big buck private was drunk and disorderly, an MP detachment arrived to maintain order. Trying to avoid violence in favor of reason, a young white lieutenant went into the saloon, hands down, and was shot dead in the doorway. This brought about some reforms. The eventual integration of the armed forces helped immeasurably. But as it has in Las Vegas, Miami, Chicago's "Calumet City," Los Angeles' East First Street, to mention a few, the honky-tonk beat blossomed forth on Okinawa. Today, incongruously in the area surrounding the Nami-No-Ue shrine, there abounds block after block of nothing but bar after bawdy bar. Ironically, Nami-No-Ue was a shrine at which arrivals and departures of distinguished travelers were celebrated in ancient times. Also enshrined there is a sacred phosphorescent stone supposedly picked up in a fisherman's net in Naha harbor ages ago. There is a Shinto shrine building at the top of the stairs. Behind a second gate and off to the right is a Buddhist temple surrounded by bells and appropriate small shrines. The annual celebration on Adult's Day, shortly before the Lunar New Year's, is held there. This is the day when people go up in fancy costumes to decorate the shrine. A shame of latter-day Okinawans is that the area around the shrine has deteriorated as it has. Annually a hundred thousand people have to pick their way through all kinds of Americanized night clubs and whorehouses in order to get to a religious shrine celebration. This is one of the enigmas of Okinawa today. And because so much money is involved in the area, nothing is going to alter this condition.

I was amazed as I wandered through this neon-lit nirvana for Neanderthals at the number of establishments, some even boasting the "A" sign of military approval as a restaurant fit to serve Americans. On any given night the routine is the same. Armed forces jeeps at the ready patrol the streets, which teem with enlisted service personnel of all branches, colors, and sizes, in and out of uniforms. Pawnshops interspersed in the blocks break the monotony of bar doors. Whenever some GI runs out of ready cash, he can always go next door and hock his watch or bracelet. Occasionally, if a boy has spent enough on drinks and pays a girl's "out fee," the two may then retire to one of the "hotels" in the area, after which he will sweat out the next two weeks hoping he hasn't gotten VD. To accommodate those stationed too far from Naha, there is a similar "amusement" zone in Koza city.

The Corps of Chaplains, which stopped the earlier in-service "arrangement," can do nothing to touch this big private enterprise now. The military makes no effort to declare any but specifically bad individual spots "Off Limits." I was unable to ascertain if this were a Mafia machination, or even mob-managed by local or Tokyo syndicates. No one seemed to show any real concern. On paper, at least, the individual licensees appeared to be upstanding Ryukyuans.

One rainy Saturday I went over to the USO on Naha's main avenue. For nearly two hours, as I watched, no one entered. Later that evening, while the tenderloin district teemed with men, there were only five in the USO building. One was reading, one wrote a letter, two played table tennis, while the fifth sipped coffee and spoke to a mild-looking local girl in sensible shoes.

Daytime living in Okinawa is similar to that in any large semiprosperous California or Gulf Coast community. To quote a U.S. Information Agency pamphlet (aimed at attracting civilian employees):

"Although there are several local bus companies as well as many taxicabs to facilitate getting about, most personnel have their own automobiles. Almost any type and model of car from the old "Model A" to the latest "Super-Duper 8" can be seen on Okinawan highways. Automobile agencies represent a great many of both foreign- and American-manufactured cars. American car prices are on a par with those in the States, plus shipping. Foreign-car prices are far lower than those in the States. There are enough automobile repair shops to handle any type of repair—from changing a tire to rebuilding a motor. Due to the combination of rain, humidity, salt, and coral dust, cars should be completely undercoated. (This means removal of all upholstery and undercoating doors, hood, trunk, roof, and any other metal subject to rust.) Gasoline at the Post Exchange costs 22 cents a gallon, and a little over 23 cents on the local market.

"The Commissaries, of which there are four in number, can supply practically any item of food available in large supermarkets in the States. The numerous Post Exchanges can supply almost all other items available in large stateside department stores. At the larger PXs, concessions can furnish men's custom-made clothes of the finest British fabrics, tailored in Hong Kong. Women can be fitted in silk saris from India, brocades from Japan or Hong Kong, or almost anything else the ladies may desire.

"For social life and entertainment, there are enough facilities to satisfy all tastes. Besides the Rest Center at Okuma, there are other beaches for swimming, sun-bathing, and beach parties, and for those who prefer chlorine, there are six swimming pools. There are several skin-diving clubs for the submariners, as well as yacht clubs for those who prefer riding on top of the water. If you like sport cars, there is a club for you too.

"Sports of all kinds are available, from ping-pong through tennis, baseball, football, basketball, to horseback riding. For those who take their sports in a milder way, there are plenty of bowling alleys. The golfer is in his glory here—the Awase Meadows Country Club provides an 18-hole course, and another 18-hole course is under construction. For others, there are several libraries which feature current best sellers. Radio and television programs are provided by AFRTS. For those who enjoy a good game of bridge, the Officers' Club has duplicate games, where the competition is keen.

"There are three officers' clubs and two civilian clubs. These clubs furnish nightly dining and dancing, and compare favorably in decor and cuisine with many of the larger night clubs and hotels in New York, while the prices are nominal. Regular breakfast and luncheon menus are routine. Military clubs close at 11:00 P.M. but this does not mean your evening is at an end. Clubs run by indigenous people stay open 'til the wee hours of the morning. Other clubs offering food and entertainment are American Legion and V.F.W. For movie-lovers there are enough theaters to sate the appetite of the most avid fan.

"Personnel employed at the office and receiver site reside on Kadena Air Base. Conditions and facilities are equivalent to stateside. Utilities such as electricity, telephones, plumbing, etc., follow U.S. standards so there will be no need to bring a myriad of paraphernalia such as transformers, odd plugs, etc.

"Two and three bedroom houses are equipped with normal basic Government furnishing. Utilities consist of a 50-gallon hot water heater, electric stove and a 16-cubic foot refrigerator-freezer combination with individual doors.

"The living room contains built-in bookcases, sectional couch, chairs, coffee table, end table, rug and drapes. The dining alcove has a sectional table with eight chairs and a buffet. Bedrooms have built-in closets, night table, vanity, drapes and a choice of beds (double, single or twin). Adequate air-conditioning units are installed in bedrooms occupied by Americans. A utility room contains laundry tubs, space for a maid's cot, if she wishes to sleep in, a storage closet and a servant's bath.

"Competent maids are available who can perform household chores including laundry, limited cooking and caring for the children. Salaries are commensurate with ability and duties, but are also contingent upon conditions of employment such as whether she sleeps in or goes home at night, whether meals are furnished or she supplies her own. If the maid sleeps in, she will usually prepare breakfast.

"A continuing and effective insect and rodent control program, operated by the Military, limits the population of these pests to an acceptable level in the housing areas."

But everyone isn't always content with a GI house, and many cannot afford to pay these prices. Recently, a highly placed friend who wished to bring his family to Okinawa was obliged to pay twenty-five thousand dollars for a modest house in Awase via the Ryukyuan Development Loan Corporation. Not all the civilian establishment serves the Service (although it is there solely because the armed forces are). The majority of its people live in and among the military people (D.A.C.'s or Department of the Army Civilians), whether they are with USCAR or not, or they live on "private economy" in small Yankee communities strategically located for maximum security, shopping convenience, and utility service. Cultura Americana has sprung up in quantity to satisfy the taste of the most compulsive of joiners. For the superannuated soldiers, there are the American Legion and the Veterans of Foreign Wars. For the business-community minded, there are Lions and Rotary, which, unlike the military-oriented clubs, have the added feature of including the Okinawans toward a more integrated community. Rotary, in fact, has almost completely become a Ryukyuan organization, meeting mainly in Japanese. I know the weekly luncheon meeting I enjoyed addressing was 80 per cent local, for which my remarks were translated by Sam Kitamura of USCAR Cultural Affairs. Also, a group of adult volunteers has made Boy Scouts a great activity for integrating the youth of both nationalities. The YMCA has wisely become almost completely an organization to serve Okinawans rather than the American community.

Shui Ikemiyagi, president and publisher of the Ryukyu *Shimpo*, one of the two big Okinawan daily newspapers, is president of the board of governors of the YMCA. The "Y" on Okinawa was just six years old in 1968, and was supported originally by basic donations from thirty prominent business firms in Naha, each contributing only twenty-five dollars a year. They also receive aid from the U.S. church organizations on Okinawa, and the chaplains' groups of the U.S. forces. They also get some aid from the Japanese YMCA Union and further sums to round out their needs from YMCA World Services. Thus far, they have only one hundred native boys and girls. This is the maximum they can take in membership, which has always been full, plus a waiting list. They take all hundred camping in the summertime to get them away from the difficulties of city living. They do plan to expand as time and money allow. Oshiro Higa (whose full-time occupation is as professor of chemistry at University of the Ryukyus in Shuri) is the executive secretary. In addition to its regular physical education and child guidance programs, the "Y" is teaching English classes and even beginning typing classes, since it received a donation of twenty Japanese typewriters from a Japanese industrial firm in the main islands.

Thus typing is taught in Japanese. Americans never have donated any American business machines, consequently, although English is being taught as a language, English typing is not being taught as a skill. The YMCA in its homemade headquarters upstairs from a bank on Kokusai (International) Street, the main thoroughfare of Naha, is enjoying its present location. They do hope to move soon to a place where they can get some gymnasium facilities and eventually will help to expand with a Y Men's Club in addition, so that businessmen also can look forward to some constructive afternoon activity. Perhaps with more active support from World Services, the Oki Y may become an islandwide thing before twenty more years slip by.

A lot of effort goes into the spoken word in the Ryukyus. And much time and expense go into the make-up of daily radio programs aimed at attracting the attention of the locals about religion, politics, and commercial products. Apart from the video (local or microwave from Japan), the Japanese-language radio from afar, and Radio Okinawa locally, there is the ubiquitous Voice of America. From eleven transmitters at Okinawa, two megawatt units (one short and one long wave), VOA operates on a clear channel in the standard broadcast band in many languages for all Asia to hear. Many of the functional staffs are Japanese. They also listen; the receiver site is located on a high bluff overlooking the East China Sea near Onna village, incongruously in an area designated as a shrine. It is visited by locals on picnics or pilgrimages, or by sight-seeing Americans.

Christian missionaries broadcast from Okinawa to mainland China longwave in Chinese nine hours a day from KSBU Okuma, completely church-supported through Far East Broadcasting Company. FEBC owns sixteen stations, three of which are on Okinawa. Jack C. Lenz, the director, recently put on a drive for as little as 20¢ per day from any one thousand people in the Ryukyus for support of KSBU, KSAB broadcasting locally in English, and KSDX reaching the full Japanese-speaking Ryukyuan population. To augment the transmission, the FEBC gives away pretuned, battery-operated, transistor radio receiver sets to the natives in outlying areas, to act as "portable missionaries."

The health of all in the islands is taken care of diligently. Out-island natives receive hitherto unknown service to keep them well and alive. Typical dramatic newsbreaks several times a year tell of 'copters going to Miyako or other out-islands in response to urgent radio calls for help. Patients are airlifted to any one of several class A hospitals in the Naha area for whatever emergency and follow-up treatment is necessary. For about seven million American taxpayer dollars, a five-story, thousand-bed hospital was built at Camp Kue in May of 1958. Completely self-contained in case of power or utility failure, it has the capacity to handle nearly any known case type. By June 1966 a news release proclaimed the fact that Filariasis, a dreaded semitropical disease, which had always been rampant in that area was reduced from 34 per cent of the population suffering to a scant 3.1 per cent, and these are under observed control. Filariasis should be gone from Ryukyus within another three years.

Ryukyuan lepers never crouch, nor are they alone. Founded long ago by an old German physician, the Airaku-En leper colony on Yagachi Shima just north of Motobu Peninsula, was supported as a house charity of the Japanese ruling Meiji family. Before the war, it was the particular pet of the Empress, and since the American era, patronage has passed to Congressman Otto Passman, Democrat of Louisiana, in whose baliwick, the Carville leprosarium flourishes. The seven-hundred-inmate Airaku leprosarium has received appreciable U.S. aid since Representative Passman's visit and concern. Four hundred are classed as cured, and their complexions are good, but they are forced by archaic Okinawan public opinion to remain away from society. So they stay to help cure the other three hundred.

Lawrence Blochman's enlightening book *Alone No Longer* (Funk & Wagnalls, N.Y.) tells the touching, dramatic story of Stanley Stein, a man who overcame Hansen's disease to again become a useful member of society. Were parts of this sage book to be serialized in the Okinawan press, it would help Representative Passman's cause considerably. There is now a highway bridge leading onto Yagachi Island from Okinawa, but earlier, one either went by boat or, as I did, drove over at low tide.

Within a Japanese shrine-like structure at the colony there hangs a replica of the U.S. Liberty Bell, which was given to the people of the Okinawa leprosarium by the people of West Berlin in 1959 to celebrate the activities of the early German *doktor.* This gift tended for the moment to create some international interest in what was going on with the lepers on Okinawa, toward whom, except for their own people, most others in the world today show understanding.

Treated as even more contagious, and less understood by all people, are the various canons of the law in the Ryukyus. I met with Irving Eisenstein, Chief of Legal Division, Legal Affairs Department, USCAR: Ever since he came to Okinawa from the Judge Advocate's General Staff in Tokyo at the close of the war, Mr. Eisenstein's litany of laws did provide the structure for order as it is today.

Criminal cases involving the military are tried in courts-martial in accordance with military regulation. Civilians in military employ may be so tried or tried in USCAR courts at the determination of the Hi Com. Any action involving a Ryukyuan, whether on a criminal or civil complaint, is tried in GRI courts, as are cases involving any Japanese national. Cases involving an occasional "foreigner" or any U.S. civilian are all in the USCAR courts.

This multiplex juridical system is valid and binding despite some outcries of "kangaroo courts." The validity of the USCAR courts was upheld in a spring 1966 decision by the U.S. District Court, Washington, D.C. Judge Oliver Gasch granted a summary judgment for the United States Government in a case in which a U.S. citizen (and dependent wife of a D.A.C.) filed an action against then Secretary of Defense McNamara. She sought to nullify her 1963 conviction in a USCAR superior court for attempted evasion of GRI income tax. The plaintiff alleged that the USCAR superior court had no jurisdiction over her since it was established by Executive Order 10713, and not by Act of Congress. The plaintiff was indicted by a USCAR grand jury, tried and convicted by a jury in USCAR superior court, and lost again in USCAR appellate court before finally appealing to the Washington bench. The Gasch judgment reaffirmed that the USCAR court system, as currently operated, does not possess unconstitutional features. USCAR courts have jurisdiction over any U.S. citizen who has committed a crime within the Ryukyu Islands, and are set up like any other American tribunal.

The GRI courts follow the Japanese system (as of 1945) with changes by Hi Com ordinances and GRI laws. It is, actually, a Ryukyuan-operated legal system for and by Ryukyuans. Eisenstein said that only patience and forbearance by all have helped the courts to reach this point safely. In a nonintegrated society where separate facilities cannot by their basic elements be equal, the Ryukyuans have freedom and autonomy beyond any prewar concept or standard.

Courts and laws are established under government agencies which exist on two semi-overlapping levels in this "nonintegrated society." Under the Hi Com is USCAR, which is all civilian, to administer over U.S. nonmilitary citizens in accord with Executive Order 10713. The native population is "self-governed" by GRI, all of whose functionaries and personnel are local. Both organizations have co-operating departments, some of which overlap, but in general each deals with its own people. The objectives of USCAR (as completely divorced from the military, whose sole job is defense preparedness), are to: promote effective government; develop a viable economy; and improve the standard of living of the Ryukyuans, while providing for the health and welfare of the Americans in the process.

The senior American civilian, who is civil administrator, is a career diplomat, Gerald Warner. Warner said: "Reversion will come in due time. If it weren't for the military mission, we'd be out tomorrow." When I asked if he felt Americans were doing the Ryukyuans any good while we were supporting the military mission, he agreed that the people were better off materially, due to U.S. services and social welfare. "The island population has doubled since the war, and the Japanese will never be able to replace the annual two hundred million dollars," Warner said.

"Okinawa's big need now," he stated, "is stability of government and development of economy." An annual Ryukyuan per capita income of $700 by 1972 from the 1965 high of $365 is the objective of GRI. This will be the result of a five-year plan for joint U.S.-Japanese co-operation, an outgrowth of the 1962 J. F. Kennedy goals for the Ryukyus. To insure that the resources of all three governments are channeled to achieve this end, William Clyde Burns, originally an engineering graduate of South Carolina's Clemson University, is the strict USCAR controller. "Okinawa exports one hundred million dollars and imports two hundred million dollars. The hundred million dollar imbalance is made up by presence of American bases. Now, if the United States left, then Japan would have to cover this amount, which will become two hundred million dollars by 1971." Burns told me frankly, "I don't think they can do it." Meanwhile, his group strives to attain optimum economic development with cultural advancement, and helps to keep up public health, education, and other services.

James Victor Martin, Jr., was political adviser to the High Commissioner. He was the Hi Com's link with the Department of State. He consulted on matters of external relations of Okinawa, and internal problems affecting the United States. Martin seemed to feel that "Expansion of autonomy is the road to reversion," as they say in Japan. He believed the Japanese-American mutual security pact and Article 3 of the Peace Treaty tie Japan and the United States in mutual security, and that Okinawa is in U.S. control because Japan wills it so. Martin was replaced in 1967 by William H. Bruns.

Liaison between USCAR and GRI is handled by Edward O. Freimuth, who is also the link with the past, having served on Okinawa since 1946. He engages in a broad area of unlimited activity to maintain a favorable climate. The trouble shooter, Freimuth is supposed to anticipate problems and try to find their solutions. He believes the locals live within a "typhoon psychology"—

"Have it today, and it's gone tomorrow." Freimuth seems to feel that reversion depends a lot on Japanese public opinion about American military operations: Premier Sato has in 1965 recognized the importance of Okinawan bases to Japan.

Americans operate two sets of schools in the Ryukyus. Dependent children of American military and civilian people on Okinawa are educated in a primary and secondary school system comparable to any good one in the States. Once he has a high school diploma, a youngster may go anywhere to college, or avail himself of many college credit courses given in extension by the University of Maryland. It is also possible for him to enroll for full credit in the University of the Ryukyus if he can read and speak Japanese fluently. (The university is also open to any qualified Ryukyuan with a high school diploma.) The completely separate educational system for the Ryukyuans operates under GRI with assistance and aid from USCAR.

All education in the Ryukyus is under the highly competent Dr. Jeanette K. Fink. She points with great pride to a graph which shows that in 1950, 165,000 local children attended elementary school. In 1955 it was 176,000, and in 1965 it had reached 271,000. The number of children in school has increased by greater proportion than the number of children. In 1945, at the end of the war, there were only 562 classrooms in all the islands; in 1955, 3670. By 1965, there were 7202.

Curricula in the primary and secondary schools are strictly Japanese in system, subject, and language. It is interesting to see the young boys and girls in their dark blue uniforms with the little black briefcases, going and coming. The American authorities blundered in 1950 by withdrawing English as the language of Ryukyuan schools and by not even leaving English in the teaching plan. English is taught to adults as part of a thriving adult education program. The total annual GRI Education Department budget runs about 22 million dollars. This also covers a commercial institute, which gives management, sales, and secretarial courses to meet the demand by local industry for these skills. Since 1960 nearly one thousand special students have been sent abroad under a Third Country Training Program. The expenses, sponsored by the U.S. Department of the Army, cover training in Taiwan or the Philippines in highly specialized technical callings, to improve the over-all economy.

The American influence on the Ryukyu Islands and their people is far greater than money. Actually the United States has given the Okinawan excesses of everything except the one thing they think they most want, emotional security by "belonging." To aid common understanding, the University of New Mexico in the late 1950s offered an on-campus resident program of scholarships for qualified young Ryukyuans. The result hopefully will be closer relations between the two peoples. So far it has proved worth while, but it is a sneeze in a typhoon compared to what remains to be done. The University of New Mexico has done a great job at better than the grass-roots level.

The new University of the Ryukyus is a major entity unto itself. Before the war, there was such an institution somewhat north of Naha. And Shuri was the site of the ancient kingdom's capital. The castle and Buddhist temple were completely demolished in the war, along with the huge landscaped formal gardens, and the Shurei-No-Mon gate (gate of courtesy), originally built in 1200 and restored at its former location, with most of its original members, in 1958. Along with a museum housing other regal remnants, the new university site was wisely chosen. The Administration Building is on the site of the old throne room, not far from where Commodore Perry stayed in 1853. Over five hundred bachelor's degrees are awarded annually (the total to date exceeds five thousand). To aid the program, a special team from Michigan State Univer-isty has set up shop in the Koshin Shikiya Memorial Library to advise, teach, and administer. Dr. Jack J. Stockton, professor of microbiology and public health, is party chief. The others are Dr. Robert Geist, who teaches English, Professor Frank Roop, Jr., mechanical engineering, and Professor Harold Foster, agriculture extension. There is also a high-level staff of over a dozen Okinawans who have taken stateside degrees and have returned to aid their homeland, but in general are not pro-American.

There are a few English-language magazines in Okinawa. One, the pocket-digest type, *This Week on Okinawa* (established in 1955 as *This Month on Okinawa*), is quite successful, and offers complete coverage of radio, video, cinema, clubs, business, and island activities—and an "off-base phone directory". The only English language daily in the islands is the *Okinawa Morning Star*. Robert Prosser has been its editor for thirteen years, starting from scratch. He now has a thirteen thousand daily circulation at 10¢ a copy or $2.50 per monthly subscription. Obviously, editorial policy reflects the military establishment: the paper is seldom critical of its readers. The local *Okinawa Times*, a Japanese-language daily with a weekly English supplement, is antiestablishment, but pro-U.S. The outside world gets the Ryukyuan "rumble" from the Public Affairs Division (PAD) of USCAR.

To return to the U.S. position, in 1948 the Navy and the Marines were out of Okinawa. By 1950 the Korean War had brought them back. Since then, there has been a gradually increasing build-up of all American armed forces, until the 1964 escalated involvement in Vietnam created the need for more "permanent" facilities to accommodate the hundred thousand or more military and naval personnel who cadre or pass through this base at any given time. Okinawa's value as a staging area is unchanged since America's first evaluation of it in 1944, or Kublai Khan's in the late thirteenth century.

The District Engineer did not discuss the extent (tangibly, geographically, or financially) to which the United States has penetrated the Ryukyu Islands with fortifications and military facilities to defend against, or to launch, an attack. But seventy million dollars annually (or to be liberal, even half that amount in earlier times) for twenty years is quite a stake the American tax-payer owns in concrete, steel, wire, and black-boxes in that far-off island.

It is also naive to consider any patchwork plan to let only the native areas "revert" while the United States continues to keep title to the bases. Any sovereign control other than American brings up the same question which caused our leaving such air bases in the United Kingdom. Just imagine the difficulties in mounting a retaliatory bombing mission while awaiting the sanction of the Japanese Diet; or still worse, how the lack of personal permission from the Japanese Prime Minister could hamstring a "scramble" to get a defensive force airborne to meet an attacking flight. And, not a single live missile could ever be launched from a Ryukyuan site without the same kind of assent.

In the words of the former U.S. High Commissioner, Lieutenant General Albert Watson II, "U.S. administration must continue in order to carry out U.S. commitments for the defense of Japan and the other free nations in the Far East and elsewhere."

Thriving Tomari Port in 1966. Highway #1 is the traffic artery, and newly reclaimed land is at upper left.—*USCAR photo.*

Kokusai International Street in Naha in 1953 before it became a busy metropolitan artery. In 1943, there were sweet-potato fields here.—*USCAR photo.*

Okinawa urban life today.
—*M. D. Morris photo.*

Street scene in Koza City.
—*M. D. Morris photo.*

The tenderloin district near Nami-No-Ue-Gu Shrine, Naha.
—*M. D. Morris photo.*

The Hiroshima repertory road company performance at the Okiei Theatre, Naha. —*M. D. Morris photo.*

The old Police Academy, which survived the war, is now a Kendo-Judo Gymnasium.—*M. D. Morris photo.*

Japanese memorial shrine to General Ushijima dominates Suicide Cliff. *—M. D. Morris photo.*

Nami-No-Ue-Gu Shrine as it was just after the war. *—M. D. Morris photo.*

The Battle for Shuri Christian Church in 1945.*—U.S. Army photo.*

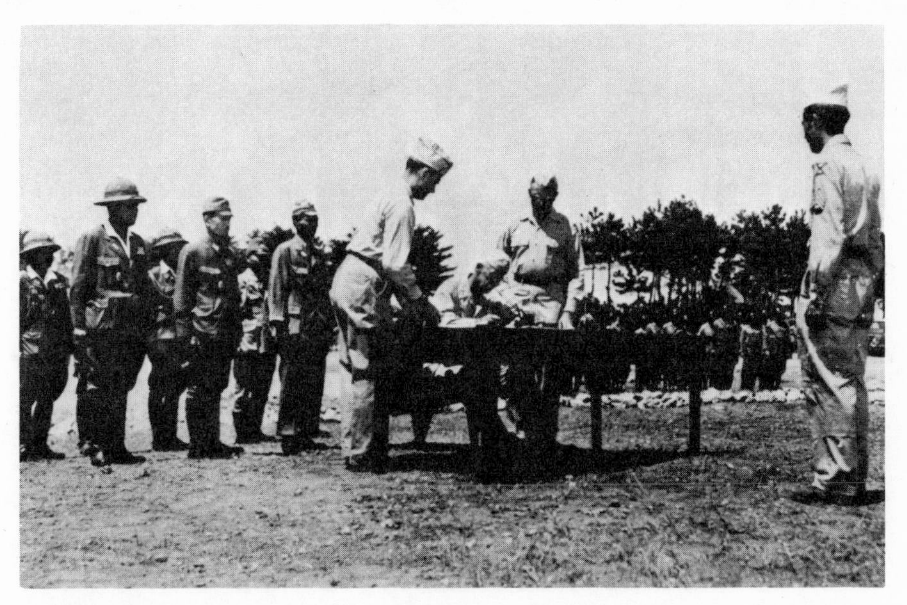

Lieutenant General Joseph Stilwell accepting the Japanese unconditional surrender of the Ryukyus at Kadena Air Base September 7, 1945.
*—U.S. Army photo.*

Seiho Matsuoka, Chief Executive, Government of the Ryukyu Islands, 1966 interview.—*M. D. Morris photo.*

—*M. D. Morris photo.*

Government Plaza, site of United States Civil Administration of Ryukyu Islands, and Government of Ryukyu Islands building complex.—*USCAR photo.*

Donald C. Wilson, Colonel, Infantry.
—*U.S. Army photo.*

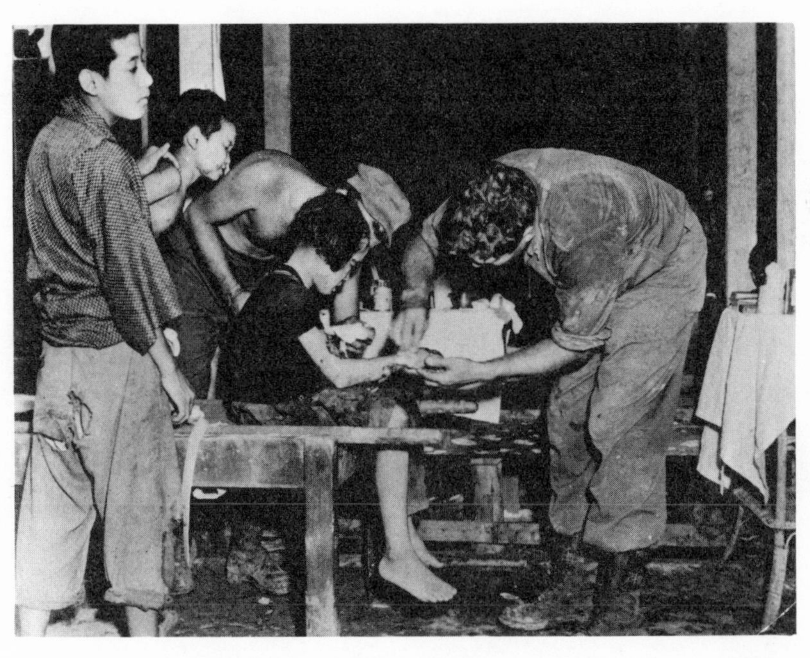

U.S. combat aid station in 1945, where wounded Okinawan children were also treated.—*U.S. Army photo.*

American style Ryubo Department Store in Naha with its Japanese style rooftop playground.—*M. D. Morris photo.*

An Okinawan sweetshop offers universal delights.
—*M. D. Morris photo.*

Modern Naha on a spring afternoon
—*M. D. Morris photo.*

PART IV

# The Horses and the Riders

# CHAPTER 8

# The Grudging Land

Okinawa was a green and brown country when I first saw it. American soldiers were everywhere in suntan uniforms and green fatigues. Quonset huts were either olive drab or just raw and rusting metal. All vehicles were army olive, also. The native Okinawans who plodded along the roadside and smiled warily at the passing military were brown people in shabby, old, tattered brown clothing. They lived in sod and wood huts topped by natural straw.

Except for an occasional asphalt or concrete top, roads were mostly brown coral and dirt. After a rain, the countryside greenery would turn lively. But soon the moisture drained into the porous soil and the military vehicles again strewed endless dust clouds onto the roadside. Only the blue and birdless sky relieved the green and brown pattern.

The kaleidoscopic color of today's Ryukyus makes a stunning contrast. From neon-lit Naha, across pastel-painted hillside housing developments, over patchwork quilts of native farms, Okinawa is a polychromatic panorama which everyone has put on the land surface.

The people of the Ryukyus have been so molded by their land that they seem to have grown out from it.

"In the beginning": The Omoro (Okinawan Bible) says that the island of Kudaka Shima was the place where the creation of the world occurred. Pedo Ko, the Okinawan version of the Book of Genesis, says that Shini Reku and Mamiko, the goddesses of wind and sea, joined forces in a momentous effort to carry stone, sand, and earth to one location. Then they hewed logs, planted trees and grass, and finally they stopped the floods which regularly inundated their island of Kudaka. Finally they lifted flame from the fire-breathing sea dragon. After meditation with the wind, they decided to produce mortal men to enjoy the land and fire they had created and won. After a time, the descendants of these first inhabitants migrated a few miles eastward to the island of Okinawa, a much larger place, which had also been built by the deities after the successful Kudaka prototype. The legend is based on fact. Floods did inundate the islands, which later emerged from the sea. In truth, prehistoric beasts walked from the Chinese mainland to Okinawa, yet at no time could any land-living creature ever have walked to Okinawa direct from the Japanese Islands.

Geologists deduce that four diluvial epochs occurred between six hundred thousand and one hundred thousand years ago. According to this theory, there was a land connection between the Ryukyus and the continent of Asia during the first three of these periods. Shinjun Tawada, a noted specialist in Ryukyuan geology, says that the first of these "land bridges" appeared about six hundred thousand years ago. A hundred thousand years later the depth of the ocean increased and the Ryukyus were submerged except for the tops of the higher mountains in the north. The second appearance of the land bridge to Asia occurred some four hundred thousand years ago. The islands were again submerged fifty thousand years later. The third and final land bridge linking the Ryukyus with Asia appeared about two hundred thousand years ago but, again, fifty thousand years later, the Ryukyu chain was submerged except for the highest mountains. Maybe this was a foretelling of their eventual unstable political and socio-economic life.

As the oceans gradually subsided, the islands reappeared for the fourth time and are still above water. When the fourth diluvian epoch ended nearly one hundred thousand years ago, the Ryukyus were no longer connected to Asia. And since then, the islands have remained at about the same level above the sea. Through the Ryukyu Islands there are prominent coral reef formations at various elevations, some hills as high as six hundred feet above sea level. Coral at these elevations proves that the surface of the ocean had reached that height during the various submersion periods. The coral reef formations, or coastal terraces, appear as terraced hills sloping gradually to the coast. The ancient neolithic men lived on these terraces and built shell mounds, of which nearly two hundred have already been found and explored.

Mr. Tawada, writing later in *Shuiei no Hikari* magazine, states that an ancient stone ax which had chipped stone cutting edges on both sides was dug up from a large shell mound near the holy city of Aza in central Okinawa. Stone axes excavated from the Kiyuna shell mounds (not far from the Aza find) were polished on both sides, shaped in the form of a square, and fashioned with a cutting edge at only one end. He believes that those ancient people used this single-bitted-type stone ax much the same way as today's woodsmen might. A fragment of human skull and an old chipped stone implement were recently dug up on Ie Shima, Tawada tells us. The skull is believed to be of an Okinawan primitive man who lived during the glacial period, anywhere from about two hundred thousand years ago to one hundred and fifty thousand years ago, when early men could well have crossed over from Asia via the "land bridge," just as the animals did.

Migrations of wild beasts did occur from the Asian continent over the land bridges into Japan and separately into the Ryukyus. There are some marked differences between the fossils of prehistoric Naumann elephants excavated in Tokyo and a Naumann elephant dug up in Miyako. These differences are believed to indicate that a variety of animal migrations had occurred via these separate land bridges over many centuries, parallel and independently. From the type and shape of the chipped stone implements found with the skull of that ancient Okinawan—its thickness, its weight, its curvature—it was deduced that the primitive Okinawan man was of a race closely related to the Peking man (*Sinanthropus Pekinensis*). But since this rustic might conceivably represent a new race of ancient man, a new scientific name (*Okinawanthropus Iejimensis Tawada*) has been created to describe it.

Due to the presence of the deep Tokara channel in the Pacific Ocean floor north of Amami and south of Yaku (the southernmost island of Japan), it is evident that the two island groups have always been separated from each other, even during prehistoric times when other parts of Japan and other parts of the Ryukyus were connected by land bridges to distant parts of the Asian continent. This theory is further corroborated by the fact that certain plants indigenous to southeast Asian countries have been found throughout the Ryukyus as far north as Amami but never found on Yaku and other Kyushu districts of Japan.

What finally emerged from the four dousings was the present Ryukyu Island chain, peaks of submerged mountain ranges separated from Asia proper by the East China Sea, and separating that sea from the Pacific Ocean. New Ryukyuan land is constantly forming by the endless building activity of the coral. The average depth of the Pacific Ocean in that area is about fourteen thousand feet. The Ryukyu trench running somewhat to the east of the island chain has been sounded to a depth below twenty-nine thousand feet. By comparison, if Mount Everest were to be sunk into this vast undersea trench, it would miss showing its pinnacle above the water. There are seventy-two islands in the group, forty-eight are inhabited, and twenty-five of these are considered important. The islands are divided into three subgroups: Okinawa gunto, Miyako gunto, and Yaeyama gunto. These three guntos, and innumerable rocks, reefs, and other oceanic-floor outcroppings comprise a total *land* area of only 541,632 acres, or 847.86 square miles, not even two thirds the size of Rhode Island. All the rest within the metes and bounds is ocean.

The chain of Ryukyus, surrounded by the major powers of East Asia, has become the most strategic outpost in the Far East. Okinawa, which the military calls the "Keystone of the Pacific," is the most important of these islands. It is

970 miles southwest of Tokyo but actually only 400 miles south of Yaku. It is just 390 miles from Taipei, Taiwan, northeast to Naha, but it is almost rowboating distance between Taiwan and the southwesterly limits of the Yaeyama subgroup. The airline distance southwest from Naha to Hong Kong is 840 miles, and flying almost due south from Naha it is 900 miles to Manila, Philippines. Seoul, Korea, is 830 miles almost due north. Mainland China is only some 400 miles from shore to shore across the East China and Yellow seas. Okinawa is the hub of a vital area of East Asia and provides a definite spearhead for the United States with regard to any Asiatic activity.

As the largest land mass in the group, Okinawa has 454 of the Ryukyus' 848 square miles. This is not really much when converted to its 290,555 acres, considering that some Texas ranches cover more than 300,000 acres. The richest soil, a mixture of alluvial clay and organic matter, is found in parts of central and southern Okinawa and to a lesser extent on some of the outlying islands. The moderately fertile limestone plains comprise approximately fifty thousand acres and are used extensively for truck farming and sugar cane. Now some 30 per cent of Okinawa's farmland is used by the U.S. armed forces for military and related installations. Natives use the deep, fertile, but poorly drained soil on the coastal flats extensively for growing rice. Next in value to the island are about thirty thousand acres of uplands lying mostly at the south end of Okinawa, which are shallow and crumbly clay soil over bedrock, and are used for small farming of the upland crops, sugar cane, sweet potatoes, and greenleaf vegetables.

The remainder of the potentially arable land is the acid red soil of the mountains in the north and their hilly uplands, just recently found to be ideal for pineapple and tea cultivation on a large commercial scale. From this land come the three mainstays of the Okinawan diet—rice, sugar cane (both items brought from China in 1374), and, also from China, the sweet potato.

During the reign of King Shō Nei in 1605, Noguni Sokan brought the sweet potato to the Ryukyus from China, on returning from one of the countless trips to take over tribute money. This poor man, whose personal identity has vanished, nonetheless is a very celebrated person in Ryukyuan history and life. They owe much to him, since sweet potatoes saved the Okinawans from starvation several times. In those early days, people of lower than samurai class were not permitted family names. Therefore, the name "Noguni" was that of the little village of the man's birth and the word "Sokan" was the title for the trade of one who burned incense at Buddha's shrine in the fantail of a tribute ship which plied its way across the China Sea from Naha and back. So this was an incense burner on a tribute ship, from the village of Noguni, who had the amazing foresight to recognize the sweet potato as an item of good food value as well as an attractive plant. It was he who brought sustenance back to the homeland, then passed on, contributing much to Okinawa's perpetual struggle for survival.

Many varieties of oriental vegetables, such as cabbage and leeks, grow in small Okinawan gardens. Grasshoppers are eaten as a delicacy. Shrimps, crawfish, and other sea foods are consumed in great abundance, since Okinawa, generally, is a fishing community. There was never too much meat, and dairy commodities were all but unknown before, and even shortly after, the war. In my recent visit, I was a guest of an Okinawan-American who took me to a fine Okinawan restaurant called "Miei" ("beautiful prosperity"). Among the dishes served were a soup made of pork innards, mushrooms, and long weeds, next an "energizer" of pickled vegetables, soybean curds, and a special variety of pork, roasted and treated with shogu sauce. On the side there was a type of taro potato, and a local cabbage, pickled and served cold. These foods were served as a matter of course by wealthy old Okinawan families, and in the royal castle at Shuri until 1879. Another night, in 1946, I dined with an Okinawan family on rice, sweet potatoes, and a sort of skewered grasshopper abdomen, all fortunately doused in weak green tea.

Mention of Ryukyuan foods cannot be complete without noting the cycas palm (sotetsu), which has so often also served as the staple food of the Ryukyuan people during periods of famine. This was also brought up to them from far southern Pacific islands and is an extremely primitive plant. The Okinawans today drink awamori, a hard rice liquor, and sake, a Japanese rice wine, generally served warm. Beer has come into the island's life more recently from Japan and the United States. Tea is served with everything. It is pale green, with very delicate flavor and aroma, much like Japanese tea. An average Okinawan breakfast today is a Japanese breakfast: Misushiro, a bean curd soup with some spinach greens, a bowl of rice into which a raw egg has been dropped, and tea. With the introduction of dairy foods and vitamins by the Americans over the last fifteen years, the diet of the average Okinawan is being balanced and his health and strength are improving. This is attested to by statistical measurements on each succeeding generation of children as they pass a given comparison age.

Marine life is in great abundance around Okinawa. Today, fishing is enjoyed almost anywhere in the great range of surrounding waters, both for sports and commerce. At times, in the streams and along the shore, night spear fishing by torchlight is a dramatic sight. Annually, early in February, there is a large-scale invasion by porpoises at Nago Bay. Nago's yearly "battle of the porpoises" is quite a spectacle. Why the porpoises come or what the exact timing is, no one knows. A constant round-the-clock watch of the bay waters is kept by people from hillsides and boats. The population is poised ready, and at a given signal from any lookout that the schools of fish have arrived, almost the entire town swarms out into the bay with hammers, adzes, picks, spears, and nets. Men, women, and children take part in this sumptuous slaughter which turns the blue waters of Nago Bay to deep vermilion. This colossal carnage must all be accomplished with alacrity, because within a day the surviving fish are gone and do not return for another year. Despite this butchery and loss, the poor creatures continue to return annually to Nago Bay for "the" day. In Nago, the porpoise meat is flavored with garlic and ginger and is eaten either raw or cooked. Much of the catch is smoked or sun-dried and preserved for later occasions. The whole bloody event is aptly described in the words of Mikio Higa, a Nago student:

"In a moment a wild game begins. The whales are now in complete embarrassment surrounded by hundreds of small boats, and some of them rush to the shore in full speed without knowing the direction, and they are caught by the people on shore. When anyone hits a whale with his harpoon he pulls it by the rope to the shore. The water of the sea changes its color completely to red, with blood flushing from the huge bodies of the whales. Everyone has a right to shoot and help others, and he gets his share. People watching on the shore are in great excitement and joy. It doesn't take more than an hour to capture almost all whales, and then people are busy in dividing their shares. It is one of the great resources to get wealth in my town; and it is so important that there are some old people who judge whether the mayor of the town is a good or bad man by how many whales are captured in a year."

I could never get myself to eat any porpoise dish because they smile so happily when they are alive, but I had consistent good luck with lobster. During the early occupation, natives would trade very good ones for cigarettes. Lobsters, always abundant in the islands, are a Pacific variety and look like an ordinary declawed Maine lobster. Crabs inshore are unsafe to eat because they devour all sorts of flotsam and jetsam. Shrimps abound and, with eels, are very famous Japanese delicacies.

In recent years, an older Okinawan had a small, live, yellowish bird of the finch or warbler family stuck on a long, thin bamboo shoot. This captive Judas-bird was unwittingly used to lure his fellows to the traps the old man had set nearby. He was catching birds to sell locally, in little bamboo cages, for household pets. This was rather a recent turn of events, because in my earlier time there, there were no birds. The total devastation from the invasion, the subsequent lack of living trees, and lesser flora and fauna killed or drove off the entire bird population for several years. Except for the unchallenged flight of both insects and U.S. aircraft, the Ryukyuan sky was unnaturally empty. During my entire tenure until 1947, I never saw a bird. But on my most recent visit I saw many, even in January. I was told that they had returned gradually, starting from 1949, although at first not in large numbers and varieties. Each year now more return. The larger birds of prey live in the northern, wilder, mountainous regions where hunting is easier for them and there are fewer humans to interfere with their activity.

The absence of any aviary adversaries has permitted unchecked the expanded growth of other creatures such as reptiles, amphibians, and insects. There are several types of harmless lizards, small turtles, and one rather poisonous snake on Okinawa, the habu. Habu runs to about four feet and is not often seen in the south end, although one gets there from time to time. There are hundreds of sizes and shapes of both tropical and semi-tropical orders of insects which are present all year round. Flies and mosquitoes pester even through the winter time. Butterflies and moths are beautiful, abundant—and ruin clothes. None of the countless insect and spider varieties is particularly harmful except for an occasional scorpion. But now that the birds are back, the pest population, which has long since become inured to DDT, is beginning to return to a more reasonable natural balance.

There were a few dogs in the prewar days; postwar there were none. During the early days of the occupation if a dog appeared it generally had to be kept on a leash because Okinawans at that time would steal them to eat as meat in their extreme hunger. Since 1950, though, dogs have begun to reappear. As late as 1963, it was observed that Okinawan dogs bark very little and seldom chase cats. In the mid-1960s, because of great American influence, dogs became very common. There are now six kennel clubs and a good number of commercial kennels, some of which cater even to poodle clipping. There is no Okinawan dog catcher. Until 1945, domestic animals were of the usual variety—a few cows and some goats on occasional farms, also some bulls (a local type of bullfighting, pitting bull against bull, was practiced until the war). From the war until recently there has been complete absence of cattle. Now GRI is trying to encourage a cattle industry through the Ryukyuan Development Loan Fund with aid from the Department of Agriculture. The outlying island of Ishigaki was the one selected by U.S. husbandmen as best for cattle raising.

Wild animals of the Ryukyuan chain are hares, pigs, wild boars, flying foxes, shrews, and mice. The original sources of these animals were tropical and northern Asia, and they probably arrived by way of the "land bridge." These animals are far more limited in variety and number than those of Taiwan, to the south, or Japan, farther north. There are also a variety of sea cows (dugong), fruit bats, rabbits, and far too many rats and mice. The Ryukyuan climate encourages growth in every living order. The lush, semitropical abundant plant life, which came originally from the East Indies-Philippine-Polynesian areas, exists in an estimated fifty thousand different varieties of ferns, trees, and shrubs. For comparison, the entire North Atlantic region of the United States supports no more than six thousand types. Molds specifically are a great nuisance on Okinawa. Clothing, shoes, books, and other things sprout growths of mold overnight. This necessitates keeping everything in a closet with an electric light going, which gives off both light and heat. It dries the air and eliminates the conditions supporting mold growth.

Surrounding the islands, a whole world of plant life exists in the ocean itself, where many of the smallest and largest plants are found. Billions of submicroscopic plants float through the ocean waters, serving as food for fish and other smaller marine creatures. Many ocean plants help to build up the coral reefs which are the very substance of the islands. Occasionally some marine fauna are edible. Farther to the north, Pacific kelp (a kind of seaweed), has been known to grow over 250 feet long. From some orders of these seaweeds, we get agar-agar, a gelatinous material widely used for scientific research in hospitals and laboratories. The ocean may someday provide the food for the Ryukyus if the population exceeds the land's ability to sustain it.

Ocean currents determine the local weather anywhere in the world. Okinawa, within the North Temperate Zone, nonetheless has a semi-tropical climate due to the influence of the Japan current, which warms and humidifies the trade winds from the south. The mean daily minimum temperature for February, the coolest month, is about 50° F., but I have been there in January when it got down to 35°. July is the warmest month, when the mean daily temperature hits around 90° F., but it does occasionally get up near enough to 100° with high humidity. The highest recorded temperature was 96° F. marked at Naha on July 21, 1916, though records of those days are now questionable.

The humidity is excessive, averaging 80 per cent relative throughout the entire year. One alleviating factor is the constant monsoonal winds which blow from the west and perhaps northwest during the winter, and from the south and east during the summer. These bring heavy rains at times. Precipitation is extremely heavy, ranging through the islands from 53 to 118 inches per year. Naha has an annual rainfall of 83 inches. May and June are the heaviest precipitation times which constitute the so-called "rainy season," yet November is an extremely rainy month and, extraordinarily, during January 1966 when I was there it rained every day but three. An important factor is that the Ryukyuan chain lies within the typhoon belt of the East China Sea. As many as forty-five typhoons form within this area each year, much as the hurricanes begin in the Caribbean area. Annually from three to six can be expected to affect Okinawa directly. The typhoon season is long, running from April through October, and it is exceptional but not unheard of for a typhoon to strike between November and April. Nevertheless, even during the heaviest periods of damage, Okinawans seem to live through; now, so do the Americans on the island.

This endless weatherbeating with its strong effect on the people has not appreciably affected the land, which has survived four natural catastrophies in its geological history. It still survives and supports its people, yet, from its depths it has grudgingly given up only the meagerest mineral resources. Beds of hard-packed limestone are found in Okinawa and Ishigaki, which indicate that the islands are truly of primordial undersea origin. Low-grade coal deposits of no industrial significance on Irimoto indicate former eras of flourishing tropical vegetation and subsequent natural cataclysms. There are deposits of sulphur, phosphate, granite, as well as scant traces of gold, iron, and copper which have been found scattered throughout the islands. None of these materials exists in commercially exploitable quantities, except in the area of Motobu Peninsula just west of Nago. A great find of natural limestone and other aggregates has led to the formation of a hopefully very profitable cement industry. Okinawa is no exception to the ancient basic, prereligious concept that the land is the mother and nothing comes except from it.

# CHAPTER 9

# The Gentle People

But for the lack of leaders, the Okinawans might have been the masters of the Eastern seas, and Okinawa the Venice of the Orient. Such a leader need only have been someone capable of instilling among the Ryukyuans unity of purpose and inspiration. At present, the Ryukyuan chances for producing perhaps several such types are better than they have ever been, due mainly to the improved conditions enjoyed by native children of the current generation.

For a time in the fifteenth and sixteenth centuries, the Okinawans themselves were the creators of an enterprise which could well have established them as a strong, free nation. But instead they chose to build ships and sail under the absentee domination of the Chinese. Ryukyuans were able and daring seamen. This, combined with a favorable geographic location, moved them to develop a very profitable seaborne trade throughout the entire southeast Asian area. *Theirs* was the first nucleus for the Great East Asia Co-Prosperity Sphere. Actually, during the fifteenth and sixteenth centuries, Okinawa did have the economic power which, under the guidance of some more able and astute statesmen (with or without the help of military leaders), could very well have turned Japan under Ryukyuan dominance. There came no such person, propinquity went wanting, and the chance was lost forever.

The average adult Ryukyuan stands about five feet tall, is a bit bowlegged, rather brown, and is lean and wiry. He has black hair, and rounder eyes than the Japanese. Okinawans tend to be friendly and nonaggressive. With diet and vitamin improvement, postwar babies tend to be straighter-boned, heavier-set, and lighter in pigment, but the brownish rather than yellowish skin cast still predominates.

Somewhat more than a million of these people live in the Ryukyu island chain; over 900,000 of them on Okinawa. This population density is comparable to Baltimore. The capital city of Naha now spreads out in typical twentieth-century fashion through its suburbs and exurbs, which have swallowed up the old city of Shuri. Naha goes down nearly as far south as Itoman and boasts a population exceeding 260,000, as many people as in Wichita, Kansas.

The original Ryukyuans descended from those Peking men who wandered out over the prehistoric land bridge from South Asia. They were early Mongolian types soon joined by Malaysians and Micronesians after the fourth geological upheaval left the chain as islands. Even today, the Micronesian element appears in the thatched hut and pot styles of the rural Ryukyuan areas. Ethnologists claim there are no basic Ainu strains in Okinawan folk.

Before men thought of sails or boats, they drifted on logs or rafts wherever the ocean currents carried them. After having crossed the Pacific just above the equator, the North Equatorial Current turns right at the Philippines, becomes the Black or Japan Current, and flows north, channeling the tropical Pacific waters up to warm the eastern shores of the Japanese islands. Along this permanent northward course, the current passes on both sides of the Ryukyu chain. In Kon-Tiki fashion, this is how the Malays and Micronesians migrated to Okinawa, but, conversely, this is why no early venturesome Japanese could ever have drifted south to the Ryukyus in time to be a founding father. In that area even now, occasional boatloads of bearded, weary, and hungry Filipino sailors get beached on Ryukyuan shores, having drifted up from their home waters after losing a sail, engine, or rudder.

Okinawa is the place where the winds divide and blow north and south. The bulk of the air mass which arrives at that Okinawan split blows from the west, due to the rotation of the earth. All the storms of China blow out over the East China Sea, the majority hit the Ryukyus and cause havoc, or else they bifurcate and dissipate. Primordial sailors lacking such simple sophistications as "tacking" or "jibing" could only sail the way the winds blew, which was again from Okinawa toward Japan. Eventually, though, they caught the trick of sailing into the wind and against the currents, and then Japanese did get to Okinawa. A very early one of those, who made his mark in history and the arts, was Tametomo. The legendary advent of Minamoto Tametomo signaled the prelude to recorded Ryukyuan history. Okinawans regard the prior time, beginning with the "creation" of Kudaka until the equivalent of the Western year 1187, as an Elysian era. Old tales tell of twenty-five Tenson kings through that extended epoch, all of whose names had been lost in antiquity—along with all trace of their accomplishments. Then Shunten, the twenty-four-year-old son of Tametomo, forcibly overthrew the last of the Tenson kings, collected taxes, established his own dynasty with some law and order, and began to record local history.

Okinawa had a promising new era started that year of A.D. 1187. In that same 1187, another war had ended in the Middle East when Jerusalem fell to Saladin and his Islamic world, thus ending in defeat the first of the Crusades. England was in political turmoil without Richard; and under Prince Igor, the Russians were having at it with the Tartars on the steppes of Central Asia. On Okinawa, Shunten came by his dynamism naturally. His father, Tametomo, landed at Unten-Ko, a little cove opposite Yagachi Shima, where the leper colony is now. He soon became notorious for his many legendary deeds, disturbing the days of the Tenson King. Legend credited him with amazing feats of strength and miracles of archery. Soon Tametomo was sought after by the Okinawan lords attempting to destroy him. (The Japanese entourage with which he landed had either gone back to Japan, assimilated, or been killed off.) Against the tide, Takamine, an Okinawan lord of a manor standing close to what is now Machiminato, made him a guest. Tametomo soon married his host's beautiful daughter, and their union quickly begot a son. Shunten was born in 1163.

Shortly after, Tametomo, still a fugitive from the King's in-group, seized a chance to return to Japan to recoup his health and fortune. He left his wife and little Shunten on Okinawa. The princess waited daily on the beach at Machiminato Inlet in vain for his return, and her vigil is said to have been the genuine origin of the "Madama Butterfly" story of a later century. On the death of Takamine, his grandfather, young Shunten became lord of the manor at fifteen. As he grew, he developed so many strong traits from his hybrid, noble breeding that between the age of twenty-two and twenty-four he was able to overthrow the Tenson King and establish the first significant "new" order on the island, which lasted half a century.

Although the general pattern of Shunten's fifty-year reign held up for thirty-six kings until the Japanizing in 1879, Shunten's dynasty itself was able to last a mere two kings through twenty-two years after his death. His grandson Gihon yielded to the all-Ryukyuan Eiso Dynasty in 1260, thus ending both the Shunten line and any Japanese claim to blood relationship with the Okinawan throne. The chart on page 126, prepared by Dr. Shunzo Sakamaki, Professor of History at the University of Hawaii, lists all five dynasties and their thirty-six monarchs, none of whom, stories or history relates, really had an easy time.

From 1337 to 1349, the island was divided into three zones, each with its own king, no one strong enough to absorb another. As time went on, there were several combinations and détentes among them, but it was not until 1429 that Shō Hashi actually was able to prove that final reunification was a fact. Midway through this period of civil strife, Satto, unable to defend his schizoid domain, kow-towed and began to send cash tribute to the Chinese throne in 1372, a practice which continued on and off for five hundred years, until the Japanese forced a stop by taking it all for themselves. This was not done at once, but gradually, and over centuries.

The Satsuma clan of southern Japan was diverted from advancing politically

## THE SUCCESSIVE RULERS OF CHŪZAN (RYŪKYŪ)

***The Shunten Dynasty***
Shunten (1187–1237)
Shunba Junki (1238–1248)
Gihon (1249–1259)

***The Eiso Dynasty***
Eiso (1260–1299)
Taisei (1300–1308)
Eiji (1309–1313)
Tamagusuku (1314–1336)
Sei-i (1337–1349)

***The Satto Dynasty***
Satto (1350–1395)
Bunei (1396–1405)

***The Shō Shishō Dynasty***
Shō Shishō (1406–1421)
Shō Hashi (1422–1439)
Shō Chū (1440–1444)
Shō Shitatsu (1445–1449)
Shō Kinpuku (1450–1453)
Shō Taikyū (1454–1460)
Shō Toku (1461–1469)

***The Shō En Dynasty***
Shō En (1470–1476)
Shō Sen-i (1477)
Shō Shin (1477–1526)
Shō Sei (1527–1555)
Shō Gen (1556–1572)
Shō Ei (1573–1588)
Shō Nei (1589–1620)
Shō Hō (1621–1640)
Shō Ken (1641–1647)
Shō Shitsu (1648–1668)
Shō Tei (1669–1709)
Shō Eki (1710–1712)
Shō Kei (1713–1751)
Shō Boku (1752–1794)
Shō On (1795–1802)
Shō Sei (1803)
Shō Kō (1804–1828)
Shō Iku (1829–1847)
Shō Tai (1848–1879)

at home by being "given" the rights to exploit the islands to the south. In 1609, the Satsumas in a force of three thousand landed at Unten-Ko (just as Tametomo had) and dealt the Chinese influence on Okinawa a mortal blow. Yet this moribund Chinese hold lasted some 250 years more in an incredible Ryukyuan period of dual subordination. The effective control of foreign affairs and the internal administration of all concerns in the Ryukyus were completely handled and dominated by the Japanese Satsumas simultaneously with the increase of Chinese cultural and commercial influence. The Ryukyuan people continued to use Chinese habits, culture, customs, and the court language of the Chinese. Shuri continued its tributary relationship to Peking, while it continued to permit the Satsuma clan to exercise the internal and foreign affairs domination. Japan's active role led to her ultimate success; China lost out because she stayed at home and waited, or hoped to prevail by cultural influence alone. Actually Japan had no more armed strength than the Ryukyuans, if only the Ryukyuans had had the courage and leadership to refuse or defy. But they never tried, preferring to believe their condition was not the result of the doings of mortal men, rather it was the will of the deity.

The principal religion in Okinawa is Buddhism, which was introduced through China and Japan. It came originally to Japan from India, through China and Korea, during the middle of the sixth century A.D. Buddhism not only flourishes as a religion among these trusting and gentle folk, but it has given much to enrich Okinawan arts and learning. Shintoism, which cannot be regarded as a religion in the strict sense of the word, is a Japanese indigenous cult. It is concerned with the worship of the imperial ancestors, with the family ancestors as a lesser consideration. During World War II, Shintoism was considered a state religion and was encouraged by both the Emperor and the Japanese military government. Under the new constitution in Japan, Shintoism no longer receives any special official encouragement or privileges; however, it exists side by side (and sometimes overlaps in the popular mind) with the practice of Buddhism. Many Okinawans today go through Shinto rites when they marry, though Buddhist rites are preferred for funerals. In many shrines on Okinawa today, such as the Nami-No-Ue-Gu shine, there is a Buddhist temple and a Shinto shrine side by side at the top of the hill, behind the three arches.

Christianity is embraced by relatively few Ryukyuans, though somewhat more in the last twenty years of American influence. It began there with the Reverend Father Matthew Adnet, an apostolic missionary from Paris. He lived in Naha with a few colleagues and converted some Okinawans early in the nineteenth century. After death, Father Adnet was buried in the Tomari International Cemetery, July 1848, five years before Perry's arrival at almost that very spot.

Commodore M. C. Perry steamed into Naha Bay in late May 1853, but was not officially received by King Shō Tai until June 6. Then he and a small group went up to Shuri Castle and wished prosperity to the "Lewchewans"

(Ryukyuans). Perry offered friendship, trade, and aid, and asked for the rental of a naval base. The last item was denied him by Shō Tai because he felt it would attract too many enemies of Japan. Perry guested until mid-August 1853, and then went on to open Japan to the ways of the Western world. Not everyone who came to Okinawa with Perry in 1853 or on his return visit of 1854 left with him. In the same little International Cemetery with Father Adnet lie seven American casualties of that peace mission. Though they buried the "Gai Jins" (foreigners) in Western fashion, they buried their own with a home tradition.

The most unique sight throughout the Ryukyus is the indigenous turtleback tomb called the Gan; or the square tomb named Hafu. These tombs are everywhere on Okinawa—along the highways, in back yards, over the hills, and throughout the fields. There are over thirty thousand specimens of the turtleback variety on the island, and there is claimed to be an equal number of the old square-cut type.

The Gan is an Okinawan innovation, evolving from the mounds used by the old Chinese in Kume village, combined with the ancient cave-type Okinawan tombs which give the turtleback appearance. The Gan is also called turtle shell or Kane-No-Ko. Many Okinawans feel that the shape symbolizes a woman in childbirth and link the design to the idea of returning to the source or womb. Another theory is that the dome, usually built into the hillside, was patterned after the turtle shell because the turtle is the symbol of long life. The cultural affairs division of the U.S. Civil Administration believes that the design evolved fortuitously among a primitive and isolated island people. Another story claims the Gan to be the tomb designed for the famed Lord Gosamaru of Nakagusuku castle in 1460. The popularity of Gosamaru added to the popularity of the turtleback tomb. Many people visited the Gan, liked the arrangement, and perpetuated it. Despite the quantity, Hafu, the original type of Okinawan tomb, was only for nobility. It was much simpler than the turtleback. The Hafu has a square stone entrance and a top which lofts into a hillside. In recent years, the Hafu has again become popular because it is far less expensive than the turtleback to build.

All tombs are very expensive. Many Okinawans go deeply into debt to buy a family tomb. The Japanese Government before the war and now USCAR have both waged verbal campaigns against this costly practice. Thus many families since the prewar days have turned to the Japanese custom of cremation. Even so, the tomb is a strong symbol of filial piety in Okinawan culture. Tombs take up much needed space from the living. In August of 1965, the New York *Times* reported that ". . . as Okinawa's cities push outward and land values soar, the traditional . . . tombs that dot the island's fields and hillsides are becoming an increasing impediment to its expansion.

"Thousands are being demolished as families transfer the bones and spiritual resting places of their ancestors to quieter, and less valuable, surroundings. . . . Naha and its widening suburbs there encompass some 6000 tombs which must be removed or relocated under the city's plan for expansion to be put into effect this year.

"The national cemetery, established on a hill west of Naha in 1949, has room for about 3400 additional tombs of the uniform, compact design now becoming popular. Officials are trying to obtain an additional 50 acres of land from neighboring communities. In purchasing the land now occupied by tombs, . . . the city allocated about $1500 per tomb, or a total of 9 million dollars for the entire project."

Gosamaru, to whose tomb the Gan is attributed, was an Okinawan hero. His legend developed in August 1460 at Nakagusuku castle, which had just been built after three years of backbreaking labor—every stone had to be carried to the summit. History says that Prince Gosamaru built the castle in order to defend his King, Shō Taikyu. It was rumored that Amawari of Katsuren castle was raising an army to march against the King at Shuri. Both Gosamaru and Amawari were still in communication with the King. Gosamaru tried to warn the King that Amawari was plotting against him and consequently built Nakagusuku to defend him, while Amawari resorted to trickery. He lied that Gosamaru was raising an army to attack Shuri, to cover his own skulduggery.

Amawari wanted the new castle for himself. He marched his army against Nakagusuku in the name of the King and carried the King's banner, without hte King's knowledge or consent. Gosamaru, defending his own castle and forewarned of the treachery, nevertheless refused to fight against an army bearing the King's banner. On the stone steps leading to the castle built in defense of the King's realm, Gosamaru and all his warriors committed hara-kiri on August 15, 1460. Knowing that Amawari would take his head to the King, Gosamaru, the legend says, left a vital message in his own mouth. The king found the paper, Amawari's trickery was discovered, and justice prevailed. Another version of this tale allows that Amawari's wife was the King's daughter. Believing that filial piety superseded the marriage vows, she fled to Shuri and told all in person. The King gave Gosamaru the regal tomb which has since become the national mode.

A custom related to the tomb is the cleansing of the bones of the departed. When a deceased has been entombed for three years the bones are then cleaned and polished and placed in a burial urn. These urns are then refurbished each year; they are extremely colorful, some being art treasures. Unfortunately, too many tombs were laid waste during the war. U.S. occupation forces did much to desecrate a good many of the rest.

One can often see Okinawan families gathered at a tomb with picnic food spread out on a white sheet. These parties are held for the spirits of the departed ancestors and are important affairs to the families. Those who are poor bring only oranges—no one goes empty-handed. There are special days for such parties, but they are also held whenever a family feels so inclined. The first of these special days comes close to March 21. Shunbun, the day of the vernal equinox, is a legal holiday. The Seimei season is observed in the third lunar month, marking the start of the tomb-cleaning and bone-washing season on Okinawa. Tanabata comes on the seventh day of the seventh month of the lunar calendar. On this day, a family, or its representative, visits the tombs, makes offerings of sake, and cleans the tomb again. Obon, the second most important festival for Okinawans, occurs on the fifteenth and sixteenth days of the seventh lunar month, shortly after Tanabata. Ryukyuans believe that the souls of the dead return to their earthly homes during the Obon festival to see how the descendants are getting along. Obon, with its many beautiful lanterns and variety of dishes, is a colorful holiday devoted to family reunion and recreation so that the departed may see unity and joy.

According to Shinto legend, Amaterasu, the sun goddess, was having trouble with her brother, who was wrecking her gardens. She hid herself, thus there was only darkness. The Council of the Gods decided to put up a bird perch outside her door for the rooster to call the day. This might well coax her out and bring back the light. "Bird perch" is the meaning of the old Japanese word, "toreii." The rooster crows three times in a morning, therefore three Toreii gates lead to the Shinto shrine. As the rooster prepares for the day, the three Toreiis prepare the heart of the worshiper as he passes through, approaching his shrine. The Toreii gate has been adopted as the symbol on the shoulder patch of the U.S. military establishment in the Ryukyus. The Americans have chosen to use this sacred oriental symbol for their Okinawan forces, but it has never been ascertained whether the Okinawans really approve of this. The actual Toreii gate, which now exists in the port of Naha, is the old gate to the island and the one for which Okinawa is most noted. It stands at the very back of the military port at Naha Bay. Immediately behind it, the Americans have built a large sports center in which they play football. However, behind the stadium still stands the Yomochi shrine, and the Gokoku shrine. These shrines were originally located at their present sites prior to the war and have since been reconstructed. The Toreii gate managed to withstand the war and is in its original state, with some minor patches.

The architecture of Okinawan houses is a mixture of the Micronesian thatched roofs, with Japanese and Chinese building design. Through it all, there are modifying Ryukyuan influences. Many of them have tile roofs on which one can see the "karashishi." This is a traditional ceramic Chinese guardian lion. These lions sit on the roofs to guard the house against ill winds and evil spirits.

Setsubun is a bean-throwing ceremony which comes early in February. It is held mainly in Shinto shrines and Buddhist temples. The rite of bean throwing is annually intended to bring in fortune and drive out evil. And Muuchii is the time, usually the eighth day of the twelfth lunar month, to pray for the health of all the family. Rice cakes wrapped in broad fragrant leaves of a local plant are taken this day to drive away the devil.

Juri Uma, a ceremonial parade held on the twentieth day of the first lunar month, is observed only in one area of Naha, in the neighborhood of the Nami-No-Ue shrine. It involves a parade of the geishas, intending to bring good luck to the teahouses in the area. Hina-Matsuri is the doll festival which falls in March and is observed only by little girls. On this day many sets of dolls, all in ancient Japanese court costumes, are displayed in the best room of anyone's house. Children's Day on May 5 is a public holiday widely observed. It used to be celebrated only by boys, but it is now a big day of the year for all children. Large paper replicas of carp are hoisted over the houses as symbols of longevity, while other dolls representing heroes of legendary days are put into the best rooms of the house.

Since 1950, American-Ryukyuan Friendship Day is held on the anniversary of the arrival of Commodore Perry's fleet, May 26, 1853. And now the Emperor's birthday, April 29, has again become a legal holiday just as it is in Japan. May Day is also celebrated to fit the European traditional Labor Day. Now all members of trade unions, left-wing or not, gather for mass rallies and parades through the streets of Naha and other large cities. There is a holiday on January 15, Adults' Day—the day when all young fellows whose twentieth birthdays fell within the preceding year go out to sow their oats. Tokachi is the day of celebration for all those eighty-eight years of age. It falls on the eighth day of the eighth lunar month. This day is called "beiju" in Japanese, or "rice longevity," since the kanji character for rice also appears in the kanji character for eighty-eight.

Tsunahiki, a gigantic tug-of-war to commemorate the harvest, falls on the twenty-sixth day of the six month of the lunar calendar. The best known and most widely attended celebration of this is at Yonabaru, where the whole town is divided into two teams, East and West. The teams tug on a huge rope five feet in diameter at its center, tapering to about three feet in diameter at its ends. The strands come out to be held by each participant. The fun comes from the side betting.

Tsuki-Mi is the last big celebration of the lunar year. It means "moon watching." This event is held toward the end of lunar August and it is from this that the term "August Moon" has come. Moon-viewing parties are common, and the lion dance, Gibo-cho, is performed under bright moonlight in Shuri. "August Moon" has come to have other meanings to Americans, as does Yuletide. The final holiday of the year is Christmas. This has been brought in by the Americans, but because it has taken on such a festive air, the Okinawans have now adopted it and like the idea, although they do not believe in the Christian meaning behind the actual celebration. Instead, they observe Hana-Matsuri, the flower festival which is held on April 8 in honor of the birthday of Buddha. Buddhists go to their temples and pour sweet tea from tiny ladles over small statues of Buddha. It is a serene and sacred day.

Of all the celebrations in the Ryukyus, Haryu-sen, the dragon boat races, is the most exciting. Races are held on the fourth day of the fifth lunar month, generally early in June by the Western calendar. This holiday calls for heats of boats competing for the honors. The races run at the fishing port of Itoman with the overflow at Tomari port. Okinawans race in thirty-foot canoes, each manned by twelve paddlers. Boats are brilliantly painted to represent racing dragons. All fishing boats are also decorated on lunar New Year's, of course, but never quite as elaborately as they are for Haryu-sen. The idea for the feast originated in Itoman, the largest fishing village on Okinawa. Itoman is unusual in that women there, since the beginning, have always enjoyed equal rights with men. And here, as nowhere else in all the Far East, polyandry (having multiple husbands), is practiced. Moreover, the women control the finances of the family. The principal shrine is Hakugin-Do, dedicated to the sea god, where, at a side altar, Itoman women also worship the fertility god.

Legend says that long ago an Itoman landowner, in order to try to emancipate himself from his position of being beholden to his wife and her wealth, borrowed mony from a Japanese lord. He was doing fairly well and approaching prosperity when the samurai returned from Japan to Okinawa and demanded his money back; the time was due for it. The Okinawan was unable to pay, the samurai was furious, demanding only the man's head. To this the Okinawan said, "If you cut off my head, you may then have satisfied your ego, but it will not get one yen of your money back. On the other hand, if you allow me to continue as I am going, I will be able to give your money back in a short while. Besides, I shall give you some handsome interest. For whatever it is worth, you get a bit of wisdom which my sage gave to me only this morning."

The samurai, still furious, said, "Well, all right, I should lop off your head but I shall listen to you just one more time. Then your answer is no money, no head. I give you this one chance. I shall be back in a year for my money." In the meanwhile, the Okinawan, grateful for the chance to go on with his pursuits, said, "For your indulgence now, I pass along this sage advice. Do not under *any* circumstances act with haste or impetuosity. Pause carefully and think twice, or three times, before you do anything drastic."

The samurai just stalked off, boarded his boat, and returned to Japan. Upon his arrival at his home estate late at night, he entered very quietly, not wishing to disturb his wife. In his own bedroom, by the light of his little candle, he could very well see his wife there, safely in bed, and right beside her was a sleeping companion. Angrily he drew his sword, about to do in the sleeping pair, when from the depths of his memory came the advice from his Itoman debtor. Rather than act in haste, he took the point of his sword and whipped off the covers. Indeed his wife was in bed, and the person whom he thought was a man beside her turned out to be the samurai's own mother! Awakened by the fuss, she told him that in his absence she disguised herself as a man, and slept beside the young wife. Thus no nighttime intruder would ever see the wife "alone."

Because the samurai had heeded the Okinawan's advice, he spared himself the anguish of matricide. Feeling completely grateful to the Ryukyuan, he decided to return to Itoman and tell the man he was to be absolved of his debt. Excitedly, at Itoman, he told the story to his debtor, who advised that one of his investments had turned over well and he then had the money, ready to pay. "You must keep the money," the samurai insisted. The Okinawan again refused. Finally they agreed, since neither would accept the sum, to use it to build a shrine to the sea god. Thus the Hakugin-Do shrine came into being—from the independent spirits in the Orient's most unusual village.

The Itoman legend, and other tales of Ryukyuan folk lore, change some while passing verbally from generation to generation and from village to village as stories and songs. In recent centuries, historical events have been more accurately preserved and perpetuated via the living theatre and in the graphic arts. During the fifteenth and sixteenth centuries, techniques for weaving, dyeing, and stenciling fine fabrics, additional arts and crafts, music, dance forms, and other cultural customs were all imported from the Chinese. Through the Okinawans' extensive sailing, Siamese, Malayan, and East Indian customs and arts also found their way into Ryukyuan life.

The most characteristic of all items of Okinawan art is the bingata. No one, if he has once seen the bingata, will fail to recognize it as exclusively a Ryukyuan product. Among things typically Ryukyuan, the bingata is the easiest to recognize as a hand-dyed cloth with patterns in bright colors—reds, yellows, blues, and maroons. Intermediate colors are seldom used. The bingata is unique for the bold floral designs which completely disregard the seasons they are supposed to depict. The bingata is like a juvenile drawing in which chrysanthemums, cherry, and plum blossoms are in full bloom while snow is falling. No one really knows when bingata printing started on Okinawa, but it must have begun some five hundred years ago, after hand-printing techniques were introduced from Japan. Printing techniques have stayed virtually unchanged through the centuries, but the Ryukyuans have added their own colors and designs of local taste. Bingata printers in Shrui say that their liking for bright colors descends from tropical people, while the designs are a combination of those from China and Japan. For many centuries, most bingata painters lived in Shuri under patronage of royal families, where their techniques were handed down from generation to generation. Generally a design cutter must be agile, adroit, and have several years' experience before he can be employed as a full-fledged cutter.

Having been rejuvenated after the war, five bingata plants are now in operation. Bingata kimonos once worn for important occasions were made only for upper class women. Today, print cloth is available in many forms, including tablecloths, wall hangings, screens, obis, kimonos, and even handbag covers. A bingata artist describes the process: "Designs are cut with a needle-sharp stylus on a thick mulberry paper which has been dipped and hardened with persimmon sap, shibugami. Pigments are mostly indigenous, blue from indigo produced in northern Okinawa, yellow from fukugi-tree bark, and the maroons come from takasharinbai, shrub bark. A clay pigment is imported from southeast Asia whenever possible. Sometimes our knives are made from old hacksaw blades. After the cutting, a young lady generally will dub pigment on a cloth, using blunt brushes. The colors are repeatedly rubbed in to gain uniform texture. Then the cloth is soaked in water for about two hours before enough rice-bran paste remains on it. The rest is washed away. Finished designs are placed on cotton silk or hemp cloth and then the rice-bran paste is put over the shibugami design. Parts to remain are painted and covered by the water-resistant paste. Finished bingatas are sold at many stores on Okinawa. But today a collector looking for a real work of art may visit the works at Shuri for good ones."

Good folk songs are hard to come by. Today, generally, all that remains are the Japanese songs and a few Okinawan songs. Little remains of Chinese music. Musical instruments are mostly the Japanese samisen and the little bamboo flutes. There is now a resurgence of interest and consequent formal instruction in koto, due to the efforts of such soloists as Kiyoko Miyagi and musicologists as Mrs. Samuel Kitamura. The koto (a two-hand, plucked stringed instrument closely resembling two large barrel staves about six feet long and two feet wide with all thirteen strings along the top) and its music were introduced into Japan from China and Korea in the ninth century, and from Japan to Okinawa.

In 1966, during a visit, I asked Shō Sen, the managing director of Radio Okinawa (a private enterprise), if all Ryukyuan folk music had been destroyed by the war or by the commercial rock-and-roll forms from Japan and America. He responded with a gift pair of original LP records, all four sides cut live in his studio especially for me. From time to time at home now I listen to this personalized slice of Ryukyuan folk life. The roughly typed program notes, given me in both Japanese and English, tell an eloquent story for themselves, and are presented in their original state:

1. (a) KAJADE-FOU-BUSHI
ARTIST: KOCHI Kamoshiyo, well-known authority on Ryukyuan music
INSTRUMENTS: Samisen and Koto

This is a classic song, traditional at happy gatherings. The words express the general idea that the day celebrated can be compared to buds coming into full flower.

1. (b) (1) ICHI-HANARI-BUSHI
ARTIST: FUNAKOSHI Kiyo (Mrs.) and ITOKAZU Kamo (Mrs.)
INSTRUMENTS: Samisen and drums

This is a sort of complex song . . . the mingling of a love affair of a girl from the small off-island of Ikei with a man on Okinawa and the scene of the off-islands viewed from Okinawa, the main island. It is a sort of patriotic song using the symbolism of a love story.

1. (b) (2) TANCHYA-MEA-BUSHI
ARTISTS: ITOKAZU Kame (Mrs.) and FUNAKOSHI Kiyo (Mrs.)
INSTRUMENTS: Samisen and drums

This is a song that accompanies a traditional dance. It is the dance-story of a swarming of small bait-fish at the beach at Tanchya village and the gathering of young men and women to net them and the fun had at this impromptu party. (Young men and young women were traditionally segregated and their conduct closely watched in the old days, when caste was important and marriages arranged. An event like this was too seldom and naturally very popular.)

3-b HIYA-MICACHI-BUSHI
ARTISTS: The five Misses IHA
INSTRUMENTS: Samisen, castanets (samba—local name), and drum

This is a modern song, composed by YANAGUCHI Seisen, and the title means "Let's Raise UP," a sort of musical encouragement to his compatriots to face the problems of reconstruction after the war (WW II). YANAGUCHI is well-known in Oriental musical circles.

4-a TOBARUMA
ARTIST: OHAMA Yatsuomo (an authority on Yaeyama folk music)
INSTRUMENTS: Samisen and pipe (a sort of Ryukyuan fife)

This is a love story, told in geographical symbolism. The separation of Yaeyama and Okinawa by miles of open water is the theme . . . a real tear-jerker in Yaeyama.

3-a KARIMATA-NU-ISAMIGA
ARTISTS: Miyako Folk Song Group (professional people dedicated to collecting and preserving fast-vanishing traditional music)
INSTRUMENTS: Samisen

Katrimata is the name of a village in Miyako and Isamiga is Miyako dialect for "young girls." It tells the story of a traditional party when the girls of the village went as a group to gather shell fish and the nice time they had and the catch they made. (Such excursions were bright spots in the year, back in the old days).

2-a (1) (2) KANNA-YOO & AMAKAWA
ARTISTS: Cannot be identified
INSTRUMENTS: Samisen and drum

Music to a popular quick-tempo folk dance. Kanna-yoo means a general pet names for girls and Amakawa means, roughly, "girl-watching" . . . and often singers improvise lyrics to suit the occasion.

Ryukyuan theater arts combine features of the Chinese opera and the Kabuki Theater of Japan. They are sagas usually taking many hours, during which the audience eats. The costumes are beautiful; the settings are works of colorful art; the live performance on stage includes music, the dance, singing, and dramatic acting; actually all forms of theater arts including locating the musicians on stage. They either take part in the performance or sit on the side of the stage to play and theoretically be ignored by the audience. In the early days of occupation, I enjoyed seeing rather makeshift performances. Later, theater was produced by traveling Japanese companies, especially a marvelous and devoted one from Hiroshima. They were true professionals, being Japanese by nationality but giving performances in the Ryukyus in the same original Shuri Okinawan dialect in which the old native playwrights had written them. Oriental formal theater defies description, and one must experience it personally to know what it is like.

The big things on Okinawa today are movies and bars. These American institutions have taken over for the most part, though there are also six television channels. Fortunately some customs of old are still observed which reflect Okinawan culture and traditions. Though theater performances are brought in via fine professional companies from Japan, there are also many local theater groups in the high schools and amateur theatrical companies. In general, nearly all the festivals are accompanied by music, and costumes are from old tradition; but these are dying off and not being refurbished or replaced. Shō Hiroshi, the grandson of Shō Tai (and cousin of Radio Okinawa's Shō Sen), now spends half his time in Tokyo and half in Naha. Shō Hiroshi is the owner in Tokyo of the largest and finest collection of Ryukyuan art in existence. Happy not to have to be king, he is active on Okinawa, not in political or commercial life, but in trying to bring about a renaissance of Ryukyuan art and culture, to keep it from turning completely Western.

The history of Okinawa is an interweaving among the incursions of the Japanese and the Chinese, and a desperate maintenance of national tradition within the islands. The Ryukyuans had had a fine chance in the "Golden Age" and let it get away. In 1511, an Okinawan mission arrived at Malacca on Malay Peninsula just after the city was besieged and occupied by the Portuguese. This was the occasion of the Ryukyuans' first contact with Europeans. Through the Ryukyus the Portuguese extended their Western maritime trade to the Far East all of which Portugal eventually took over. This marked the beginning of the decline of Ryukyuan seaborne commerce before it really reached maturity. The Spaniards, the British, and the Dutch followed the Portuguese, aided by the European Renaissance, which brought about new techniques in navigation, improved ship design, and the perfection of firearms (which was made possible by Marco Polo's originally taking gunpowder from the Chinese to Europe). The Chinese had gunpowder for ages but used it only for celebrations. But the Westerners returned it to the Orient for use in death-dealing instruments, a practice which still has not ceased, even in 1968.

Okinawans, although able at seamanship, did not have the leaders and the wealth the Europeans had. The beginning of the seventeenth century saw the transition from exploration to the establishment of Western settlements in the Orient. It also marked a finish for the Okinawans as a maritime power. Once they had within their grasp the possibility of being the central nation in east Asia, but they failed to take advantage of it. They chose the role of subordinate to the Chinese Empire, later falling farther under both China and Japan. Eventually the Ryukyuans let themselves be swallowed whole by the Japanese, where they remained quietly until the close of World War II.

# CHAPTER 10

# China, the Befuddled Dragon

Legends about "Islands in the Eastern Sea" southwest of Korea appear in Chinese records as early as the third century B.C. But concrete reference in the Ryukyus (or the Loo Choos, as they were called in China) appears in the archives of A.D. 605. Chinese annals for A.D. 607 mention an unsuccessful expedition to these islands. The following year a Chinese force did reach the island of Okinawa and demand that the people acknowledge the Chinese Emperor as their suzerain. The difficulty was in communication. None of the Chinese could speak the local Okinawan dialect and naturally no Okinawans were able to speak Chinese. Consequently a battle ensued and the invaders withdrew taking back to the Chinese mainland about one thousand captive Okinawans.

In 1187, while Shunten organized the first united kingdom on Okinawa, the southern Sungs were ruling in China in the eleventh dynasty. The regime of the southern Sungs lasted 152 years, to 1279, but had very little to do with the Okinawans. Late in the thirteenth century Kublai Khan made repeated demands on the Ryuku Islands, attempting to bring them under Mongol rule, insisting that they help him provide a force and a staging area for an invasion of Japan. To enforce this there was a Chinese invasion of Okinawa and again a battle and withdrawal. More Okinawan captives were removed to mainland China. But neither the Japanese invasion nor the alliance with Okinawa ever materialized.

The new Ming dynasty in 1368 began the thirteenth epoch in China. In 1372 Emperor Hung-wu sent the third of the Chinese missions to the Ryukyu Islands. They approached Shuri with gifts and demands on the incumbent central kingdom. Satto, the King at Shuri, acquiesced. Thus finally the Chinese were successful and a tributary relationship ensued. Chinese customs and culture began to flow into the central Okinawan kingdom and later throughout the entire island and other islands of the chain. Chinese settlers grouped in a section of Naha and established a trading community, which was known then as Kume Mura. It later became Kume village, and the Chinese people there eventually assimilated into Ryukyuan life. Okinawans today, including the Shō family (of the dynasty), take pride in their Chinese heritage, though Kume village was annihilated in World War II, and never re-established.

Many Okinawans, traders and scholars alike, would go to China in the official annual tribute missions from Shuri. They were allowed to stay there and engage in business. It is not known if they were ever able to trace the Chinese descendants of those Okinawans taken away in the two earlier unsuccessful invasions. The Chinese permitted the Okinawans only in their coastal cities, and many young Okinawans from patrician families were sent to study in China's fine schools.

The Mongol influence of the early fourteenth century finally crumbled. With it went China's control of the overland trade routes through Asia. Then Vasco da Gama, the Portuguese, discovered an all-water route to the Orient. Thereafter foreign commerce and international intercourse went via sea lanes instead of going overland. The Chinese were either unable or unwilling to become a maritime nation and, therefore, withdrew to their homeland and considered all other areas as tribute territories of the Emperor. It was beneath the dignity of the Chinese to travel to outside areas in search of commerce; rather, they insisted the Ryukyuans come to them. With extremely limited natural resources, the Ryukyuans provided few products for tribute and trade with the Chinese, and thus Chinese interest in Okinawa waned. The Ryukyuans themselves built up maritime trading, and through the entire fifteenth and sixteenth centuries Ryukyuan vessels played a significant role in the commerce of that area. They ran as far south as Siam and the Indies, and Naha resembled Venice, a transshipment port for a great many items passing through to other areas. For a long time it was the clearinghouse for indirect trade between China and Japan.

Chinese emperor Hsüan-tê did nothing when in 1429 Okinawan King Shō Hashi reunited the three kingdoms. The unification of the Okinawan kingdom meant acceptance and continuation of the tributary status. Ryukyuans also continued to be middlemen in lucrative trade which brought great profits to all Okinawans especially to the Chinese Kume village. The tribute came out of the profits. As a result, through no effort of China, its culture and art came to the Ryukyus, along with the three items which remain a part of the staple Ryukyuan diet, rice, sugar cane, and sweet potatoes.

Ties with China continued to strengthen. Chinese literature, educational processes, and all their administrative forms were taken to the Ryukyus and modified to meet local needs. In spite of the tributary relationship, the two centuries until nearly 1570 were known as the Golden Era of Ryukyuan history. The onus of Chinese authority was hardly felt though its influence was great. But this situation was a partial cause of China's undoing. During this era formal relations developed between Okinawa and Korea, and between Okinawa and Japan. Also there was some interchange of envoys with Siam, Java, and Sumatra. In 1609 the Japanese lord of the Satsuma clan began making incursions on Okinawa, and thus began the Japanese influence in the Ryukyus and the waning of the Chinese. For the following 260 years the Satsumas exercised control over the foreign and internal administration of the Ryukyus, while the Chinese exercised their absentee landlordship and received their tribute. The clan realized, too, that Okinawa was the place for the illegal trade between China and Japan.

Chinese Emperor Wan-li failed in 1609 to make any serious defenses in the Ryukyus to expel the Japanese. Consequently when the Meiji restoration came on in 1868, the Chinese had no claim to the island group. Gradually Kume village became assimilated into Okinawa, and from 1871 until the end of World War II there is no significant record of Chinese in Okinawa.

The next Chinese to come after 1871 were members of a pioneer squad who established a camp on Okinawa in 1946, not far from the site of the main U.S. contractors' interim construction base, Camp Kue. The name of the working unit which eventually grew out of this advance group was B.O.S.E.Y., *B*oard *o*f *S*upply, *E*xecutive *Y*uan (yuan, the oldest Chinese "dollar," like Japanese "yen," is used in the sense of "exchequer"). B.O.S.E.Y., was, in effect, a purchasing office. This installation was considered by the U. S. Real Property Control Office as Chinese territory, and over it flew the red, white, and blue flag of Nationalist China. These people, all agents of the moribund Kuo-min-tang government, were experts on machinery, business, international military protocol, and logistics (of course, as in any army, some were incompetent). By this time the Japanese war of attrition in China was over. The Chinese could finally move from the provisional hill capitals of Chungking and Kunming to the old republican southern capital at Nanking and attempt to re-establish the Old Chinese Republic, which might possibly have thrived had not the warlords interfered from within and the Japanese invaders from without.

Shortly after the Island Command Headquarters on Okinawa had issued permission to establish the temporary enclave of "Chinese territory," I went there to survey the installation and evaluate it for the usual report form. Fortunately as I arrived, I was recognized by David Anjen Hsiung, a major of the Chinese Air Force. Major Hsiung had been a prewar student at the University of Southern California during my one year there. He recalled our early acquaintance, and through him I was able to communicate with the entire B.O.S.E.Y. organization. I was also able to complete my survey mission report in three days, though my warm friendship with those people lasted for my entire stay on the island. There were many dinners of sumptuous Cantonese cuisine which they considered ordinary. The "special" U. S. Quartermaster fare for officers was meager recompense, as was our green beer for their jasmine tea.

I remember in particular Captain T. J. Fan. He taught himself English, and had a New York accent (rather than Brooklyn, as most of the New Yorkers in that part of the army world had). Captain Fan had the tremendous sense of humor the mission needed. Fan was able to "con" almost anything for his installation, since he was a charmer who at the same time was amazingly, disgustingly honest. The commanding officer of B.O.S.E.Y. was a general of the Chinese National Army, and a personal friend of the Generalissimo's. The general was silent, aloof, and dignified. Yet when I asked one favor of him—to Okinawa was to have been the staging area for the Allied assault on the Japanese wished to study at the prestigious Ling Nan University in Canton—he gladly agreed, and did it.

The purpose for the B.O.S.E.Y. mission in the Ryukyus was simple. Since Okinawa was to have been the staging area for the Allied assault on the Japanese home islands, a tremendous amount of military stores accumulated for the invasion. There were jeeps, tanks, trucks, half-track vehicles, many and various pieces of heavy field artillery, small arms, provisions, duwks, other types of landing vehicles, etc. All this, convoyed brand new from U.S. war plants, was stored in many depots about the island. Naturally there was some deteriorating and pilferage. The colors were U.S. dull-finish olive drab, and everything had the white five-pointed star painted on it. B.O.S.E.Y. people were on Okinawa to look over every supply depot, select and earmark by serial number all inventory items in excellent working condition. These were to be shipped to the Chinese homeland for use in Chiang Kai-shek's Nationalist defense campaign against conquest from the north by Mao Tse-tung and Chou En-lai.

The United States Government was selling the goods to the incumbent Chinese government for 20¢ on the U.S. dollar, and the 20¢ was to have been given to the Chinese as Marshall Plan-type aid.

To transport the items to China, the B.O.S.E.Y. mission decided they would hire a British transport contractor named Marston, rather than an American, to handle crating, lugging, and loading them aboard ships bound for Chinese coastal ports. He was paid 100¢ on the dollar. This money too was "loaned" to Chiang Kai-shek by Washington.

It wasn't until 1951, at a lecture by Dr. Knight Biggerstaff, chairman of the Department of Oriental Language and History at Cornell University, that I learned the end of the story of the Okinawa equipment transfer. It seemed that the Nationalist Army was able to operate and maintain the matériel as long as it had assistance from service personnel of the English and American forces. But in rural areas, equipment would either run out of fuel or break down. Vehicles were abandoned in the fields or on the streets. Some would rust. Local people would cart away parts for their own vehicles or homes.

In time, small squads of soldiers from the north would come to work on the abandoned vehicles. Soldiers of the People's Army repaired the equipment with expertise—and painted the white star red. The local people had great respect for this new type of soldier. According to Dr. Biggerstaff, not only did the People's Army acquire all the equipment and matériel by default, but they reworked it, fixed it on the spot, to the admiration of the people. In addition, Dr. Biggerstaff observed, the soldiers were neat and shaven, did not come to loot, rape, and burn. Instead, they gave small gifts to the people. In short, they were entirely different from the unruly warlord armies these people had suffered under for thirteen centuries.

In each new area the People's Army would immediately set up a communications center, and a school to which the local children were sent. While they had to learn the party line, nevertheless they were also taught to read and write. In turn they were required to repeat at home the new ideas they learned. These are some of the strongest reasons why the Army of the north was able to run Chiang Kai-shek off the mainland to Taiwan. These are also some of the reasons why Communism fared so well at that time. The fate of the equipment store was ironic. The war matériel brought from America across the Pacific—in such bulk and at such expense—was intended to crush Japan and free China. To the ultimate possessors, the Chinese People's Army, the matériel actually served its original purpose. Had the Okinawan stockpile not existed, it is virtually certain that the United States would never have sent such mountainous stores of equipment to aid the Chinese Nationalists. What Chiang thought was a windfall at a very low price turned out to be what helped drive him into the sea. With the cessation of hostilities in China proper, the B.O.S.E.Y. mission in 1949 struck its camp and retired to Taiwan, and again the Chinese flag ceased to fly over Ryukyuan soil.

But even the Taiwan Nationals cannot agree among themselves. In Naha, early in 1966, for instance, I tried to check on the date of closing of the B.O.S.E.Y. installation. I found that no fewer than four separate and independent offices each alleged to represent the Taiwan Chinese interests. Though only two claim "official" Nationalist Government ties, not one of the four even knew the meaning of the letters B.O.S.E.Y., nor the dates the mission existed; and none of the four will recognize or communicate with any one of the others. A representative from the Central Trust of China (Taipei) has an office in Naha for trade promotion. It also distributes forms and handles traffic in both directions for goods shipments and for commercial travelers. No tourism in either direction exists or is encouraged although CAT (Civil Air Transport), the Taiwan Airline calls at Okinawa on the Tokyo–Taipei run. The Chamber of Commerce of Taiwan has a Naha office which purports to do the same things as the Central Trust; and two commercial offices, the U. S. Summit Corporation (belonging entirely to the Leong family) and the Lungan Trading Company, maintain a fair-sized import-export business. There is no consul general, per se, and no treaty.

Within the last decade, the Chiang Kai-shek regime has decided to abandon its efforts regarding a territorial claim to the Ryukyus (which old China in its time, due to the palate difference, called the Loo Choos [or Lew Chews]), even though both Okinawa and Taiwan were lost to Japan in the same 1895 treaty. Today Nationalist Chinese policy favors a rapid reversion of Okinawa and its out islands to Japan. Interestingly, Taiwan's existence depends in large measure on the proximity of the U.S. Seventh Fleet—a shield which conceivably could disappear if the United States were to leave the Ryukyus. Further, the Nationalists, in this regard, are in complete agreement with the mainlanders. The Mao Tse-tung regime gave up its earlier and unsuccessful claim to the Ryukyus.

Since Japan and the People's Republic of China have commerce and intercourse, Peking has made a vigorous attempt to dominate the Communist and Socialist parties of Japan. The OSP (Okinawa Socialist Party) is registered as the Okinawa Prefectural Headquarters of the Japan Socialist Party and accepts instructions from Socialists in Tokyo. The OSP, after abandoning the Chinese claim to the Ryukyus, for a brief period advocated an independent Ryukyuan nation.

The only course left for Peking is to support the now popular tide of Japanese residual sovereignty. This policy at least offers faint hope for an end to an American spearhead so close to their shores. Thus the "two Chinas" are united on the singular point of the Ryukyus.

# CHAPTER 11

# Japan, the Hungry Ermine

"Even with devils, we prefer the ones we're used to," says an old Japanese proverb. This may in part explain why Okinawan politicians, writers, industrialists, and labor leaders turn to Tokyo for advice and counsel, in spite of the American omnipresence and the fact that Japan has no official authority. At least they have known the Japanese longer, although their relationship has always been one of the Ryukyuan horse and the Japanese rider.

Ninety years after the first Chinese invasion of Okinawa in A.D. 608, a Japanese mission was sent to claim the "southern Islands" in the name of the Emperor Mommu. While Mommu originated the concept of Japan as the nucleus of a great empire, apparently this expedition never got as far south as Okinawa. Official records from the period refer only to the islands north of it. Later, representatives of the northern Ryukyu Islands visited Japan, bringing gifts. The Japanese considered the visits as tribute missions. The gifts were offered at the Grand Shrine at Ise, and misconstrued as tokens of recognition of imperial Japanese authority. Through the next four and a half centuries, there were numerous Japanese incursions on all the Ryukyu Islands. Minamoto Tametomo, the legendary samurai warrior, landed at Okinawa in 1165 and sired the first documented dynasty there. Thus the Japanese considered themselves the originators of the royal house of the Ryukyus, even though that direct dynasty ended in 1259, twenty-two years after Shunten's death.

With the 1429 reunification of the Kingdom of the Ryukyus under one Shuri King, all the islands, including the northern subgroup, Amami Oshima, were brought under Shō Hashi's rule. This became a significant factor in the

Japanese division of territory after the Meiji restoration and in the post-World War II return of some northern territories to Japan. The Satsuma clan, of the southern Japanese Island of Kyushu, grew large and powerful at home. Believing him an internal threat, the shogun bestowed upon the lord of Satsuma the meaningless jurisdiction of all the "southern islands" (the Ryukyu chain) and then encouraged him to assert his claim and divest control from the Chinese. The Satsumas did not challenge the Chinese until 1609. Their first expedition, a force of a hundred ships and three thousand men, put an end to the Chinese influence, then they returned to Japan with captive Shō Nei, the Okinawan King whom they soon restored to Okinawa, where he ruled until his death in 1620. Japanese domination and the period of dual subordination had begun. Since the Satsumas were blocked in Japan proper, they turned their aggression to the subjugation of their newly acquired southern islands. Naturally the shogun was pleased to have his major rival working *for* him by increasing Japan's area, sphere of domination, stature, and coffers. But Satsuma did not eliminate China from the Okinawa scene for reasons which closely parallel the situation vis-à-vis China and England in Hong Kong today.

After another Japanese war in Korea (actually directed at China), the Chinese Emperor refused to trade with Japan. Okinawa was then the only trade link between the two countries. The Satsuma clan, as "agent," reaped tremendous profits. And the Chinese, enjoying the business, ignored the Satsuma domination. Neither side wished to upset the commercial balance. However, such a relationship (in some ways resembling the Japanese-American position in Okinawa today) could not continue indefinitely. The Okinawan administration became so thoroughly institutionalized in the Satsuma Japanese way that the personality or presence of their own King became "unimportant." Authority rested with a Prime Minister aided by a council of state ministers and fifteen administrative departments, all patterned after the Japanese rather than the deposed Chinese system. Representatives of this central authority were stationed in all the islands' districts. There was a law court consisting in a chief judge and fifteen associates and local "organizations" directly subordinate to the lord of Satsuma, and under his constant supervision.

The Golden Age of Ryukyuan commerce declined with the advent of European commercial sea routes. The lucrative trade in the East dwindled and the Okinawan economy shrank to the production of sugar for export and sweet potatoes for home consumption. Funds above the barest sustenance level dwindled, and most of what was left went to the Satsumas as tribute—this had to be paid in full, and on time. The Shuri government, though reduced to figurehead status, also collected. Later, the local lords in Okinawa (permitted by the Satsumas and the house of Shuri) took their cuts. Since the Chinese had no agents in Okinawa, their tribute evaporated; they had no way to enforce their demands.

The Chinese also lost their spiritual and cultural hold on the Ryukyus. The

Satsumas brought potters in from Korea to teach ceramic techniques. Tiles also became a native industry. Temples and shrines were built by the Japanese, who, for their own convenience, also improved roads and other public works. The final coup de grâce came with the Meiji restoration. When Emperor Meiji rid Japan of the shogunate in 1868, he also ousted the war lords and their clans. He changed all the family or political subdivisions of Japan into prefectures, to which he appointed all local governors. The subjugation of the Ryukyus became a governmental rather than a private enterprise. Tokyo discarded any pretense about indirect rule over the Ryukyus. All the islands were incorporated into Japan proper, and in 1879 Shō Tai was asked to come to Tokyo to visit the Meiji family—a trip from which, unlike Shō Nei in 1609, he never returned. Thus ended forever the reign of the Shō kings on Okinawa. Shō Tai finished his life in royal exile in a gift palace in Tokyo which has now become the Shō family estate. His islands remained secluded from the rest of the world for the next sixty-six years. In the administrative reorganization which followed the breaking up of the Satsuma clan (once again Amami Oshima was taken from them), all the islands in the Ryukyu chain north of Okinawa were incorporated into Kagoshima prefecture. The southern portion of the islands became the separate Okinawa prefecture which was directly responsible to the central government in Tokyo. There was some token opposition from small groups on Okinawa about the formal change in status and the complete exclusion of China, but it faded rapidly. At first Okinawans feared Chinese retaliatory measures. When none came, China lost face with the Okinawans, who then turned to the Japanese. The first few years after annexation marked a period of trial and error, enervation and neglect, referred to as the "do nothing era." The treasury was, as usual, empty, and local resources too meager to support the ever-increasing population, which then, as now, was concentrated in Naha, Shuri, and Nago. Finally, in 1894, after a Japanese war with China, the Emperor's central government moved with some efficiency and started development programs for the Okinawa prefecture. Ultimately a good number of qualified men was sent from the home islands to study the situation and come up with recommendations and a system.

Japan suddenly became interested in expanding and strengthening central government control over all aspects of Ryukyuan life. They sealed off the islands from the rest of the world. To insure total assimilation of the Ryukyuan community into the Japanese pattern, Japan purged the islands of the ancient Okinawan culture and all the residual influences of the Chinese. This was followed closely by improved economic conditions and the development of a tax structure designed to bring Okinawan money to Japan. (This idea haunts the Japanese today in their bid for residual sovereignty.) Japanese became the only language for Okinawans and the only one taught in the schools. The people had to dress in the Japanese style and acquire Japanese customs, culture, and names. When the imperial yen became the coin of the realm, Japanization of the islands was complete. The Chinese learned from the Japanese success that one nation cannot dominate another for long through culture alone. Okinawans were considered social inferiors. They were used in the Imperial Army only in labor battalions, and were sent to the Japanese homeland only in subservient capacities. Okinawans seldom attained high government positions, and most posts, even those of rural schoolteachers and local police prefects, invariably were filled by Japanese who were less capable than those holding comparable jobs at home in Japan. Soon Nippon fortified and garrisoned the Ryukyus to use as its southern defense block. Okinawa also became a principal naval operations base for most of Japan's aggressive campaigns. All this ceased abruptly with the end of World War II.

In the eyes of the Okinawans the Americans, (who actually went after the Imperial Japanese Army, not the native civilians), bombed their land. Japan, a vanquished nation, was not looked upon by the Okinawans as responsible for their devastation. Nevertheless, General Stilwell's surrender document brought Japanese influence to a legal, if only temporary, end.

Those Japanese who did not become Allied prisoners of war (PWs) either eluded capture or did not know of the surrender or peace.

According to official USCAR chronology, the late surrender of all Japanese forces in the Ryukyus was due to "delay occasioned by continued resistance by isolated Japanese units." General Ushijima's last official order was for his men to quit organized fighting, infiltrate the American lines, work their way north, and continue indefinitely in guerrilla action. The order resulted in day-to-day flare-ups in the Ryukyus which continued for nearly two years. It is said that even now there are some isolated Japanese who have not been ferreted out and repatriated. These superannuated soldiers live with Okinawan families, and are so assimilated that they really are no longer soldiers of the Imperial Army. Of course, they will never be repatriated—they are no longer the same men.

Almost immediately after V-J Day, units of the broken Imperial Japanese Army began to be repatriated by the Allied powers, though many PWs were retained on Okinawa as late as spring 1947. They worked in various labor gangs, construction crews, maintenance groups, and as kitchen canaries, and were well treated. Some PWs believed they might never be returned home and spent a great deal to "buy" their way back. Others tried various escape plans, and the few who were successful discovered they would have been repatriated in a month or two anyway. Among littoral Okinawans there was strong sympathy for the Japanese, and there was a going "underground railroad." On dark nights, Japanese PWs who had paid their way out of internment compounds would get aboard a small sampan in groups of six. They sailed the China Sea a little beyond sight of the coast to meet a larger vessel from Japan, which would then take the PWs home. After many successful trips, the enterprise was discovered and quashed. As the PW population dwindled, some would make such items as watch bands, lamps, ash trays, junk jewelry, etc., from scrap and old shell casing. Openly, yet illegally, these handicrafts were traded with the Americans for cigarettes, chocolate, small convenience items, and sometimes money. Mass repatriation in mid-1947 abruptly ended the Japanese presence in the Ryukyus for nearly a decade.

The immediate postwar occupation, rehabilitation, and U.S. interim construction periods were relatively calm; it was the American epoch of cautious adjustment. The Ryukyuans and Americans regarded each other with suspiciously guarded optimism. Neither was resentful, and both managed well without the presence or assistance of the Japanese. There were a few isolated public health emergencies, which called for the aid of specialist Japanese physicians. They were brought in, performed their missions, and returned home appropriately compensated.

The interrelationship among Japan, the United States, and Okinawa was clearly detailed in the three major legal documents in effect—the treaty of peace with Japan (1952), U.S. Executive Order 10713 (1957), and a statement by President John F. Kennedy (1962). Chapter II, Article 3 of the treaty states:

"Japan will concur in any proposal of the United States to the United Nations to place under its trusteeship system, with the United States as the sole administering authority, Nansei Shoto south of 29° north latitude (including the Ryukyu Islands and the Daito Islands)". Further, "Pending the making of such a proposal and affirmative action thereon, the United States will have the right to exercise all and any powers of administration, legislation, and jurisdiction over the territory and inhabitants of these islands, including their territorial waters." It is quite clear here that although this treaty article provides room for further disposition of the Ryukyu Islands, it neither mentions nor offers any Japanese "residual sovereignty."

Executive Order 10713 dated June 5, 1957 (as amended by Executive Order 11010 of March 19, 1962) is not a diplomatic agreement. It is a U.S. internal document which is, in effect, the "constitution" for the government of the Ryukyu Islands, setting up administrative details and also providing for the general welfare of the local people, but no mention is made of any contact with Japan.

President Kennedy's 1962 statement began: "I have today signed an amendment to Executive Order 10713, dated June 5, 1957, providing for the administration of the Ryukyu Islands. [based on] recommendations of the Interdepartmental Task Force appointed last year to investigate current conditions in the Ryukyu Islands and the United States policies and programs in force there."

"I recognize the Ryukyus to be a part of the Japanese homeland and look forward to the day when the security interests of the free world will permit their restoration to full Japanese sovereignty." But the President continued with: "In the meantime, we face a situation which must be met in the spirit of forbearance and mutual understanding by all concerned." The phrase "Japanese sovereignty" caught on, while "forbearance and mutual understanding" have been swept under the carpet. The statement was taken up by a lobby group which previously had been only an amorphous movement within Japan. Although this group had only an objective, it functioned surprisingly well. For instance, three hundred Japanese Rising Sun flags were shipped to Okinawa on December 19, 1955. They were distributed to primary and high schools, and youth organizations. The 4- by 6-foot flags (not toys) were gifts from the Japanese people. The organizers certainly were promoting "reversion!"

The phrase from President Kennedy's statement, ". . . restoration to full Japanese sovereignty," when taken out of context indeed becomes electric. But reading on to points 4 and 5 of his statement, clarifies his intent:

"4. Entering into discussions with the Government of Japan with a view to working out precise arrangements to implement a co-operative relationship between the United States and Japan in providing assistance to promote the welfare and well-being of the inhabitants of the Ryukyu Islands and their economic development.

"5. Carrying on a continuous review of governmental functions in the Ryukyu Islands to determine when and under what circumstances additional functions that need not be reserved to the United States as administering authority can be delegated to the Government of the Ryukyu Islands." (To GRI, not GOJ.)

And the six amendments to the Executive Order, (point 6) refer to the power of the Government of the Ryukyu Islands (GRI) and its relationship with the U.S. Government. The relationship between the GRI and the Japanese Government is made unofficial. Although in Tokyo, Okinawa is alleged by Japan to be "home territory," Ryukyuan questions are not handled by the Japanese Home Office, but by the Foreign Ministry. (Yet even if the United States would permit a Japanese embassy, legation, or consulate on Okinawa, this would be a Tokyo admission of "foreign status.") Because the Japanese deal only with the United States on Okinawan matters, they do so through their Foreign Ministry's North American Affairs Bureau.

The only "official" Japanese Government representation in the Ryukyus is the Southern Liaison Office (Nampo) under the administration of a director general in the Executive Branch of the Prime Minister's office. The Ryukyus are getting top-drawer attention in Tokyo. For better communications, the North American Affairs Bureau maintains an observer in the Nampo Office in Naha. But in deference to the liaison officer, and for the sake of the Japanese image, there is neither duplication of efforts nor divided responsibility. Through the co-operation of Masaki Yagi (deputy chief of the Overseas Press Section of the Japanese Ministry of Foreign Affairs), not long ago in Tokyo I was able to visit with Nobyuki Nakajima, chief of North American Affairs Section, and his aide in the U.S. Affairs office, Makoto Watanabe. The meeting was long and cordial. Watanabe San, a tall, handsome, young graduate of Swarthmore College, personified the new era in Japanese diplomacy. Nakajima San too is of the new order. A graduate of Tokyo University Law School, he left his first post in the Foreign Ministry in 1942 to enter the Imperial Navy. Now he is a seasoned career diplomat, whose home is in Kagoshima Prefecture, Kyushu, (the southernmost section of Japan and the closest to the Ryukyus).

We spoke that afternoon of the "abnormal condition" existing in Okinawa as a by-product of an "abnormal" international situation, and of how reversion could not be rushed due to Ryukyuan need for the United States. In spite of the Okinawan longing for "reversion," the two men felt those advocating it were opportunistic. Japan will cross the defense bridge when it happens, though there was no comment on a defense forecast. They also offered no solution to the "take-off permission" for U.S. aircraft in case of split U.S.-Japanese authority. Nakajima said: "No one at present is ready to answer this question." Both men thought that the needs of the Ryukyuan people were psychological as well as material, and that the Okinawans wanted "independence" in the sense of not always being directed by America and having closer ties with Japan. Lately Okinawans have attempted to run for seats as members-at-large in the (upper) House of Councilors of the Japanese Diet. They have all been defeated due to lack of knowledge of the ways of Japanese politics, and to their inability to organize a proper political campaign.

They suggested I talk to Tokuji Tokonami, the Conservative representative of Kagoshima Prefecture in the Diet and the chairman of the Committee on Okinawa. Their conclusions were there is "no magic medicine of one dose," and that, hypothetically, the Meiji restoration pulled in all feudal lords' lands to the Emperor's government, and there they must eternally remain.

I then visited what once was the Imperial Army Headquarters and, by law, is now the Japanese Self-Defense Force (JSDF). There, Hidemichi Kira, counselor for the defense agency, arranged for me to meet Major General Ryoichi Tabato, chief of Intelligence, and military adviser to the Government of Japan. At this meeting, black coffee, not tea, was served. General Tabato was experienced in both military and diplomatic affairs. At the time of Pearl Harbor, he was an instructor of armored tactics at Sobudai Military Academy, which is now Camp Zama, the base of U.S. Army Engineers Operations in the Far East. He remembers he "could not imagine how Japan could face the U.S. armored might." He fought on the Manchurian front and never faced any Americans. He remained a career soldier, since Japan would still need at least a few professionals to help maintain some sort of self-defense force. He has since become the military historian for the agency.

In 1959 Tabato led the first organized Japanese military group to visit Okinawa after the surrender. Thirteen young officer candidates viewed the war's devastation. "Now it happens every year. Groups of officer candidates visit Okinawa with the object of studying old battle history, and to view the new U.S. installations. Article 9 of the New Japanese Constitution forbids war except, and solely, for self-defense," he said. "Now young officers have no concept of what war can be like, and to keep them in check we make this annual Okinawa visit to bring it into clear focus—to play down war by portraying a horror picture.

"We go to Okinawa because it is closest to Japan in distance and in spirit". General Tabato continued, "Okinawa was the only battle ever fought on Japanese 'sovereign territory,' and it was the largest strength we brought to bear in the war's decisive battle. But today's new U.S. tanks are the best to be invented by the United States. Kublai Khan from Mongolia tried to invade Japan at Kyushu and his force was annihilated. Naturally, Japan would assume defense of Okinawa as a part of her 'sovereign territory.' But at present there is no plan for reversion. This will develop as the situation warrants. As you Americans say, 'don't spin your wheel' for hypothetical situations. The United States would not depart until all chance of external danger was passed."

I later found out that Article 9 of Japan's new Constitution allows the JSDF a standing total force of some 210,000 men, including a ground force of 141,000, a maritime navy of 32,000, and 37,000 in a self-defense air association. C. M. Magee, press officer at the U.S. Embassy, told me that the United States provided this force with $20 million for armaments in 1950. The annual budget for the force, is $31.97 million, which seems low. General Tabato ended our interview by saying: "Many Japanese lost chauvinistic feelings, except Okinawans. Okinawans are faithful to Japan. No ill will against the Japanese army. The thirteen young officers in the first 1959 visit felt much toward the Okinawans."

The taxi driver who took me back to my hotel was too young to remember the war. He had heard of the Ryukyus, but did not think them important enough to disrupt Japanese-American relations. Americans, he said, spend much money in Tokyo. The "B" girls in the expensive night clubs shared his view. An English-speaking conductor I met at the Odawara station of the new Tokaido railroad line did not believe more territory and people would help the Japanese home situation at all. An old farmer, whose conversation the conductor briefly interpreted for me, quite embarrassingly confessed he did not know where or what Okinawa was. Ito San, a business man in Tokyo, who had been in the Philippines at the time of Pearl Harbor, thought *no* problem should be allowed to disrupt international trade, which he believed could be the successor to wars. Kuroemon Onoe, a prominent Kabuki actor, said Okinawa is less important to Japan "than the serious problem of decline of Japanese culture, tradition, and national identity, which is being submerged by universal mediocrity."

I discussed these grass-root findings with Saiji Hasegawa, the managing director of Jiji Press, Japan's major international news wire service. He thought public opinion was of little value, since there are too few educated people who see things in a clear way without their clouding the picture with the taint of their wishful thinking. "Whether Okinawa likes it or not, U.S. will go in fifteen or twenty years. U.S. is not wanting more land. After they go, there must be an adjustment," said Hasegawa San. "Mao will go and next generation more mature, not so proud, and more practical."

Going further, Hasegawa said, "The Communist world is divided. The U.S. and the U.S.S.R. are best together to oppose China, but not in shooting war. We must all develop *now* an economic-industrial program as we Japanese call 'san-kai.' " But don't worry about the narrow opinions of the people, he cautioned: "In Hokkaido, the laborers all cried 'go Yankees,' and Yankees went, then they cried for jobs!

"If you really want to know about Okinawa, you must talk to Diet member from Kagoshima, Tokonami San." He was not the first person to suggest this to me. With a bilingual cub reporter as my guide-interpreter, I went to the Diet building for an interview. Actually, Tokuji Tokonami spoke English quite well and he has always been in government. At the time of World War II he was working for the Welfare Department in Tokyo. As the incumbent Diet representative from Kagoshima (the closest Japanese land to Okinawa), and former chairman of the House Committee on Okinawa and Amami, he is interested in the Ryukyus. Although he was recently moved up to chair the political investigating committee for the Liberal Democratic Party, his reversion plan remains *the* only solidly documented plan (although unofficial).

"If Okinawa reverts," he said, "it will be a separate prefecture as it was before the war. Okinawans could now be in the Diet independently without reversion, but only in the upper House. According to present election law, there are no votes for Okinawans, therefore no representative in lower House. For instance, now for upper House, President Ohama of Waseda University has a good chance where others failed. He will lead a delegation to Washington soon, it is not yet official, but should be; it is a good idea. There is no difference between Japanese and Okinawans, except *they* must have things done for them. Every day a ship goes from Kagoshima to Okinawa now, and there are three local air trips per week to Naha independently of any flights from Tokyo.

"Japan must rely on U.S. for defense. Okinawa is the most important base in the Japan-U.S. mutual security treaty. The U.S. cannot just *leave.* It must keep the hub of the Japan-Korea-Taiwan-Philippine wheel. The aircraft 'take-off problem' cannot be changed for the time being, but it must come eventually. Now though, we do not have an 'official' plan. Meanwhile, the U.S. should attend to Okinawan will for Japan. Nipponese efforts for reversion must not be let up because there may be a chance of resolving the 'take-off problem' diplomatically and keep U.S. forces there. I am pleased with your High Commissioner's activities; it alleviates our anxieties, because keeping the base on Okinawa indefinitely invites war. Transformation should be gradual, department by department, not the full government at once. But this change-over should begin now. The U.S. cannot hold status quo without expecting trouble from the left." He gave me a copy of his plan for immediate though gradual reversion of the Ryukyus. "It must work," he said. "It works on Amami, Amami has reverted, and is in my prefecture."

Amami Oshima, the northernmost subgroup of the Ryukyus, historically has bounced to and from Ryukyuan and Japanese hands. Those islands hardly were affected by the war itself and did not come under American control until March 1946. Until this time, although prohibited by the Japanese document of surrender of the Ryukyus, the islands of Amami gunto were part of Japan's Kagoshima Prefecture. The U.S. Military Government which came in allowed the prewar Prefectural Branch Office to remain as the civilian government organization, except the name was changed to Provisional Government Northern Ryukyus. Municipal elections were held on July 1, 1946, seventeen months *before* the same elections were held in the other three guntos of Okinawa, Miyako, and Yaeyama. For the first time in Ryukyuan history (except in Itoman), women participated on the same basis as men. Also for the first time, mayors of municipalities were chosen directly by the voters.

Many natives of Amami were dissatisfied about the U.S. occupation and wanted to go north to Japan but found this was illegal. Mitsuteru Miyuki tells: "Amami Oshima had belonged to Kagoshima Prefecture Japan until February 1946, when the U.S. Navy Military Government was set up in Amami Oshima. Since Amami Oshima was separated from Japan, the proclamation made it unlawful to freely travel and trade with Japan.

"Accordingly, the people had to be confined to a limited area, actually to the Ryukyus, and the number of the unemployed increased more and more. A great number of the youth was led to give up the continuation of higher education in Japan. In fact, most of the young people before the war would be sent to Japan, Manchuria, Formosa, or somewhere else to take higher education, or to find a job, instead of staying in Amami Oshima where no employment was available.

"But there are so many people who are engaged in trading with Japan, knowing it is a violation against law, and one merchant was unfortunately captured by the police authorities on suspicion of illegal trade with Japan. He confessed that it is one of the most important problems to open free trade with Japan; otherwise, Amami Oshima will be left behind the times. One of my friends who was a college student in Japan returned home to see his parents, and one day when I met him, he said he found that, compared with the Japanese high school student, the Amamian youth lacked knowledge of social science.

"Now, the status of Amami Oshima has not been determined yet, whether to return to Japan or to be controlled under the U.S. trusteeship. But I personally feel that there will come the day again when Amamian people and the people within the Ryukyus at large will be able to freely travel and trade with

Japan, and it will be the shortest way to solve many problems derived from the aftermath of the war." On the other hand, many Amami citizens were pleased with the new arrangement, since all Amami has little economic or strategic value to pay for its maintenance costs.

Colonel D. C. Wilson of MG at Okinawa foresaw in 1947 many of today's problems. He helped conceive a great plan which unfortunately was lost in an airplane crash. Wilson's plan would have provided for the disposition of the Ryukyus by returning Amami to Japan (which was done eventually), giving Miyako and Yaeyama to Taiwan (now out of the question), and keeping Okinawa and its surrounding small islands for the United States. On December 25, 1953, the United States decided to set up a trial situation with Amami as a giveaway prototype. It signed an "Agreement Between the United States of America and Japan Concerning the Amami Islands." To quote Article I, Section I:

"1. With respect to the Amami Islands, the United States of America relinquished in favor of Japan all rights and interests under Article 3 of the Treaty of Peace with Japan signed at the city of San Francisco on September 8, 1951, effective from December 25, 1953. Japan, as of such date, assumes full responsibility and authority for the exercise of all and any powers of administration, legislation and jurisdiction over the territory and inhabitants of the Amami Islands." This agreement unfortunately set a postwar precedent, which Japan hopes eventually to expand to include many more islands now held by the United States and the Soviet Union.

But everything works both ways. West of Highway 1, between Tomari Port and the Machiminato area, below road-grade, there is a little seaside community called Aja village. Although not publicized and officially illegal, many local inhabitants are disenchanted émigrés from Amami, who chose to live with the Yankee dollar. By ignoring this sub rosa migration, both sides gain. Japan avoids losing face, and the United States avoids delicate legal chores. Indeed, to quote an old Japanese maxim: "Every extra thing you own is extra trouble."

The man who most has to move with caution and trepidation to avoid any trouble is the Japanese (Nampo) Southern Liaison officer. His post has no diplomatic status officially (whereas he must be an ultra diplomat), no public information office, no bulletins, and no clearly defined duties.

The incumbent I interviewed was Yoshio Yamamoto, who told me the purpose of his mission officially was to exchange memoranda between the United States and Japan about Okinawa (a job which could really be done in Tokyo). The rest was as nebulous as a post possibly could be, but his bent was good will and whatever he found to do; in his words, "Public service to all three peoples." He thought the Okinawan economy was both advanced and underdeveloped, depending upon the aspect. The U.S. High Commissioner, he believed, was "a symbol of the true spirit of American democracy. Hi Com Watson operates according to basic principles of human society and knows the difference between freedom and autonomy."

I asked about Ryukyuan needs, benefits from Japan, politics, taxes, details, battle memorials, and his opinions in general. He replied:

"Okinawa most needs combined aid from both the U.S. and Japan, which it deserves for the involuntary sacrifice of 1945. There is a maldistribution of wealth—even the rich are poor by Tokyo or New York standards. The poor need more. They need autonomy, not freedom. They need moral support—to belong—not to feel isolated or alone. After Prime Minister Sato's visit, Japanese aid to Okinawa doubled and is now 5.8 billion yen (or 16.114 million dollars) per year. Japan buys sugar at bonus prices to help Okinawan industry, and Ryukyuan pineapple is treated as a duty-free domestic product. A small amount (eighty million dollars from the war's end to now) goes as private welfare to war-bereaved families. It is difficult to say what more might be done after reversion. Maybe the Tokyo-Osaka-Nagoya area, a big tax region, might be made to distribute some of its wealth to cover lesser areas; perhaps raise the annual aid to Ryukyus to 20 billion yen. The pre-World War II half million population has doubled, and we cannot deny U.S. assistance in support of one million Ryukyuans today despite immigration to Peru, Bolivia, Hawaii, Argentina, and Brazil.

"Past Prime Minister Yoshida made tablets with antiwar inscriptions to be placed at shrines at Okinawa battle places. This is good to promote unity of spirit and religion, to foster tourism, and banish war feelings. I think all three peoples should celebrate the battles jointly to bring them closer together and avert future war. Premier Sato's recent visit was to further unity and resulted in increased aid funds. It is economically impossible for Ryukyus to be independent because it depends too heavily on subsidy and U.S. support.

"Small details such as money, traffic direction, postage, and exchange might easily be ironed out with reversion. I believe all problems must work out by mutual understanding. No one should be one-sided, must appreciate views of others. Try and continue to try to understand all." Yamamoto San has since become Japanese Consul General in Honolulu.

Prime Minister Eisaku Sato made four speeches during his visit to Okinawa in August of 1965. The important things, though, were the response he evoked from the Okinawan people; the attentive ear he got from the American press, echoing as far back as Washington; the doubling of Japan's tangible aid; and the double-knotting of the old ties. The Prime Minister's position was all embracingly summed up in an informal statement he made at Kokuei-Kan: "Japan, allied with the United States by the mutual co-operation and security treaty, has co-operative relations with her as a partner. And the Ryukyu Islands are playing a very important role for peace and security of the Far East. I firmly believe that without the security of the Ryukyu Islands, the security of mainland Japan is not guaranteed, nor without the security of mainland Japan are the Ryukyu Islands secure." This indicated clearly that Sato San's primary interest is in having Japan defended by the United States, with a principal base of operations in the Ryukyus, and so long as there is any hint of a threat to the security of "mainland Japan," nothing ought disturb the defense status which must remain at quo.

Despite this attitude, the chemistry continues to boil in Tokyo. Japanese government circles want the Ryukyus back in the "home" fold, because Okinawans are a good, honest, hardy, and docile people. For all the years of closed-door domination from 1879 through 1945, there is not one single recorded incident of subversion or insurrection in the Ryukyus. Yet the average Japanese person hears little about the Ryukyus. Not long ago a middle-age Japanese woman went to Okinawa to visit her son then living in a Ryukyuan village with a local wife. In her baggage Mama San took with her fish-hooks and frying pans.

# CHAPTER 12

# What It's All About

The only time in their history the Okinawans ever said "no" was to the only outsider who came unarmed, offering peace and prosperity. Perhaps the error was in presenting a choice. The Chinese, the Mongols, the Japanese, and the Europeans all successfully thrust their wills upon the Ryukyus without opposition. But the United States in the mid-nineteenth century offered peace, trade, and friendship as conditions for opening the closed oriental doors, and was denied. Commodore Perry arrived June 6, 1853, commanding an armored fleet of steamships which could easily have blasted the entire Japanese Empire into colonial submission, along with Okinawa. Until he left a year later, Perry tried to establish a reciprocal trade relationship with the Shuri court, and to rent space for a U.S. naval base at Naha or Tomari port. (He could easily just have taken the port as the British took Hong Kong from China eleven years earlier or the Portuguese took Goa from India.) Yet in deference to the Japanese, the Ryukyuan reply was an unqualified "no."

Today a huge two-sided memorial for Perry (one side in English, and the other Japanese) stands inside the little International Cemetery at Tomari port, ironically a few paces from his proposed naval base. Beside the graves of John Barnes, Hugh Ellis, Jesse L. Carter, John Miller, William Board, Eli Crosby, and John Williams, the seven unsung naval heroes of the first American mission to Okinawa, Perry's tablet seems to mark a future which "might have been." No one will ever know if such an American base would too have been swallowed up by the flood tide of the Meiji restoration or if it might have preserved at least token independence for Okinawa. For it was the same negative King

Shō Tai who later lost his Ryukyuan realm when he quietly went into exile in Tokyo twenty-five years after Perry's offer. Subsequent to Perry's visits, there was no significant contact between America and the Ryukyus until the aerial bombardments of the fall of 1944.

When the United States captured these islands in the spring of 1945, the Japanese yen became valueless. In the earliest postwar days, the barter system was the only means of exchange. Military payment certificates were issued by the armed forces "for use only in the United States Military establishments by United States authorized personnel in accordance with applicable rules and regulations." Americans could not use this money locally, nor could any natives use it. These certificates were recalled March 10, 1947, replaced by a special issue of "B" yen at 120 yen for one dollar. The change was made so U.S. establishments could pay their native labor force without setting up two independent currencies. Thus the American and Okinawan economies became intermingled. While the "B" yen remained stable at 120 to 1, the Japanese yen inflated to 360 yen to the dollar by 1965. But the "B" yen was worthless except in the Ryukyus. On September 20, 1958, the "B" yen were recalled and genuine U.S. dollars were issued in return!

The third phase of postwar reconstruction in the Ryukyus, as I learned from Samuel C. Oglesby of the USCAR, is characterized by rapid development of private enterprise and institutions and facilities typical of a normal society. Postwar economic, social, and political growth had been gradual but continuing. Several important 1952 policies and the results of their implementation mark that year as the beginning of a new phase of postwar reconstruction. Policies adopted during this phase had four prime objectives: establishing a central native government organized along democratic lines; a sound public financial system to make this government self-supporting; a system of education and other institutions characteristic of a democratic society (without submerging local culture and customs); and a free enterprise economy which would provide a decent standard of living for the people (at least comparable to the prewar one). These objectives, as well as the policies for implementing them, were first set forth in the directive for the USCAR on December 5, 1950.

As its name implies this directive also created a civil administration in lieu of the MG organization which had been responsible for civilian affairs in the islands since 1945. During the earlier phases of reconstruction, the MG assumed many operational responsibilities and maintained a large staff of U.S. and "foreign" personnel. Prior to the directive, the Military Governor lacked the authority to act on some matters related to civil affairs.

This directive represents one of the most significant events in the history of the Ryukyus. The people, whose status, according to the Rules of Land Warfare, was still that of enemy nationals under military occupation, were granted and encouraged to express a voice in the determination of their local affairs greater than they had ever before enjoyed. They were also given financial assistance to establish and own enterprises in a free, competitive economy and were subjected to *no* tax or tribute on behalf of an outside power, a condition which never existed in the Ryukyus before 1954. Also prior to the directive, the Ryukyu Dollar Commercial Account, later named Ryukyu Foreign Exchange Fund (RFEF), was established as a depository for dollar earnings from the sale of services and goods to the U.S. forces and the limited government-to-government export trade. The going single rate of exchange of 120 to 1 was maintained. "Foreign Exchange and Trade Procedures in the Ryukyu Islands," MG Ordinance No. 26, was promulgated in November 1950 in anticipation of the re-establishment of private foreign trade.

More than any other action, the opening of this dollar account to private foreign trade in February 1951 is responsible for the subsequent rapid economic development and improved income level in the Ryukyus. The immediate effect of this on the local economy was the appearance of vitally needed personal and household goods which had been inadequate or unavailable for more than ten years. The local currency rapidly attained the full purchasing power intended by the adoption of the single rate of exchange. Cash wages alone were sufficient incentive to Ryukyuan workers employed by the U.S. forces. The direct monetary saving to the U.S. Government in carrying out its military construction program largely with Ryukyuan labor, and to a significant extent with Ryukyuan contractors, amounted to many millions of dollars. The value to the United States and to the other nations of "free" Asia, by the completion of these projects at the accelerated rate, cannot be measured in terms of money.

The Bank of the Ryukyus was designated as the central foreign exchange bank for the administration of the Ryukyu Foreign Exchange Fund in accordance with quarterly foreign exchange budgets prepared by the Board of Trade (later the Economics Department of GRI) and approved by USCAR. Customary foreign exchange and commercial banking procedures are followed in administering all foreign trade transactions through the RFEF. Foreign exchange limitations and other controls were provided for by MG Ordinance No. 26. Since the beginning, however, free convertibility of type "B" yen into any foreign currency through the medium of United States dollars, for the purpose of foreign trade, under an automatic approval licensing system, has been permitted with very few exceptions.

On three occasions, temporary limitations were imposed on the import of sugar, soy sauce, and flour to protect a newly established Okinawan industry. The private import of food, rice, and petroleum products is still not permitted. These materials are imported and distributed by the government through designated agents in a licensed monopoly. Some imports, such as firearms and narcotics, of course, require certification by the responsible government agency. Controls over these items are not related to economic policy. Finally, the U.S. Foreign Assets Control regulations are enforced against goods of Communist origin. (It is too early to judge whether this restriction is good for the economy.) A more restrictive import policy would have been unsuitable.

With their limited and underdeveloped prewar productive enterprise completely destroyed at the end of World War II, the Ryukyuan people, by 1951, could produce only a few items for their own use, much less export in significant quantities. But, at least, considerable money was earned through labor services to the U.S. forces. The upward trend of such earnings was anticipated safely because the military program was expanding at that time. MG did not use U.S. funds and facilities to "force draft" an industrial establishment because the economy still lacked many of the facilities and resources essential for its operation.

The rather limited government procurement and distribution of foodstuffs, lumber, and a few other essential materials (given under the grant programs) proved an inadequate substitute for private commerce, even there and then.

While some items required for the economy could be manufactured locally, Ryukyu private enterprise by 1951 could assume responsibility for their importation and distribution. By making the RFEF available for this purpose, the important elements of a free competitive economy developed rapidly. Wholesale suppliers, retail stores, repair and service shops, and other domestic commercial facilities were established throughout Okinawa and subsequently in all islands of the chain. This commerce stimulated further expansion and improvement in water and land transportation, communications, utilities, and construction. The prices of commodities and many services have declined steadily since 1951, while those in the United States and Japan have risen.

Many Ryukyuan importers and wholesalers of imported goods soon turned to export. As they developed capital strength and business experience, others invested in industries and production enterprises to supply items for both local use and export. In 1952 this export trade had tripled. Since the quantity these industries exported increased only moderately during this period, the sharp rise in export earnings is attributed primarily to the greater efficiency of private foreign trade over the government-to-government system. Export earnings have continued to increase since 1952 (twenty million dollars in 1957), despite a decline in the price of the principal export item, sugar, to a more stable and equitable level. The disastrous typhoons in the summer and fall of 1956 destroyed the major part of the sugar crop, thus export earnings in 1957 were adversely affected. The decline in total exports for 1958 is attributed entirely to the sharp curtailment of scrap shipments.

Ryukyuan postwar foreign trade has developed primarily with Japan due to geographic proximity, long established trade relations, and the many characteristics the two peoples have in common. In 1951 and immediately after, private imports were almost exclusively from Japan, but as Ryukyuans have increased their business contacts with other countries and expanded their services to U.S. forces, they have become diversified. There is greater emphasis in recent years on direct import of some items of Western origin such as soybeans and wheat from America (originally brought in via Japan). Goods from the United States, the largest supplier after Japan, have increased considerably since 1953, and the trend is still upward. A significant amount of imports is also obtained from Burma, Hong Kong, Thailand, Taiwan, and, more recently, South Vietnam.

This diversification has not happened to the Ryukyuan export trade. Practically all exports during the postwar era have been to Japan. By special act of the Japanese Diet, products of Ryukyuan origin enter Japan free of all taxes, duties, and foreign exchange restrictions imposed upon goods from foreign countries. Japanese importers are automatically allocated the U.S. dollar exchange to buy Ryukyuan products. These special considerations were extended to include pineapple grown in Taiwan and canned by Ryukyuan companies in Okinawa and Yaeyama. (This pineapple also competes with the Ryukyuan product.)

The sizable increase in Ryukyuan export earnings since 1951 would not have been possible without these Japanese trade privileges. But Japan profits too. The principal items imported from the Ryukyus are not produced by Japanese private enterprise in quantities adequate to meet even the minimum local demand. The Ryukyu Islands are, and will continue to be, an important market for Japanese goods. They are, in truth, one of Japan's few "cash dollar" customers. The value of goods purchased from Japan by local private enterprise rose from nearly forty-five million dollars in 1952 to seventy-five million dollars in 1967. (These figures do not include the many millions of dollars earned each year by Japanese insurance companies, steamship lines, contractors, and suppliers of the U.S. forces, and from other transactions with customers in the Ryukyus.) Japan's trade balance with the Ryukyus is a more favorable one than that enjoyed before the war with any foreign country or colonial area. The prospects for Japan's continuing its special treatment to products of Ryukyuan origin are about as dependable as any trade agreement in effect today; they cannot afford to be otherwise.

While U.S. seed money generated the Okinawan economy, from there the Okinawans helped themselves. Originally, there was the Ryukyu Reconstruction Finance Fund, which grew into the Ryukyu Development Loan Corporation. Aside from private banks and loan agencies, there came the Central Bank for Agriculture, Forestry, and Fisheries, the Peoples' Finance Corporation, and the Ryukyu Overseas Emigration Corporation.

Because private financial institutions were incapable of channeling savings into productive investments, the Ryukyu Reconstruction Finance Fund was originally established by MG on April 10, 1950, to provide long-term credit for economic development. Commercial loans were decreased, while increased emphasis was placed on industrial development, expansion of power and water facilities, and the urgent need for domestic housing loans. The Ryukyu Development Loan Corporation (RDLC) was established by HICOM Ordinances on October 10, 1959 as the descendant of the Ryukyu Reconstruction Finance Fund. The RDLC assumed all assets and liabilities of the RRFF on January 1,

1960. Although the regular loan terms vary according to the category of the loan, the majority are extended in the amount of 50 per cent of project cost for a term of five to fifteen years with interest rates of 4 per cent to 7 per cent. In order for RDLC to make a maximum contribution to the growth of Ryukyuan investment, more liberal terms are extended for specific industrial development projects in the form of reduced equity requirements, lower interest rates, and longer payment periods.

In addition to the regular loan program provided for by charter, RDLC was designated representative of the GRI for purposes of implementing the agricultural commodities agreement of 1963 with the United States. This agreement provided for the long-term purchase of designated abundant U.S. agricultural

RYUKYU DEVELOPMENT LOAN CORPORATION
COMPARATIVE PROFIT AND LOSS STATEMENT
(In Thousands of Dollars)

| | *F. Y. 1964* | *F. Y. 1965* |
|---|---|---|
| Earnings | *2166* | *2298* |
| Interest Income | 1972 | 2110 |
| Other Income | 194 | 188 |
| Expenses | *278* | *293* |
| Operating Expenses | 256 | 271 |
| Bad Expense | 18 | 17 |
| Depreciation Expense | 4 | 5 |
| Net Income | 1888 | 2005 |

RYUKYU DEVELOPMENT LOAN CORPORATION
LOAN DISBURSEMENT
(In Thousands of Dollars)

| *Classification of Loans* | *F. Y. 1964* | *F. Y. 1965* |
|---|---|---|
| Domestic Housing | 3886 | 4158 |
| Agriculture and Fisheries | 285 | 365 |
| Commerce | 110 | 63 |
| Industry | 1865 | 1801 |
| Transportation | 517 | 296 |
| Utilities | 850 | 1446 |
| Municipal Government | 287 | 700 |
| Tourist Industry | 494 | 50 |
| Disaster Projects | -0- | -0- |
| Small Enterprises | -0- | 102 |
| | 8294 | 8981 |

commodities and for the use of the proceeds generated from local sales of such commodities for the extension of loans for economic development (particularly the livestock and poultry industries). RDLC has for this purpose established a special "Public Law 480" loan program through which loans for grain-handling facilities, livestock purchase, livestock production and processing facilities, and other projects are to be available in amounts of 80 per cent to 90 per cent of project cost. Repayment terms range from two to fifteen years at a 4 per cent interest rate. RDLC is administered by a board of directors appointed by the civil administrator. Two directors are selected from the staff of USCAR, two from the staff of GRI upon nomination of chief executive, and one from the public.

The civil administrator appoints one of the USCAR members chairman of the board and one of the Ryukyuan members to be president. In 1966, the acting chairman of the board of directors was Sam Oglesby.

The Central Bank for Agriculture, Forestry, and Fisheries was established by the legislature of GRI in 1952 to provide financial resources for local co-operatives formed by farmers, forestry workers, and fishermen to promote production in their respective fields. The officers of the bank are president, managing director, five or more directors, and three or more auditors. CBAFF has total assets of twenty-two million dollars (U.S.) versus thirteen million dollars in liabilities. It shows over two hundred thousand dollars in profits, and receives some contributions from Japan.

The People's Finance Corporation, wholly owned by GRI, was established by Legislative Act No. 40 in 1954, to lend necessary business capital on a short-term basis to people who find it difficult to obtain loans from banks and other financial institutions. Its governing body, the People's Financial Council includes representatives from the GRI departments of Administrative Services and Economics, from the fields of commerce, industry, agriculture, maritime activities, and banking, and three persons from the general public. It makes decisions and offers opinions on important matters concerning the operations of the corporation, whose officers are president, vice-president, three directors, and two auditors. PFC total assets are close to four million dollars, versus only half a million in liabilities. Its annual profit is about twenty-five thousand dollars.

The Ryukyu Overseas Emigration Corporation, wholly owned by GRI, was established by the legislature in September 1953 by Act No. 85 to provide financial assistance in the form of term loans to Ryukyuan emigrants settling abroad under the government's emigration program. The affairs of the corporation are managed by the chairman of the board, five directors and two auditors appointed by the chief executive. Total ROEC assets are close to two million dollars, versus a seven thousand dollar liability. Contributions come from the Government of Japan and from America via USCAR and AID.

In 1966 I spoke to Sam Oglesby, then acting director of economic affairs for USCAR and chief of its Commerce, Industrial, and Financial Division. Oglesby, often called the "father of Okinawan industry," was largely responsible for the "Report on the Ryukyus Islands, Pre-war and Post-war (through June 30, 1958)." He feels that the Okinawan economy is hurt by the unfavorable ratio of land to men. There are nearly a million people on 847 square miles of land, of which only 27 per cent is considered arable (and much of that is not too fertile). Nor is the arable land in one place. Actually, forty-eight of the sixty-five outer islands are uninhabited. It is difficult to get to them to provide essential public services. The distances are great between the Ryukyu Islands, unlike the close island community of Venice. Ryukyuans also have problems with the distribution of drinking water. Hardly any exists in the out islands, and though it is abundant in the north of Okinawa, it is badly needed in the south. There are plans to pipe water from the copious northern areas to the south. For some time, rather than bring the water to the people, the attempt was made to take the people to the water. Attempts at internal resettlement were made by the Japanese from 1900 until 1945, and by MG and USCAR between 1946 and 1960. Finally, because it was never successful at any time, it was given up.

The great trend in the Ryukyus, as in most places, is from the farms to the city. For instance, a young translator named Nadoyama came to Naha from a small village in Motobu Peninsula to study languages and clerical skills. He is now chief of Okinawan Office Service Personnel for the Public Affairs Department of USCAR. He told me that if he had not tried to better his lot by getting a city education, he would still be nowhere working on the family farm.

The influence of outside powers on the economic development of the Ryukyus was neglected by and large until the USCAR established the Ryukyuan Foreign Exchange Fund. As long as the United States was committed to remaning in the Ryukyus from 1950 on, it was necessary to promote the health and well-being of the "host" nation. Congress then appropriated several million dollars to do so. Most of this money went into basic agriculture, and a minimum to commercial fisheries and public services essential to joint U.S.-Okinawan operations. A most significant economic event in the postwar era was the opening of Ryukyuan foreign trade on a private basis. Previously, the United States and later Japan poured in about a million and a half dollars per annum with liberal restrictions—almost all the U.S. dollar expenditures went into construction and labor services. After this the internal needs of Okinawa were more fully developed to keep pace with their external development.

It was assumed that there would be a lag between the full construction income and the establishment of a firm Ryukyuan economy. The United States subsidized the latter. For example, all Army post exchange (PX) concessions were either Taiwan-Chinese, Indian, or Filipino until 1951, when the Ryukyuans also were allowed a part in the concession system. Now there are seventy-five Ryukyuan entities in operation, 650 retail outlets in the PX system, which gross nearly five million dollars per year. (This figure includes the money paid to Okinawans employed in various clerical and sales positions in the PX system.) The auto repair industry and the operation of taxis etc., by Ryukyuans brings in about 125 million dollars a year, which the Okinawans are definitely earning from the American presence. Now the U.S. over-all long-range mission is to create a viable self-sustained Okinawan economy. To those who say that this shall never happen, Sam Oglesby says that every increment in this road makes the ultimate gain less difficult and makes the need less acute. Because they must, locals are now shifting from a basic to a local economy without losing the generation of private capital. And private capital is most important for the Okinawans now.

Every Okinawan industrial giant (and there are many) started by dealing in the basic economy. As they developed capital and confidence they went out on their own. Some of the obstacles in their way were getting water, power, and good roads. As these facilities developed, it was easier to operate independently.

Oglesby suggests that between 1945 and 1949 the objectives of the military government were re-establishing the rehabilitation of basic resources and services, and from 1952 on they were re-establishing private enterprise. Oglesby says that since these objectives were attained there is no reason why, for instance, commerce and manufacturing, construction, banking, and other facilities to support private enterprise cannot proceed rapidly. He pointed out that in 1959 manufacturing was up to six million dollars per year and it was up to thirty million per year by 1965. Ten per cent of the over-all total national income now comes from manufacturing.

Referring to industry, Oglesby says that in 1951 opportunities were open for the promotion of various manufacturing enterprises in Okinawa. Many qualified Okinawans applied to Oglesby's office with ideas for starting factories, and asked for subsidized trips to Japan to learn how to do so. Many schemes were unsuitable. But a man named Gushiken, the brother of the Orion beer entrepreneur, had a very practical idea for a soy sauce and bean paste plant. Gushiken was sent to Japan, and today is running a successful concern.

The sugar industry now is as strong as it was in the past. But despite the abundance of sugar cane, a rum industry is extremely poor and shows no future. No one can explain this, though there is a small plant near Sukiran, and several other local establishments, but none of consequence. One possible reason is awamori, a local product peculiar to the Ryukyu Islands. It is a raw, distilled liquor, 35 per cent alcohol which is not sake. Awamori is sold in the native stores for about 20¢ for each one third of a quart (it is beer which is the luxury drink). There is a special Awamori bottle for tourists, much like a vase. Three of these (about a quart) cost about $1.80.

The name Orion beer was decided by a contest. Before the only brewery in the Ryukyus opened, a great publicity campaign was launched for the public selection of a name for its beer. A judging committee ultimately chose a pair of finalists which were Sun and Orion. Orion beer is strictly the child of Shosei Gushiken, a captain of Ryukyuan industry and a man deeply interested in the general welfare of the Ryukyuan people. He has also written an autobiography, privately published in the Ryukyus and Japan in a restricted number edition. I am pleased with my autographed copy, and feel it a pity I do not read Japanese because there is not a single word of English in it. My translator told me that the biographical story tells of a poor but enterprising young fellow who rose by his own sandal ties to his present position. His philosophy is, one must break eggs in order to make omelets, and this is reflected in the title of his memoir, the translation of which, extremely liberally, is "What the Hell."

I visited him at his Naha offices, where he and his staff wore American-type baseball caps on which was written Orion Beer in two languages.

Over many cups of tea Mr. Gushiken explained that the brewery began on May 1, 1957, and became operational a year later. The first lot of beer produced was so bad that it had to be recalled. The second run was much better. The original investment was fifty million "B" yen (at 120 to the dollar). He claims the money was all Okinawan, which had come from banks and the Ryukyuan Development Loan Corporation (in truth American money). The original plan was to buy an old brewery's machinery from Japan for reasons of economy, but when more investments came in, new equipment was procured instead. The site, Nago is very convenient, and near an excellent water source. Nago, in addition, is the second largest city of Okinawa, providing large numbers of people for employment and good local distribution. There is a long haul transportation center nearby, and the city is reasonably well protected from typhoons.

The first brand-new equipment was a bottling machine from America. From Germany and Denmark came other implements for the brewery and tanks. Contracts for all equipment specified a manufacturer's representative to be on hand to ensure the proper installation and initial operation. Much progress has been made since the first days, and over and above the plant and inventory they maintain a loose working capital of $417,000. As the first public corporation in the Ryukyus, Orion has 454 stockholders.

With a German-trained Japanese brewmaster under the over-all direction of Gushiken's enterprises, Orion turns out a good product. Their 209 employees work on a forty-eight-hour week and produce 180,000 units of twelve-ounce bottles of beer per day. Five million gallons per year!

Gushiken has set the pace not only in breweries, but for Ryukyuan advertising and promotion—the naming contest, the baseball caps, billboard ads, spot ads on Radio Okinawa, etc.

To preserve a favorable price for Orion beer, GRI has put a tax of twenty-one dollars per hundred liters on the three imported Japanese beers. There is no import tax on the American beers occasionally available, but they are too expensive for the average Okinawan.

Orion was interested in the expanded military market, with a hundred thousand American men buying vast quantities of beer. It was also eager to try to capture the market of beer going to Vietnam. The Navy was quite interested in giving Orion an exclusive, and the price was right. But naval regulations require that beer be delivered in cans, and Orion could provide only bottles.

As a captain of industry, Mr. Gushiken offered opinions on the local situation. Although he is, as are most, of divided allegiance, he feels that the United States should remain because it is the basis of the entire dependent economy. Although Okinawa ultimately wishes to become self-sustaining, it can only happen through exports. This will not happen soon, nor could it ever happen under Japan. He feels that 90 per cent of his market ultimately will be in the United States and its trade partners:

"Orion was Okinawa's first experience with local beer. Prior to the war, it had been a closely guarded Japanese secret. The Japanese looked down on the Okinawans, yet the Okinawans were determined to establish self-determination. The U.S. helped us to realize this. With beer and cement—both industries going concerns in Nago—the U.S. has helped launch Okinawa toward self-determination. We would appreciate it if the Americans would put a 200 per cent tax on imported Japanese beer to protect local interests. It would be much better than the twenty-one dollars per hundred liters that exists presently." Gushiken does not feel that this good economy will continue if reversion occurs. He feels also that Okinawa will not be able to compete and things will then go down under many Japanese restrictions. Therefore he thinks reversion is not the best thing. Nonetheless his secretary Yamada, a native-born Okinawan, continues to refer to localisms such as "we Japanese say . . ." and the Gushiken executives continue to ride about in Toyopet cars.

"Have one!" said Bill Matchett, president of Okinawa Soft Drinks, Kaisha, the authorized bottlers of American-brand sodas in the Ryukyus. This is a private Okinawan industry, even though the president is an American. Just like the Orion brewery, this company makes use of Okinawan materials and personnel.

Cola drinks have been on Okinawa as long as the Americans have, coming in with the third wave of landings on Love Day. Though some regard Coca-Cola as a government-sponsored monopoly, it is not. It is only big business. Dick Klepper was the first civilian to land on Okinawa on Love Day. He was not a soldier, he was the soft drink man. He is one of many such men, trained and paid by his company, who then receive limited military accreditation and work with the Military. The armed forces felt that as long as it paid its own way, a consistently good soft drink on hand at all times at the front helped morale. Immediately after landing, Klepper moved with some marines and engineer soldiers to an old Japanese water point previously selected for him by an Army Intelligence officer. First they started setting up pumps and filters for fresh water while the engineers rapidly constructed several water tanks and a Butler building to house his bottling machinery. While bullets flew and bombs zoomed, Dick Klepper had his bottling company going (near Hacksaw Ridge), and nickel sodas were sold to the troops.

By the time I left Okinawa in 1947, Klepper was still there without relief. In 1948, Klepper was replaced by William E. Matchett, Jr., a soft-spoken Georgian and a lifetime company man. Matchett was local manager until 1950 when he went to the Philippines for a while. As soon as the concession became available, Matchett went back and resumed the operation. The local company is now 100 per cent Matchett owned. (Originally he had the franchise as a joint Ryukyu-U.S. venture.) Although there is a local plant in Vietnam (much the same as his own started in Okinawa), a good portion of Matchett's production is sent there.

He employs 156 Okinawans, two Americans, one Nisei, three Filipinos, and one Japanese. Many of the Okinawan people have great job security, having worked there ten to fifteen years. The plant capacity is seventy-five thousand six-ounce bottles per eight-hour shift. They work an eight-hour day, but at times during heavy periods Matchett runs a shift and a half, bottling both cola and other soft drinks called Fanta.

Matchett's competition is Bireley's, which came with the Army in 1950, and in 1951 was legally permitted to be sold to the Okinawans via native distributors under USCAR control. In 1955 the soft-drink field in the Ryukyus was thrown wide open and Pepsi-Cola came in with a plant. Seven-Up and Canada Dry are also bottled there by a company called Best Soda. Two local Okinawan beverages, Bon and Keep, are also subsidiaries of Best but neither poses any significant competition, nor does a come-lately called Win Cola. Recently an A & W tap root beer roadside stand was set up near Camp Buckner, and has had a big reception. In 1964–65 the total soft-drink consumption on Okinawa was 3,634,032 cases of twelve bottles each.

The plant is still at its starting site, and only two years ago Klepper's original wood tanks were replaced by steel units. Matchett recently built a new home near the old site of the Hacksaw Ridge battle and intends to remain in the Ryukyus as long as possible.

Matchett says that the soft-drink industry will continue to flourish only as long as the U.S. remains in the Ryukyus, because the Japanese appetite for carbonated sweet soft drinks is rather small. He believes reversion would be a considerable blow to the Okinawan economy.

To quote a local student, Masao Hamakawa:

"In olden times, agriculture was considered the main occupation of the people of Okinawa, but since the Second World War they have come to think it more important to engage in commerce and engineering. This has caused a complete change in the economic life of the people. Okinawa today is no longer what she was yesterday.

"It is because most of the fertile cultivated fields in the southern and central parts of the island, which had produced much sugar as the main export, have been occupied by the U.S. military installations since the war's end. Besides this, as Okinawa is a small island, it cannot manufacture any manure, so that it is obliged to import all manure from Japan and the U.S., and it is so expensive that the people cannot afford most of it.

"As the people have come to be attracted by city life or military employment, the cultivated fields have been laid waste day by day, because they can make much more money by engaging in commerce or engineering than by engaging in agriculture.

"The most important and basic policy for the rehabilitation for Okinawa is how to let them return to engage in agriculture which must be the main part of economic self-support, and also how to let them emigrate from their native islands, which are too small for their economic self-sufficiency." In part young Hamakawa's wish has come true; today Okinawa has a large pineapple industry.

In the opening days of international commerce and industry, 1951 to 1953, some enterprising people set up canneries to take in Taiwan-grown pineapple, process the raw fruit, and turn out neatly packed, canned and cartoned preserved pineapple both for consumption in the Ryukyus and for export. Within two years, by 1953, agricultural engineering and economical consultants were brought in from Hawaii, and almost immediately the local pineapple industry was underway. Most of the rugged old green mountaintops in the north end have been scalped of their vegetation and short trees; the red soil has been laid open, tilled, and cultivated. This has become the area reclaimed from the lost for pineapple cultivation.

The Ryukyuan pineapple production, fifteen years old in 1968, has grown into the Ryukyu's second largest agricultural industry after sugar refining. Pineapples are grown the year around on Okinawa largely by farmers in the north and central areas on these shaved, reclaimed mountaintops. Yaeyama Island is also ideal for this because its rugged mountainous terrain lends itself to pineapple cultivation and production. There are now twenty-three canneries going in the islands, ten on Yaeyama, one on Kume Shima, and the rest on Okinawa.

The Noren Pineapple Cannery, near Nago, the site of the Orion brewery and the new cement industry, is Okinawa's largest. Peak harvest season for pineapples is July through September, but there is a winter crop harvested from November through March. The industry creates employment for more than twelve hundred persons during peak harvest. Recently this was not enough, and 245 experienced workers were brought in temporarily from Taiwan. Japan is the principal export market for this new Ryukyuan industry.

Pineapple did make one prolonged appearance on Okinawa before the new industry, though. As the story went, three or four days before Pearl Harbor a freight ship left Hawaii bound for the Far East with ten thousand cartons each containing a dozen No. 10 cans of pineapple wedges in their own syrup. About five or six days later this freighter was allegedly intercepted by Japanese naval vessels. Not sunk, she was boarded and taken to Naha where she was off-loaded. The entire cargo of pineapple in cartons was stored in a Naha warehouse by the Japanese Army Intendance Department. The ship was then turned over to the Japanese merchant fleet, where it was later reported sunk by U.S. operations somewhere in the Pacific. When the Americans invaded Okinawa, this warehouse was among things "liberated." It was still 70 per cent full of pineapple, which had been used only for Japanese officer personnel on occasion. (Japanese enlisted personnel dined on tins of steamed fishheads and rice.) The "liberation," however, was practically the bane of existence for many U.S. army installations which drew rations from Naha supply depots, because as late as 1946, all we had for lunch and supper dessert (and to start breakfast) seven days a week was pineapple and pineapple juice!

Thrust out of the sea, the Ryukyus live by its grace. Their natural first choice of livelihood has always been fishing. There have always been multitudes of fish, shellfish, mollusks, and other kinds for both home consumption and export if all conditions were favorable—weather, labor availability, sea conditions, processing conditions, and market demand. In a good year, fishing can bring considerable profit.

From USCAR reports, we note that the establishment and development of commercial fisheries had been, and continues to be, one of the important goals in the reconstruction of the Ryukyus. Appropriations of 1949, 1950, and 1951 provided a total of nearly three million dollars to start the program. The funds were used to construct sixty-five fishing vessels ranging from 15 to 150 gross tons, one large fish-freezing cold-storage plant, and five small ice plants; to rehabilitate twelve float yards and numerous fish landing ports; and to purchase fishing gear for all the vessels; plus lumber and equipment for katsuobushi (processed skipjack) factories, and some other processing plants. Many other fishing vessels, ice plants, marine processing factories, and other facilities were constructed privately during this period and continue to be so. By 1953 the basic facilities for the operation of commercial fisheries had been provided.

Ryukyuan fishermen have traditionally limited their operations to the narrow coastal belt which surrounds the islands. Many conventional methods of fishing (such as trawling) cannot be practiced because of the rough coral bottom of the adjacent banks. During the war years intensive fishing with explosives was condoned which seriously depleted the fish supply in all nearby waters. The effective progress for the commercial fishing facilities just provided was impeded by the reluctance of local fishermen to depart from the inshore waters, where their efforts were not fully rewarded.

Deep-sea fishing operations require a business organization with adequate working capital, managerial ability, and technical knowledge, as well as fishing vessels and other physical facilities. In anticipation of this need, the Ryukyu Fisheries Company was formed in 1951. This joint stock company, owned privately by members of the fishing industry through their federations and co-operatives, operates the large fish-freezing cold-storage plant at Naha port. Initially its fleet consisted of two 150-ton refrigerated vessels (constructed with early American grant funds) and one 55-ton ice boat. Since 1951 the company has gradually added vessels. It is also served by several independently owned fishing craft from all parts of the Ryukyus.

The company's first pelagic fishing activities were limited to long-line tuna and swordfish operations. Japanese technicians trained in this fishing skill and in fish freezing were employed by the company. Japanese experts in processing and other technical specialties have also been added to the staff of this company and employed by other members of the local fishing industry as new commercial firms have developed.

Mackerel fishing has provided the greatest impetus for the industry. A lack of cheap fish has always been a problem in the Ryukyus. Of Japan's total annual fish catch, exceeding three million tons, more than two million are mackerel and sardines. These constitute the cheap protein food for the masses of Japan. After the establishment of the "Rhee Line," defining Korea's limits, resulted in the loss of the valuable mackerel fishing grounds adjacent to Korea, the Japanese then began to fish for mackerel commercially in the vicinity of "their" Ryukyus. Mackerel fishing was unknown to Ryukyuan fishermen and it had never been conducted on a commercial scale in their waters prior to 1954. In May of that year a vessel, jointly operated by Ryukyuans and Japanese, landed sixteen tons of mackerel at Naha. This joint undertaking was expanded by the addition of other craft from the freshly idle mackerel fleet in Japan. Several independently operated Ryukyuan vessels are now engaged in this joint effort.

Using the facilities of the large Naha refrigeration plant and a smaller one later established at Ishigaki Island, surplus catches were salted, smoked, canned, and quick-frozen to be used as food during off-season periods, and as bait for other deep-sea fishing activities. Total fish landings during 1957 were approximately fifteen thousand tons, more than double the catch in 1951, when fishing activities were still confined to coastal waters. By 1965 totals reached 20,407 metric tons, providing a return of $7,426,000. Surprising is the variety of sea life included in the tally: skipjack, tuna, swordfish, shark, sea bream, snapper, red shad, flying fish, horse mackerel, wrasse, Spanish mackerel, dolphin, garfish, grouper, cuttlefish, octopus, crayfish, crab, precious coral, shells, seaweed, porpoise, whale, and sea snake; everything but the Loch Ness monster.

Other marine products have also been an important source of dollar earnings since 1950. Principally they are sea shells and kaijinso seaweed, which are exported to Japan for the manufacture of shell buttons and medicine (vermifuge). Finished and semi-finished shell buttons are also manufactured by two new Ryukyuan factories for local use and export, but these raw materials are raised from waters within the jurisdiction of other governments. This results in complications limiting the operations of Ryukyuan vessels engaged in these very specialized fishing activities. On the other hand, attempts are being made, with moderate success, to expand the culture of kaijinso in Ryukyuan coastal waters, and three Ryukyuan international whaling stations were licensed in 1958.

By 1964 the early shore-bound fishing philosophy had all but vanished and Ryukyuan deep-sea trawlers were operating in international, open waters off the west coasts of Africa and South America. They fish up a holdful, put into some port, sell it off, lay in provisions, cable home the profits, and cast off for another catch. In this way they work their way around the world around the year, making good money to augment the local Ryukyuan industrial yield.

To meet a local consumption level equivalent to Japan's, the present annual catch must still be increased. Beyond this local demand is a promising export market, providing Ryukyuan products can be offered at competitive prices. The marine resources available to the Ryukyus are virtually unlimited and markets are world-wide. Thus, with potential supply and demand awaiting exploitation, the realization of the commercial fishers' goal depends upon the willingness and ability of local private enterprise and the government policies pursued with respect to fisheries and the economy in general.

Edible oysters are now being grown by the "raft-culture" method. One of the locations where this "farming" is conducted has been "A" approved by the public health authorities of the Air Force to supply oysters to its personnel. This business is expected to provide another significant source of dollar income. Pearl culture, using the indigenous black-lipped oyster, has been going on since 1951, when a joint undertaking by Japanese and Ryukyuans was licensed. Six companies were engaged in this activity on a limited scale by 1958. Small pearl crops and pearl blisters have been harvested and exported. Japanese experts believe black pearls of high quality can be produced in some "inland" waters of the Ryukyus. But due to the necessarily long development period and the reluctance of private enterprise to invest in such a risky venture, it is not expected that this industry will contribute much to export earnings in the foreseeable future. Other forms of agriculture are practiced to a limited extent by local families to supplement their food supply. A Portuguese African fish, *Tilapia mossambica,* was successfully introduced into Okinawa for this purpose in 1954. This species is a prolific breeder and fast grower in ponds and rice paddies. In addition to its value as a cheap source of protein food, it has been used effectively for mosquito control in normally stagnant inland waters.

Except for a tremendous new cement-concrete industry on the south shore of Motobu Peninsula, the mineral resources of the Ryukyu Islands are meager and have only limited commercial importance. The old phosphate rock mining at Kita Daito Island, the sole significant pre-war mining operation, was commercially feasible only because phosphate ore was used by the Japanese steel industry. When Japan converted to the Bessemer process for making steel, the demand vanished completely. This mining operation was conducted under MG supervision from the postwar period until 1951, when it was confirmed that these phosphate deposits contained no ore of quality suitable for the manufacture of superphosphate or even fused phosphate fertilizer. The project was then abandoned and the equipment at the mine was sold to local private enterprise for other uses.

The Ryukyus have no petroleum resources and nearly no fossil fuels. MG was also unsuccessful in its attempt to resume the coal-mining operation at Iriomote Island. Prior to 1945, the Japanese mined some coal in this area for use as bunker fuel for Formosa. Changed economic and political conditions after the war made it impractical to sell this coal to Taiwan. Moreover, Iriomote coal is not suitable as a fuel for ordinary purposes because it is in powdered form. The cost of transporting it from the mine, loading, and shipping even to Okinawa was prohibitive. Thus this project too was abandoned by 1952. Surveys conducted since then have disclosed higher grade coal deposits in other regions of Iriomote. As the economy of this sparsely populated, forested area is developed, it is believed that these coal deposits may be of some commercial importance.

Travertine is mined in increasing quantities for use as building facing, and in the manufacture of such things as book ends and small tables. Due to high shipping costs, the travertine export or its by-products is not considered economically feasible. Old and new mining rights have been issued to private parties to mine sulphur, antimony, and gold in various locations. A small amount of sulphur is being produced at Tori Island. The limited antimony deposits on Okinawa have already been exploited to the point where the operation is no longer commercial. The gold-mining venture at Kume Island has, to now, been unsuccessful.

On the positive side, near the Yabu area on Motobu Peninsula, sizable deposits of gray clay, gypsum, and limestone were found. Further investigations disclosed enough of these materials in the proper proportions to make first-class cement for the next two hundred years. Further, the presence of good "crushing rock," sand, and water (of the quality for Orion beer) combine to make the entire south and west coastlines of Motobu Peninsula a two-hundred-year source of class A construction concrete.

I viewed this vast new industry from a helicopter. It begins at the huge new processing plant at the west end of Nago and continues nearly to the northern shoreline of Motobu. It represents the largest U.S. investment in a single Okinawan industry, some six million dollars to start the Ryukyu Cement Company. The United States holds 37 per cent of this in the Ryukyu Cement Company of Oakland, California. The over-all project manager is from Kaiser Industries; Getz Brothers of San Francisco owns 12 per cent, and the other 51 per cent is Okinawan owned. The daily yield of cement is five hundred to six hundred tons, and the facility is programed for a three-fold expansion to meet 50 to 60 per cent of the island's demand. The plant uses West German engineers and equipment for the American money.

With the postwar switch in Ryukyuan economy from agricultural to commercial, construction naturally became the largest of Okinawa's private ventures. Postwar requirements and future plans called for larger structures for military, government, and commercial enterprise, thus the emphasis was on new construction rather than reconstruction.

The prewar roads accommodated two-wheeled carts, bicycles, and a very few small Japanese motor vehicles, inadequate for the postwar years which brought military and passenger vehicles, buses, and trucks. By 1955 twenty miles of paved four-lane highways and one hundred thirty miles of paved two-lane roads, together with the necessary bridges and culverts, had been constructed on Okinawa in addition to paved road networks within military areas. Highway No. 1 extends a distance of fifty miles along the west coast from Naha Air Base north through Naha city to the second city of Nago. Another paved highway, No. 13, approximately twenty-five miles long by 1955, extended along the east coast. Those two main arteries were connected by many paved roads traversing the southern half of the island.

Construction and improvement of secondary roads and bridges, reclamation of land, and restoration of sea walls were carried out within the limits of budget funds. Much additional work of this sort was required, particularly in Yaeyama and in northern Okinawa, the regions where resettlement is still being encouraged. Municipal development was one of the most important programs undertaken in those years. After the war, private construction developed on the land which was available without regard for prewar land uses or plans for the future. New Naha city actually grew up around and beyond the U.S. forces' installations located within the prewar metropolitan area.

Here a marvelous chance for a triumph in oriental city planning might have been achieved by a minimum of American foresight combined with a modicum of Okinawan patience. But the urgency for money and new places prevailed and the platinum chance was lost forever. Instead of the city being a model for oriental urban redevelopment, it incorporated the worst features of Western gaudiness and Eastern habitual reuse of the old familiar footpaths. It thereby condemned itself to becoming the slums of the next three decades.

Yet many developments and improvements were achieved in a few of the larger municipalities, notably Naha and Nago. Naha today is as contemporary as any Californian town of comparable size. Modern retail stores, office buildings, and other commercial establishments were constructed by private enterprise, even while street work was in progress.

A considerable amount of land adjacent to and between the ports of Naha and Tomari was reclaimed and protected with newly constructed sea walls. A new housing project and a wholesale district, with approximately fifty large concrete business establishments, were constructed between the two port areas. Other public projects which have been constructed with U.S. financial assistance and/or GRI's include a civic center, the Naha Central Post Office, Police Headquarters, port terminal buildings at Naha and Tomari ports, the pier warehouse at Naha, the Okinawa Housing Corporation project of four hundred thirty-eight dwellings (all of which were rented to members of the U.S. forces), and another two hundred houses expressly for the U.S. forces which were located within military areas.

The leader of the Ryukyuan construction industry, and a dynamic public figure, prewar and postwar, has always been Kotaro Kokuba. In July 1931 at Miebashi-cho, Naha, he founded a sole proprietorship, a civil engineering and construction business, introducing the latest technical skills which he had acquired through his ten years of experience in Japan. The company has made steady progress. Its remarkable prewar works include the North and South Meiji Bridges at Naha, the Kotobukiya Butanol Factory, and the Okinawa Broadcasting Station. In 1941, Kokuba Gumi began construction of the Japanese Military Barracks and Air Base Facilities in Naha, Yomitan, and Ie Shima. Under exclusive contract with the Japanese Army, the company maintained a constant force of close to twenty thousand workers.

In March 1964, the company established a stainless steel factory, where sheet is processed, and kitchen utensils are fabricated to meet the domestic market demand. In 1951, Kokuba Gumi had a capital of $83,333 and in its report quoted $600,000 with a total investment of $1,675,400. He has worked in Japan for the government as a registered contractor since June 1963 and in the Ryukyus for local and U.S. money. Since May 1950, Kokuba has successfully completed ninety-five contracts for U.S.-owned or -controlled facilities, the smallest of which was $86,100, and the largest (Marine Corps Facilities, First Increment, at Camp Hansen) in October 1962 was valued at $11,450,000. Thirteen of the contracts were worth more than a million dollars each. The projects ran the gamut from silos for the Okinawa Flour Milling Company to silos for Nike missile sites.

In addition to such subsidiary businesses as lumbering and woodworking operations, ironworks and stainless steel processing, stone processing and asphalt sales operations, Kokuba enjoys exclusive rights to explosives, foreign liquors (Johnnie Walker and others), American tobacco products, and hunting guns.

Kokuba is also president of the Okinawa Power Distribution Company, Ltd., which was established in 1953 as a public corporation. But due to general apathy for such investments, Kokuba has come to own 70 per cent of it. There are four other power distributing companies besides OPDC. Together, they supply Naha, Itoman, and the entire south end with a maximum daily capacity of thirty thousand kilowatts. They sell to the U.S. and GRI installations at cost, and to American and Okinawan civilians at retail rates. Each of the five distributors buys electricity from the Ryukyuan Electric Power Corporation at $0.0151 (about a penny and a half) per kilowatt-hour and they retail it at $0.028/kwh, just under 100 per cent mark-up.

Any discussion of Ryukyuan industry would be incomplete without mention of the Free Trade Zone opened in February 1960. To quote the USCAR Facts Book:

"The Free Trade Zone is a designated area, located adjacent to the port of Naha, into which goods may be imported for temporary storage, display, repackaging, processing, finishing or other operations, for subsequent re-export.

"Upon entry into and re-export from the Free Trade Zone, goods are exempt from duties or taxes, import and export licensing controls, quotas, and usual customs procedures. Goods may not be transferred, however, from the Free Trade Zone into the customs territory of the Ryukyu Islands without an import license from the GRI. In the event of such transfer, all imposts applicable to imported goods become due and payable.

"Seven companies are operating within the Zone, employing approximately 700 persons at this time, of which five are engaged in assembling transistor radios, one in assembling cameras, and one in manufacturing baseball gloves.

"The total value of sales from the Free Trade Zone in FY 1965 was $4.0 million, of which $3.2 million were transistor radios exported to the United States."

Anyone may enter the zone on foot to make retail purchases. However, more retail buying is done by Americans in their PX and commissary systems, and by Ryukyuans in the open retail market. Ryukyuans had by 1958 replaced most of the "foreign" concessionaires of the U.S. PX system. The PX has concessionaire agreements with eighty Okinawan enterprises for the operation of approximately two hundred business establishments within military areas. More than eight hundred restaurants and other establishments engaged in the production and sale of foods and beverages, located outside military areas, have been approved by the military medical authorities for patronage by U.S. forces.

The traditional system of small retail shops and open markets supplied and operated by female vendors is still in existence, especially in rural areas. Naha and Nago cities and other urban centers of Okinawa have since 1953 boasted modern sales and service facilities of a number and variety seldom found in other oriental communities of comparable size. Many Western-type department stores, specialty shops, Ivy League clothiers, service establishments, restaurants, theaters, and other enterprises derive a considerable part—in some cases the principal portion—of their earnings from the patronage of members of the U.S. forces and their entourage.

"The Okinawans are a peace-loving people," said Colonel D. C. Wilson long after he retired from MG. He pointed out the absence of any crime of violence or insurrection against Japanese authority. It was humiliating to Ryukyuans when in 1895, a company of four hundred Japanese soldiers was stationed in Naha to watch for signs of rebellion. Subsequently, policemen with swords proved most unwelcome to a people who had caused a raised eyebrow from the great Napoleon when he had received a report that there was "a single island in the Orient where the inhabitants possessed no weapons whatever."

The Japanese built and maintained a police academy, which was one of the few buildings in the Naha area left standing after the war.

Most of the key positions in the prewar police force were held by appointees from other Japanese prefectures. After the war began, Japanese military security and counterintelligence units, such as the Tokko and Kempei Tai, took over the direction and actual operation of many Ryukyu police functions. The most able and experienced of the civilian police force were called into active service or given other assignments outside the Ryukyus. Of the six-hundred-odd members of the prewar civilian police force in Okinawa Prefecture and Amami gunto, only a few were available to the U.S. forces when hostilities ended.

During the initial stage of the occupation, the several MG teams on Okinawa and other islands simply designated a number of able-bodied native men to act as civilian police and furnished them with arm bands marked "CP" as their only uniform, armament, and badge of authority. With the establishment of the Central Okinawa Administration, these "police forces" in Okinawa were united into a police department which was directly responsible to the chiji (governor). In early 1946, similar police departments were established in the other three guntos.

Fewer than 20 per cent of the Okinawa Police Department had any previous training or experience in police work. The department was also severely handicapped by lack of materials and equipment, as well as communications and transportation facilities. Buildings to house policemen and their families were practically nonexistent, and the same was true about facilities for confinement of prisoners. Personnel turnover was high. To provide assistance, military units donated several Quonset huts and MG assumed some of the department's expenses. Using some of the experienced members as a training cadre, a police academy was opened at Naha late in 1946. A limited number of pistols and motor vehicles were provided by the United States during the next few years, though no significant rehabilitation of police facilities in any of the guntos or changes in the police organizations were effected before 1950.

In the ensuing years, the old Police Academy was indeed rebuilt and refurbished but now serves only as a gymnasium and place for judo and kendo practice. Headquarters are in a brand-new administration building west of the old barn, which is now dwarfed by a surrounding complex of high-rise civic buildings. The department itself has matured; applicants are chosen through rigid Civil Service and physical examinations and are subjected to eight months of broad and strict training. The problems these men now have to cope with were never envisioned in 1950.

Naha today is a city with a quarter of a million people, a lively night life, and several very large "B"-girl bar areas. There is a tremendous amount of international traffic with merchant sailors coming. Still OCP manages to maintain order. The areas of authority are clearly defined between the Okinawan Civil Police and the U.S. armed forces police. Jurisdiction over U.S. cititzens at large on the streets of Okinawan cities on their off-duty time falls into the realm of the OCP force. American nationals are advised of this, and at the same time they are advised to behave themselves reasonably as Americans and show respect and consideration for the civil peace of the Okinawan countryside. The latter-day generation of young Okinawan teen-agers, taking their cue from their Japanese counterparts, have become somewhat "mod." They go around with black jackets and gloves, epaulets, tight black pants, and sideburns. They listen to rock-and-roll music of Japanese manufacture and generally tend at times, in groups, to do a little excessive drinking and become disorderly. Nevertheless, they are all kept close in hand by the OCP force using its own devices.

Naha city sprawls its way up the hillside through all the open country which used to lie between it and Shuri. It has swallowed Shuri and moved on eastward through to Yonabaru and southward toward Itoman and to the southeast also in an area which used to be the back bay. These environs have, in just eighteen years, again become slums. The paper houses with their old tinderbox aspect are again abundant in some sections. There is a large area of teahouses which are in truth nothing more than that—just teahouses. During the day Okinawans go to their favorite locations. There is block after block of nothing but one teahouse after another in this zone. This is where most of the local business is transacted. In the evenings a few of them remain open until midnight or later but most of the activity occurs in the daytime. Beyond this is the native bar and drinking area. This is very different from the honky-tonk bistro district for the Americans, being for Okinawans only. They are the same style establishments as the teahouses, except that place after place is a native bar where perhaps the people from the daytime tea-drinking establishments go to imbibe their alcohol and meet their friends or their women.

Besides this, there is a native red-light district quartering many blocks of houses. None of these is licensed by GRI. But on the other hand, neither GRI nor the police makes any attempt to close them down since, again, they have recognized within themselves the prurient needs of the male population. There is no need for military police to patrol this area because, not only is it distant from anything the American population could get to, but it is also a section where no girl would accept an American "client." Actually in this neighborhood, there are no red lights per se, if there is someone out front she will be soliciting, if there is no one out it means that house is busy or closed for the night.

Finally there is an area of nearly total darkness which is the core slum area of the bawdy house zone and which police cars tend to avoid. It is the center of violence which is a contained permissive area, because in oriental philosophy those who wish either to punish themselves or to allow themselves to be punished would enter on their own desire for just that purpose. It never flows out of bounds.

There is no provision for public care of the insane on Okinawa. The budget is so meager that those who are considered harmless are allowed to remain at large. (The only time they were ever locked in was during the Japanese Premier's visit.) Of course, they are easily recognized in public. One called "Old Half Mast," wearing trousers which seemed about to fall off, roamed around à la Cantinflas in the area of Koza and down toward Futema. Another wore a beret and shorts without shoes or a shirt, regardless of the weather, and walked with his palm forward in a circular motion as if shining a window. There was another junk man, who always wore five or six overcoats, four or five pairs of pants, and carried newspapers in bundles. He never seemed to sell anything. While the government cannot afford to treat these people, public reaction in Ryukyuan society reflects increasing tolerance.

Since the school system as developed by MG, and later USCAR via GRI, is superior, there is little illiteracy, and a surprising quantity of books and periodicals are consumed. There are two major local daily papers, many magazines, some from GRI via Les Hardwick, and some private; besides several Japanese imports, all in addition to any English literature readily available.

Private personal and commercial messages from the Ryukyus are carried worldwide by license of such consistently beautiful and interesting postage stamps that possession of these islands' issues has become a source of philatelic pride equal to that of any European postage-stamp republic. Even from the outset, philatelic history was made fortuitously when some enterprising young Navy men assigned to an out-island MG team ran off mimeographed sheets of self-designed "stamps" for the locals, which they cut apart with scissors and applied with flour-and-water paste. Within a decade, these franks became quite valuable collectors' items, as were most subsequent Ryukyuan postal issues. Both the Okinawan Civilian Department of Postal Affairs and the Department of Cultural Affairs were established by MG Directives 152 and 153 of April 17, 1946, and the first domestic post office was oddly at Goya. Foreign postal service was declared available on May 25, 1947, though conditions were such that no mail was accepted until late the following month.

*Taira: An Okinawan Village* is a ethnographic study by Thomas W. and Hatsumi Maretzki of all aspects of the daily and nightly routines of rural Ryukyuan life. The Maretzki volume, the fifth of a "Six Culture Series" published by John Wiley & Sons, N.Y., is part of an over-all study jointly supervised by Cornell, Harvard, and Yale universities which began in 1954, to learn about distant peoples by living among them for protracted periods. Things affecting growth and development, like traditional beliefs and climate, are reported, along with household compositions, medicine, and the six separate stages of child training. It is gratifying to note that the liberal aspect of American thinking has penetrated even to the remote fringes of the illegitimati. "Since World War II," the Maretzkis tell us, "the distinguishing red ink mark is no longer used in recording these children."

# PART V

# Quo Vadis?

# CHAPTER 13

# Quo Vadis, Japan?

"We should not avoid difficulties," Kozo Masuda, a Japanese chess player of the ninth grade, said recently, "A game is won only by a player who has not only mastered detailed techniques, but has also attained a wide view of the general situation." His advice applies to Japan's situation in the "Okinawan problem." By taking a "wide view of the general situation," the Tokyo government might well be in a far better position than it is.

His Excellency, Prime Minister Eisaku Sato, on the twenty-second anniversary of V-J Day, insisted that the continued government of Okinawa and its nearly one million Japanese-speaking people by a "foreign power" this long after the end of World War II was "unnatural." He vowed to take up the issue with President Johnson during an official trip to Washington in November 1967. Premier Sato indicated a course of increased Tokyo pressure on Washington when he said that continued American administrative presence in the islands might impair future co-operation between the two nations in the defense of the Far East. This was the most far-reaching statement by any Japanese of top rank about the Okinawan matter. The occasion then was the inaugural meeting of the Okinawa Problems Council, a new sixteen-man advisory arm of the Prime Minister's office.

The most natural choice for the chairmanship of this group was appointed. He was mentioned earlier as the Okinawan most likely to succeed at being elected a member-at-large of the upper Diet Chamber, and is past president of Waseda University, Dr. Nobumoto Ohama. He is the most famous living Ryukyuan-born Japanese and is politically astute. Under Dr. Ohama's gavel, the committee should do well, but it might bear in its collective mind the chief of the North American Affairs Bureau's admonishment, "Reversion cannot be hurried, because the United States is needed in the Ryukyus." Nobuyuki Nakajima further and far more wisely said, "There is no magic medicine of one dose."

To the tempo of two days of Tokyo riots in which 130 Japanese were injured and 330 went to jail, protesting their Prime Minister's pro-American policies, Mr. Sato left for Washington November 12, 1967, saying of his previous visit, "President Johnson gave me a Texas ten-gallon hat—and this time I'd like something to go in it." What he got was a pledge for "early" return of the Bonin Islands, possibly within a year. (Other than the war prize of Iwo Jima, all the United States now maintains in the Bonins is a seventy-seven-man naval weather station and an airstrip, which makes this "return" highly possible.) But fortunately the Okinawa question was answered only with such vague diplomatic dodges as "guided by the aim of returning administrative rights" and the main item, "joint and continuous review." The last confirms the tautology of the Japanese line. In Tokyo it is always under "continuous review" toward achieving Mr. Sato's presently frustrated goal. Japan's "postwar period does not end," he said, "until foreign control of former Japanese territory is removed."

While such old-hand diplomats as Yoshio Yamamoto, former Japanese Nampo Liaison officer on Okinawa warned that ". . . all problems must be worked out by mutual understanding," the Japanese press continues its pressure. Tokyo newspapers report quotes from "unnamed sources in the Foreign Ministry" that Japan would like to regain the territory in "eight or nine years."

Yet the *Japan Times* did in 1966 publish: "Our own impression is that this era of co-operation between the United States and Japan, in the case of the Ryukyus, can become an additional bond between our two nations, and there is no need to look for difficulties. Even granted that the situation is not theoretically ideal, the practical advantages are considerable." And Saiji Hasegawa, managing director of Jiji Press, said: "Whether Okinawa likes it or not, U.S. will go in 15 or 20 years."

Today's Japanese-American relationship is the result of a remarkable postwar metamorphosis, based on a great similarity of defense, economic, and political interests. It has, to date, run smoothly in the common interest. Admittedly the American overinvolvement in Vietnam has upset the Japanese considerably, since they do maintain a relationship with mainland China. Economically, Japan must realize that althrough nearly one third of her world trade is with the United States, she in turn accounts for only one-twelfth of the American overseas trade, a distinct imbalance in her favor. There are other economic considerations. For instance, the Japanese do benefit from the fact that the United States spends close to 130 billion dollars a year, seventy billion of which goes for world defense. The total Japanese annual budget is about twelve billion dollars, with nearly nothing for defense. Their problem might become how to double this immediately to allow for the same proportion of defense spending, and still allow for about 6 per cent annual growth.

Mid-1967 saw days of angry thousands of unemployed and underfed Japanese rioting and burning in the shabby slums of Tokyo. The Japanese economy, currently suffering from overproduction and underemployment, was hard pressed to recoup the financial loss. And with home problems of this nature, one wonders how the Japanese propose to feed another million or more outside people.

Though all sixty-six years of Japan's closed-door domination of the Ryukyus were without violence, subversion, or insurrection, such a situation might not exist today. These are not the same Ryukyuans, nor should they be pawns to "impair future co-operation between Japan and the United States in the defense of the Far East," to use Prime Minister Sato's words. The *Japan Times* editorial observed: "We should regret to see this country remilitarize in anything like the old sense, but we cannot tell what may happen in the days to come. What is fairly certain is that if the United States, for any reason whatsoever, should be obliged to modify its defense commitments to Japan, it would be our own obligation to make up the leeway." Major General Ryoichi Tabato, chief of G-2 Japan Self Defense Force answered my query on the possibility of Japan's defending the Ryukyus: "At present, there is no defense 'plan' for reversion. We do not 'spin our wheel' over hypothetical situations."

In our interview, Tokuji Tokonami, the Diet representative from Kagoshima, told me that "the United States cannot just leave" the Ryukyus, and "Japan must rely on America for defense." In his published plan (Appendix) for the return of the Ryukyus he suggests that because Tokyo asserts a claim to the Ryukyus and because the United States maintains a strong military base there (supposedly through Japanese tolerance), "Thus, needless to say, Japan is serving to secure the peace in the Far East."

More accurately, the *Japan Times* editorial says: ". . . At present Japan is in a privileged position; her defense is guaranteed and her young men have not to worry about being called upon to make a major contribution in the matter of preparing to defend their country against possible aggression." The Japanese people, I believe, have had their fill of wars. Too long have Japanese young men conducted their own funeral services before leaving home for foreign battlefields. Now Article 9 of the Constitution outlaws war. Only one of every two persons in Japan today was alive twenty-five years ago to remember. In another twenty years, fewer than one of five will be able to recall the war. And when the present heroic survivors of Hiroshima and Nagasaki disappear, will Japan still remain out of the world nuclear club?

Today, China has positive nuclear war potential—so has the United States on Okinawa. If these American bases were to become Japanese territory, how could U.S. forces fire a missile or take off an aggressive aircraft without the Prime Minister's personal permission for each mission? A high Foreign Ministry official told me that "No one at present is ready to answer this question." Yet many are ready to urge "Ryukyuan reversion." America also has bases in Japan proper. They provide income and employment for many Japanese beside furnishing military protection. This too must be kept in mind when the 1970 treaty revision time comes around.

Japan and the United States have differing world responsibilities; America's global, and Japan's Asian. This affects their approaches to common problems. Japan presses for more aviation and fishing freedom as a matter of national honor, while America regards this as a minor practical matter. Too few Americans speak, read, or write Japanese, and the Japanese grasp of English seldom goes beyond the word-for-word translation, too often the source of humor.

If Japan is successful in recouping the Ryukyus, it will indeed have a tiger by the tail. Exclusive of aid, gifts, or loans, it will immediately have to find 125 million dollars a year to replace that value in American expenditures on Okinawan goods and services to maintain the military establishment and its peripheral people. Concomitant with the return of the Ryukyus the Japanese will have to support an additional million people in a standard to which they have now become accustomed. Locals will have to be eligible for Diet chairs and possible Cabinet posts. They have to be free to aspire to any position for which they can qualify without being relegated to dishwashing and labor battalions. Okinawans will want more than the barest needs and a place to belong. There is also the defense problem, and ultimately the Tokyo treasury must be prepared to buy up all the American dollars in the islands for an equivalent amount in Japanese yen without diminishing its purchasing power. This sum has been estimated from under one to over five billion dollars.

There is a very real possibility that Japan might be successful in its drive for Okinawa. Today, nations can start, pursue, and lose wars—then demand and get the return of all lost land. As if it were a chess game, after the conclusion the vanquished gets all restored to pregame status, perhaps to begin another game.

When the shoe was on the other foot, did the Japanese even remotely consider returning residual sovereignty of territory they captured from China, Korea, Russia, Ryukyus, et al., between 1871 and 1943? If this precedent is successful, the Germans may press for another "return" of the Sudetenland, Italy might sue for Nice, Sweden for Leningrad, and England for America's Atlantic seaboard from Massachusetts to Georgia in thirteen separate chunks.

Suppose, as a result of giving in to Japanese pressure for return of the Bonin and Volcano Islands, the United States also gave back the Ryukyus, what would the next move be? The Japanese will also have a basis to claim the Kuriles and other northern islands from the Soviet Union. (Japan captured and occupied the Kurile Islands in 1875, then renounced all title to them under Article 2 of the peace treaty of 1951. In 1965, because of some correspondence between the Japanese and Soviet Foreign Ministers, Tokyo feels "they are now under unlawful possession of Soviet Russia.")

Perhaps, too, the Japanese would claim Formosa, which they acquired from China in 1895. (Chiang Kai-shek's tenant domain conceivably could then find itself with Tokyo as a landlord!) Moreover, what might prevent a successful claim from mainland China on residual sovereignty over Taiwan? Why should the 1945 American Okinawa military victory be any less binding than Japan's 1895 Taiwan triumph over China? And why shouldn't China argue that their residual sovereignty over the Ryukyus pre-empts the Japanese "rights," because they held a tribute domination over the islands from 1372 until Japan forced them out five hundred years later?

Finally, if Japan does get the Ryukyus, there is no real, unified plan for the islands' incorporation. Everyone concerned to whom I spoke in Tokyo seemed to know of no existing "plan," except for Tokuji Tokonami, the Diet representative from Kagoshima, the Prefecture of Japan most likely (at the beginning at least) to include the Ryukyus. Some years ago, he advanced an over-all plan, calling for an immediate start on a gradual, transference of total administration.

New Japanese war memorials are springing up all over Okinawa, far beyond the original cluster at Suicide Cliff. Many religious memorial pilgrimages journey from Japan in large and small groups to the monuments and other shrines in the islands. Monetary and other tangible gifts appear almost daily, and recently a sizable appropriation from a Japanese teachers' union paid for a large Naha building to house a combination planetarium, science museum, and exhibition hall, all for Okinawan children. Japanese books, papers, and magazines abound —and, of course, there is now the microwave television, which brings Japan's daily news events "live" right into the bosom of the Ryukyuan homes at family times.

There appear to be a number of intermediate goals toward which the Japanese might apply their energies in a more rewarding manner regarding their relations with the United States. Japan might take a more active part in programs of the international scene. Nippon has joined the United Nations and other world councils, her industrial, technological, and artistic advancement could be of considerable assistance on an expanded scope with under-developed nations rather than just in Asian trade. Perhaps the most reasonable approach would be for Japan and the United States to work jointly toward establishing a stable, viable economy in the Ryukyu Islands which might eventually lead to their independence from both major powers. The two countries might work out a schedule for phasing out American forces from bases in Japan proper. This would involve the re-employment in the home economy of Japanese now working at American bases, and the strengthening to Constitution and treaty maximum the Japanese Self Defense Forces.

Economically, the Japanese might consider lowering trade barriers to allow a freer movement of the world's goods in, out, and through Japan's ports. Payment imbalances might then level off. Japan might drop exchange restriction on long-term capital fund movement into their business economy. These moves may quickly become reciprocal on a world-wide basis. Japan should not let American policies influence its own trade, cultural, economic, and political ties with mainland China. Japan's destinies in Asia must be her own. Goodwill and understanding on a reciprocal basis may well leave her in an advantageous future mediating position. While World War II created strong anti-Japanese feelings in South and Southeast Asia, this could be overcome. In addition to trade, Japan could help these countries develop through her own experience. The Peace Corps idea, which the Japanese have recently adopted, could be most fruitful.

Finally, communications between Japan and the United States must improve. Aside from government-to-government programs, or independent ventures of private citizens, educational foundations, schools and universities, industrial, labor and civic organizations in both countries could develop meaningful programs. As far as working with the Americans toward a compromise or possibly a free Okinawa in the not too distant future, the *Japan Times* succinctly summed up: "Even granted that the situation is not theoretically ideal, the practical advantages are considerable."

# CHAPTER 14

# Quo Vadis, United States?

On the twenty-second of any June, there is a quiet Japanese-American memorial program at the new Japanese Memorial Park in South Okinawa, near General Ushijima's suicide spot. Thus the date and place of the vanquished have become the points of record, and the unique joint commemoration reaffirms hopes for a lasting peace. The German defeat at Stalingrad was described to the German's at home "as a sacred beacon, this noble example of supreme heroism and ultimate self-sacrifice." Stalingrad became a myth to "impart a sense of obligation to all future generations of Germans." It is the sincere hope of all people that no such immolation status be imparted to Okinawa by the Japanese.

The shooting battle ended as it began—in silence. But the verbal battle for this western Pacific frontier island continues. The protagonists and subjects are the same, but the conditions have changed. In addition to General Stilwell's surrender documents, there are three other legal and binding items in effect governing both the islands and the relationship between the United States and Japan vis-à-vis the Ryukyus—the treaty of peace with Japan (1952), Executive Order 10713 (1957), and a statement by President John F. Kennedy (1962).

The surrender has unfortunately become buried, and seems superseded. Although the treaty of peace never mentions the term "residual sovereignty," Chapter II, Article 3 leaves room for further disposition of the Ryukyu Islands. The Executive Order is in effect, the "constitution" for the GRI. Only in President Kennedy's statement, which accompanied an amendment to 10713, was there ever actually mention of "recognition" of a Japanese desire for reversion of the territory; it is the first written reference to "residual sovereignty" of the

Ryukyus, although now it is impossible ever to tell if this was a politically expedient Kennedy statement, like *"Ich bin ein Berliner,"* or a serious international Kennedy stand, like the Cuban missile crisis. We shall never know, but its effect is with us.

On this reference, which it has come to believe totally valid, the government of Japan has based its case for "reversion." And while the United States says it concurs, the re-enlistment rate for noncommissioned personnel of the Army and Air Force on what was once called "the Rock" has now become higher than at any other U.S. base in the world. And Washington-ordered capital construction of permanent base facilities continues apace.

Actually the United States might never have been in this peculiar position if it had availed itself of an opportunity which is now past. In the five years between 1945 and 1950, the United States had done a tremendous amount for the Ryukyuan people. Although nonfraternization was the rule, the general will of the Ryukyuans in 1950 was reflected in a petition for American annexation for what the United States had accomplished. Some looked on this as a possibility, but the attitude of most American officials was "thanks, but no thanks." The Okinawans were politely rebuffed. Had anyone in 1950 Washington foreseen that Hawaii would become a state within the next decade or that possibly the Ryukyus could have been administered some way from a Hawaiian nerve center, things might have been different. The United States has on other occasions adopted for full citizenship islands of people with far less potential. The Okinawans have always been honest, diligent, willing followers, and in the Americans they saw money and energy.

Feeling cast off again, the Okinawans turned back to the Japanese, who were just beginning in 1950 to send a few people back to the Ryukyus. This was the turning point. America's influence declined, although its authority continued to grow.

Today the Japanese forcefully demand the outright return of "their" islands or some sort of A.C.-D.C. arrangement of Japanese administration over civilian affairs of the natives while the United States keeps control of its bases. This seems even more unnatural than the "unnatural condition" which they insist obtains at present. But a surprising number of influential Americans agree with Japan.

A September 1967 nongovernment conference, the Japanese-American Assembly met at Shimoda, Japan, to discuss major items of the interrelationship between the two countries and concluded that Okinawa should revert to Tokyo control. The principal features of the final report, written in part by Professor Herbert Passin of Columbia University, states that disagreements seldom followed national lines, but more often had "found Americans and Japanese on one side of a question opposed to Americans and Japanese on the other side."

Yet many more people in Tokyo offer opinions on the Ryukyus than in Washington. Distance plays a role; the islands are close enough to Japan to count.

Washington should persuade Tokyo to work with the United States for another decade or two, to try to develop a self-supporting viable island chain. To do so, advice, not from theoreticians, but from those who have served in meaningful capacities in the Ryukyus, should be sought and used. Reliable information is needed, as it has always been for the Ryukyus.

For instance, Edwin O. Reischauer, Harvard professor of Oriental history, and U. S. Ambassador to Japan from 1961 to 1966, said at a hearing before the U. S. Senate Foreign Relations Committee on January 31, 1967 that Japan and the United States were "natural allies." It is hard really, to see how two countries, half a world apart, with different cultures, who had no contact until just a century ago, after which they began to compete avidly for commercial control of the western Pacific, could possibly be "natural allies." At most, one might say that after the four years of bloody combat and seven years of tenuous occupation, the Japanese and American governments have become friendly. ". . . We still, twenty-one years after the war, administer through our own military the lives of something over nine hundred thousand Japanese living in these islands," stated Professor Reischauer. But surely he must know the military governs only the *military,* and the nine hundred thousand are administered by the Government of the Ryukyu Islands, an all-Ryukyuan elected body under the aegis of the U. S. *Civil* Administration of the Ryukyus, responsible to the Secretary of State. Also, the Ryukyuans are not "Japanese," even though their land was Japanized by armed force in 1879.

Then Profesor Reischauer said: ". . . their [Japan's] financial aid to the Ryukyu Islands has increased greatly, so I think now it is probably larger than what we are putting into the islands." Actual Japanese aid figures are available in the *Facts Book* published annually by the Hi Com. Japan's aid is only a fraction of America's annual 240 million dollars.

The former ambassador continued, ". . . the Soviet Union . . . did not have any right to claim the Kurile Islands. The Japanese had acquired them over history in a perfectly legal manner." In fact, the armed forces of the Meiji restoration, in their unprovoked drive for territorial expansion, landed in the Kuriles in 1875 and gobbled them into the Japanese Empire. This is no more or less "legal" than the U.S. capture of Okinawa, yet the professor advocates that *both* be restored to Japan. Moreover until a University of Tokyo survey polled a mere sixteen hundred Ryukyuans for their thoughts, in mid-1967, no one ever even remotely considered consulting the Ryukyuans. Has anyone ever checked in the Kuriles?

Senator Robert F. Kennedy said in Chicago, February 8, 1967, "We do not know . . . about our goals, our own policies, our own conception of national interests in Asia. We proclaim our intention to assure self-determination, with American lives if necessary, yet we support and defend a Formosa whose indigenous people have no voice in government." The Ryukyuans and the Taiwans alike should be entitled to a free choice, but only after they have been made internally and externally secure.

The Okinawans who could count have lost heart. They feel their future is not to be determined at home, but in Tokyo and Washington. An American general, on the other hand, said the timetable for reversion depended on "Peking, Hanoi, and Pyongyang." The United States cannot leave until all is secure. And Tokyo cannot take over the Ryukyuan defenses even though the New York *Times* reported that Prime Minister "Sato has said that it will be all right for the U.S. to pull out of Okinawa if Japan can replace the American bases with sufficient Japanese military power to protect the country." Actually, the United States doesn't just "protect the country," USARYIS is the "Keystone of the Pacific" protects the entire region. And what of Article 9 of the new Japanese Constitution vis-à-vis this "sufficient Japanese military power"?

Lieutenant General Ferdinand T. Unger, the Hi Com as of November 1966, said he had been pleased to find on his arrival that the situation was not as hostile as he had expected. He is planning to rescind some twenty-nine laws of USCAR as soon as GRI produces local legislation more in keeping with Japanese practices. This is fine if it helps the Ryukyuans, but not if it is another gradual easement of the islands toward Japan. The *Reader's Digest* in August 1959 called Okinawa "a showcase for American resolution and integrity." Francis V. Drake's article urged in it, "If we permit the Island to revert to Japanese control, the whole fortress could conceivably become useless as a deterrent to war."

Okinawans do fly the Japanese flag on Japanese or American holidays—why not? They do not have a flag of their own, and the Americans have denied them the Stars and Stripes. There was a problem with U.S. forces personnel chauvinistically tearing down Japanese flags when they first burgeoned forth in 1965, but a Hi Com memorandum spelled it out. In the words of cinemagnate Charles Dunn, ". . . an implied warning to servicemen that a superior chewing awaits any souvenir hunter who (as has been their wont) snatches one."

On the twenty-second anniversary of V-J Day, Japanese Premier Sato declared that the continued government of Okinawa by a "foreign power" was "unnatural." He makes his points well. He is a charming and polished professional politician. He is cultured, sings baritone, plays good golf, speaks German (of course), and is a master in the cha-no-yu, the ritual tea brewing and drinking ceremony. A political Napoleon, Sato rose from stationmaster in Futsukaichi village to head Japan's railroads by 1945. In 1953 he won a representative's seat in the lower Diet house, from which he had to resign over a scandal involving unreported contributions from a shipowners' association. Subsequently he headed a Cabinet Ministry when his elder brother Nobusuke Kishi became Premier. He retained this post after his brother was succeeded by Sato's schoolmate and lifelong friend, Hayato Ikeda, but then Sato San resigned to challenge Ikeda's Liberal Democratic Party leadership. To those who accused him of disloyalty, he said, "Friendship should not be permitted to interfere with a person's decision when it has any bearing on his course of action in public life." Though the challenge failed, Ikeda died of cancer a few months later and Eisaku Sato became Premier.

When Sato San returned home from his November 1967 Washington visit with only a pledge for "early" return of the Bonin Islands and a promise to keep the Okinawa question under "joint and continuous review," one Japanese newshawk observed, "The Americans are on the right track. I just hope they keep moving." I most enthusiastically agree with his statement, since the track appears to be holding onto the Ryukyus for the foreseeable future.

Americans have done much for the Ryukyus in the twenty-three years they have been "guests" in the islands—things like the schools, the public health and welfare, the engineering facilities, the comforts, the entertainment, the protection, the services, and the 240 million dollars a year above the actual upkeep of the bases. There is full employment, although it is a sort of forced-draft economy. Enterprising Americans ought to take a long hard look at the islands and the possibilities they offer for reasonably priced, intelligent, willing, honest help, good natural surroundings, and reasonable initial costs for industrial investment. This is almost a pristine world.

HICOM Ordinance No. 11 of September 1958, with two changes of July 1963 and August 1965, regulates "Foreign Investments in the Ryukyu Islands." The rules are simple and reasonable. Successful going concerns now are a major soft drink bottling company and its half dozen competitors; the American Concrete Pipe Company, a large plywood plant, an even larger cement plant combined with a concrete industry; all aspects of fishing, shipwrights; flour mills; and an assortment of lesser light industry.

Sam Oglesby says an honest, ambitious American can set up shop and beat the local import market on such needed items as vehicles and parts, clothing and textiles, construction and industrial machinery, electrical appliances, paper and paper products, chemicals (fertilizers, insecticides, disinfectants), marine products, animal feed, dairy products, and whatever else the imagination conceives. Yet too few go.

There are many ways for the U.S. businessman to get from America to the Ryukyus. If he is to be going via Tokyo fairly regularly, some thought should be given to a mode of travel tailored to suit his routine, time schedules, convenience, comfort, economy, and fringe benefits. Those who have done it once believe it takes "getting used to," but those who go regularly will quickly tell you of the "date-line syndrome." It is difficult to fly nonstop, New York to Tokyo, for the alleged convenience of not having to change planes, or "getting it all over with." The body won't take it and any time gained on a grueling through flight is lost sleeping it off at the other end. From Tokyo, normal travel to all oriental cities including Naha is routine, in most cases by Pan Am, JAL, CAT, BOAC, KLM, and Qantas, among others. Trans Pacific, JAL and BOAC run often, and Pan American offers a daily choice of short polar or long mid-ocean flights.

But *caution*: before you start for Okinawa be sure you have the proper landing clearance papers, which are easily obtainable for any legitimate purpose from the U.S. Department of State. Once there, avoid the attitude that Orientals are inferior. Unless Americans practice an attitude of friendship, and mean it, all our early efforts vanish like cobwebs before a typhoon. Using experience as a partial guide, the United States must separate the past from the future without losing track of the valuable lessons we have learned in the last century of dealing with our "natural ally." Washington cannot afford to be panicked or stampeded by the Sato or any successive Tokyo government. In all international intercourse there are both clashes and accords. The disagreements must be taken one by one in proper context, and not be permitted to create irreparable breaches in over-all relations.

In summary, the United States must not allow itself the privilege of being convinced that keeping the Ryukyus at least pro tem will result in charges of "imperialist" or "aggressor" from the Soviet Union. The U.S.S.R., too, is in a similar situation with Japan over the "reversion" of Shikotan and Habomai islands off Hokkaido, and Kunashiri and Etofu islands. Japan renounced all claims to these with the peace treaty, and now wants them back also.

Perhaps if the United Nations were stronger, a reasonable solution to the Ryukyus riddle might be a trusteeship system so provided by Article 3 of the treaty of peace. In view of current world conditions, however, this does not seem workable. Israel's Foreign Minister Abba Eban called international law "The law which the wicked will not obey, and the righteous will not enforce." In any event, international law does suggest that the United States has a positive reason to be in the Ryukyus.

# CHAPTER 15

# Quo Vadis, Okinawa?

"Better to be the head of a chicken than the south end of an ox," said Japan's Prime Minister Sato in Washington a few years ago. While he was referring to his own country's position with the United States, the statement seems just as applicable to the Ryukyu-Japan relationship. Okinawa has always been socially, economically, and geographically Japan's "south end." Though Okinawa may be only a "chicken," it should at least have its own head.

But Okinawans today seem to have chosen the path appearing to offer the least conflict. Nevertheless the Ryukyu chain cannot always be regarded as a political infant. It is old enough to think about standing on its own feet, once a viable enonomy and external security are established. This *can* happen within a reasonably foreseeable future if the Ryukyuans are willing to aspire to it. National integrity will never come from reversion. The Okinawans must decide if they wish to achieve their own long postponed national heritage.

At home, the average Ryukyuan leads a modest, quiet, domestic life. The urban people are somewhat poorer, but seem to "live" a bit more. Rural folk work hard, are far from the peasants their grandparents were, and are achieving more comforts. It is now time for a show of some internal strength. A close look at the historical record shows clearly that neither the Ryukyuan land nor the people were originally Japanese.

Japan made its first stab at Okinawa in A.D. 698, and then never ceased to hit and run. The Satsumas came in force in 1609 to stay, dominate, and milk their resources. They deprived Okinawa of its status as an independent state, while allowing Shuri the continued double indignity of paying tribute to China. Finally, in 1879, the Ryukyus were forcibly swallowed into the domain of the Son of Heaven, where they were completely assimilated by attrition. In the ninth century, Okinawans made their only venture to Japan. They went with gifts, not swords, and this was misinterpreted in Japan as a voluntary offer of tribute.

The present generation of Ryukyuans is two inches taller and ten pounds heavier on average than their forebears, the result of dietary donations for children (vitamins, powdered milk, and balanced school lunches), given since the war's end by RYIVOC (Ryukyu International Volunteer Council), comprised of the American Red Cross and various church groups. Once past the early rough days of MG, adults have been given serious dietary assistance. Their infant mortality rate has steadily decreased, and as their resistance rises, the usual run of endemic and regional diseases is being obliterated. The result is the Ryukyuan population has doubled since the end of World War II, and they are not suffering. In 1967, for instance, their economy registered an 11.5 per cent gain over 1966, due just in part to the escalation of America's Vietnam war. Besides a tremendous increase in education, Okinawan unemployment has virtually vanished.

In mid-1967, a team of sociologists and psychologists from Tokyo University polled sixteen hundred Ryukyuans, trying to find a general consensus. They found 88 per cent for reversion. But then these were the Japanese asking the questions. Actually more than half of the 88 per cent added they favored a "gradual return" similar to the Tokonami plan. A little more than half those queried thought U.S. administration of "Japanese territory" was "unpermissible," a scant half of 1 per cent more felt that the U.S. administration had been "of considerable help economically," in what was one of the poorest areas of prewar Japan. Though they freely enjoy American aid and comfort, and 41 per cent conjecture they would have been "worse off" had Okinawa remained Japanese in 1945, they still talk of "reversion."

Interestingly, the polls and discussions generally direct themselves to when and how completely the United States will withdraw—it being a foregone conclusion that America shall. Do any of them consider in depth independent status for the islands? "Out of the question!" emphatically declared most everyone of consequence I asked in Tokyo. "Happier the eve than the holiday itself," I answered, with an old Japanese proverb.

Okinawans today do have a governmental structure in GRI with all the usual political elements. Elections are held to fill all offices. The Ryukyus divide into sixty-four sons (counties), which include towns and villages, but not big cities; those are independent. There are thirty-two election districts running candidates for one seat each in the one-house legislature. Thirteen thousand Okinawans work for the GRI as civil servants and belong to a government employees' union. Each village has an elected chief (shi), and the larger cities have their mayors. Junji Nishime of the Okinawan Democratic Party won a tremendous second-term election as mayor of Naha by gaining all but one local district against the strongest united-front candidate, an incumbent legislator.

There are six parties in the full left to right spectrum generating much strong electioneering. The Okinawan Democratic Party, alleged by some to be the puppets of the United States are nonetheless the strongest party at the polls and consequently dominate the legislature. Originally, the Hi Com selected the chief executive with the rubber-stamp approval of the legislature. Later the method was reversed and the CE is now elected by the legislature, with the winner subject to Hi Com's approval. Since the ODP is in the majority, its leader is invariably elected. All opposition parties are agitating for open free election of the CE, which they feel might result in the selection of a popular man from a coalition. The Hi Com refuses to change the system used in England and Japan. Oddly the free-election system they want (so atypical of the Orient), closely resembles the American way.

Political activity is avid with fringe elements such as Okinawa Women's Federation and young businessmen who are lost to the conservatives because the elders still take a seen-but-not-heard attitude toward what they term "young hard-boiled eggs." The conservatives also lost the women this way and are now trying every device to recoup both elements.

The winner and still champion, the Chief Executive of GRI, sixty-nine-year-old Seiho Matsuoka, is the picture of calm confidence. His opponents, he contended, were against the system, not the man. Born in Kin village, and eventually enrolling at Columbia University in electrical engineering, he became director of Public Works for MG. He told me that Okinawa could not be self-sufficient if America left it to Japan unless 50 per cent of the population left. People have it too good now, and all would suffer from a drop in the economy. He described Japan today as in a greenhouse; protected from the weather by the United States, it has only to worry about growing. The big problem in the Ryukyus now is the great understanding and communications gap among four groups—industrial tycoons, university scholars, sociopolitical types, and the people at large. The poor are not so poor; they dress badly but they eat well and save. When I asked him about his two major rivals, he thought Asato was a bright man who could mature and develop. Senaga, he felt, had been stronger ten years ago; his popularity fades more each year. Chief Executive Matsuoka agreed with me when I quoted from Vern Sneider's *Teahouse of the August Moon* that if Okinawans expect nothing they are not disappointed, but what they do get is not quite what it ought to be!

I wanted to talk to both minority political leaders following the CE's comments. Tsumichiyo Asato, Chairman of the OSMP (Okinawan Socialist Masses Party), was readily accessible for interview in the Legislative chambers. I learned from him that his is the second largest party, with nine seats against the majority ODP's nineteen. A decade ago his was first, but the U.S. lump-sum real estate payments unseated them. He feels that direct elections would work well because of the small number of votes. He advocates political and legal moves to change the gerrymandered election districts, direct election of the CE, and no U.S. support of any candidate, direct or indirect. Mr. Asato majored in law at Nippon University in Tokyo and still practices. He feels reversion is a must, since it is contrary to American basic concepts for the United States to control other lands for military purposes. It is tragic to keep two segments of the same "race" separated, and their farm lands under airfields. In the summer of 1965, Asato San spent a lot of money in an unsuccessful campaign, running in Japan for a member-at-large seat in the upper House of the Diet.

Unable to reach the Leftist leader, Kamejiro Senaga, through usual channels, I asked a journalist named Miyagi for help. He got me as far as Senaga's home telephone number. The next day my man Yamashiro reported, "I could not make an appointment with Mr. Senaga. Every time I call him, he is not at home." Finally he reported: "Being called upon to make an appointment, I telephoned to Mr. Senaga. Since he was not at home, I explained to Mrs. Senaga that Mr. Morris, a writer and nongovernment journalist in the United States, would like to interview Mr. Senaga concerning political, economical, educational, and all other problems in the Ryukyus and that he is scheduled to publish them in book form during this year. But, after that, everytime I called him, for three days, he was not at home. And Mrs. Senaga's reply was always vague. So I asked her, 'Can I understand that Mr. Senaga is not interested in meeting with Mr. Morris?' The answer was 'yes.' " Senaga's OPP (Okinawa People's Party) has only one seat in the Legislature. There is one seat for the OSP (Okinawa Socialist Party) and two Independents for the thirty-two-seat total.

"Herald" is the English word for "shimpo"; oddly "progress" is its Japanese homonym. This is the name of one of the two principal Japanese-language dailies in Naha. Shui Ikemiyagi, in addition to presiding over the Board of Governors of the local YMCA, is president and publisher of *Ryukyu Shimpō.* Competing with *Okinawa Times, Shimpō*'s sixty-five thousand circulation of morning and afternoon editions sells at 3¢ a copy.

Two other postwar papers came and failed twelve years ago. "Poor editing," conjectured Ikemiyagi's aide, S. Hokama. "*We* were founded in 1893." Ikemiyagi said "that Ryukyuan papers following the Japanese tradition are politically neutral and are independent of GRI; Asato would never win a popular election; Okinawa needs capital, technology, and improvement of local administration, and can get these," he said, "by following the Nipponese way." Okinawa must revert while the U.S. bases remain. Since he left Waseda University, probably the best idea Ikemiyagi San believes he's had is for the United Nations to move its headquarters from New York to Naha to be on completely neutral ground. I went again to Radio (and TV) Okinawa (ROK), to visit Shō Sen, the grand nephew of the last king. A patrician in every sense, Shō Sen started ROK nine years ago with his own funds, which obligates him neither to the United States nor Japan. The facility, now capitalized at three hundred thousand dollars and reaching all Okinawa with ads, news, and entertainment, will not run any "Gallup polls." Though ROK is entertainment and commercial, it does give equal time to politicians without itself taking any sides. With more aid from both the United States and Tokyo, he said, "the resourceless Ryukyus could strive for a self-supporting economy." But Shō Sen rejects independence now. The tendency today is toward broader international economic cooperation, as in Europe. He prefers this to the new African wave of free nations, regardless of visible means of support or defense. Shō Sen explained that the Ryukyuan businessmen's association believes a clear effect of reversion to Japan would be an almost irretrievable decline in the local economy.

Sen's cousin, Shō Hiroshi, is the grandson of Shō Tai, the last of the Shuri kings. When Shō Tai was exiled to protective custody in a Tokyo villa he took with him a priceless treasury of Ryukyuan art, which his son and then Hiroshi have in turn inherited, cherished, and expanded. It is now the world's largest and finest collection. An aesthete, Shō Hiroshi feels he can do more for his people by leaving power politics to the politicians and by continuing his efforts for a rebirth of Ryukyuan folk arts and a resurgence in local culture. Some years ago, with the help of the *Okinawa Times,* he held an annual arts festival, but it had to be dropped when it became too commercial. As the economy improves, the interest in culture goes down. Yet it is possible to improve both along the lines of pottery, bingatas, and rock ware. Shō Hiroshi is ambivalent about reversion. The Meiji restoration began the stifling of Ryukyuan culture, yet he lives and works half of each year in Tokyo, the land of his birth.

The Shō family crest, the Tomé, is also the traditional "national" emblem of the Ryukyus. Like the dual Korean "Yang and Yin," the triple Tomé is the symbol of life for Okinawa and might be on its flag, were the Ryukyus ever to have one. I prefer to think of Tomé as the oriental symbolism (of the Christian triangle of body, mind, and spirit), which may eventually represent a united Ryukyuan republic, conceivable within the next generation.

"Eight hundred thousand Okinawans are betrayed by dealing with the United States without their consent," cries Kyan San, president of the Okinawan Reversion Council, who also claims that Okinawa has been sacrificed twice by Japan. The clearest aspect of his position is that the government of Japan must respond to the jibes from the leftists and repatriate the Ryukyus, since, having been rejected by the United States, Okinawans have no place to go except to Japan—or into the leftist camp. How could his fear miss the very inbred traits of his people as definitely unsuited to selfless Communism? The individual small farmer working his own ⅓-acre tract would never adapt to a collective farm (even though local workers all help out in the community during cane harvest time). The myriad local women in the tiny side-street stalls and shops continue to retail all sorts of wares, despite the inroads of modern stores and markets.

I looked up two contemporaries of the late Dr. Koshin Shikiya. Thomas Jugo was deputy to Shikiya in the MG days and succeeded his mentor as head of the provisional government. Now he is still active part-time as chairman of TV and ROK. He understands Americans well, "having dealt with them since they came." He also got to Washington three times—in 1953 as chief justice, in 1958 on the land conference, and in 1962 privately. He also understands the Japanese, having his law degree from Kyoto University. ". . . We cannot let sentiment displace realism," he said. "Prewar Japanese developed no commerce or industry, and we have no resources other than our human selves. We should make the most of the United States while they are here. Perhaps five or six years more, capable thinking people will emerge to help guide our country's fate. Meanwhile, we should make no rapid, rash moves to leave us in depression. Meanwhile, we must not overcriticize the Chief Executive. In my own case, whatever I did, good or bad, created a furor. CE needs better staff, and people must realize the CE works *for* them."

The other colleague of Shikiya was Higa Eigen, who was director of agriculture in MG, and earlier taught and superintended prewar schools. At seventy-nine, he is semiretired at his family home just north of Nago. Taking time off from the affairs of the Nago Steel Company (of which his nephew is president), he received me in his traditional Japanese-style home. He feels that Okinawa must revert immediately and Japan, who helps its poorer prefectures, will also decrease taxes by one third and pour in generous subsidies. Higa thinks that Japanese big business will invest in upgrading Okinawan plants. "It will happen," he insisted. "New Year's 1945 I predicted a tidal wave on the first of April and actually it did happen!" Very seriously he said that the real solution is for five hundred thousand Okinawans to move to California and start a sugar industry. Then they could send much money home to the remaining five hundred thousand, who would have an easier time because there would be more room and outside money coming in!

Old Master Gushiken of the Orion Brewery is far more in touch with reality when he contends that reversion would not help the Ryukyuan economy, welfare, or morale as much as would economic self-sufficiency. Naturally, his soft-drink "competitor," Bill Matchett, agrees, but though his industry supports a good piece of the economy, Matchett is still a "gai-jin." At a Rotary luncheon, I found out that there is in the islands an Okinawa Small and Medium Enterprise Federation under Masatsune Sotoma, which helps little private enterprises become self-sustaining to aid the local economic life, but the big local business gun is the very American concept of the Chamber of Commerce. And a giant of a man was its director.

Kunio Matsukawa is the kendo instructor at the police academy when he is not running the CC. He feels that local growth is fantastic and should not be interrupted or set back by any administrative changes until it reaches a reasonable plateau. When he was a boy, only three of ten went to high school, and it took a day to go from Naha to Nago—now it can be done in two hours by bus for 48¢. The old-line "reformists," the ultraconservatives, and the leftists all have in common the goal of anti-United States feelings and "reversion." "There is so much industrial development yet to be accomplished, so much industry begging to be developed that a great future is available in cane waste, tuna, shrimp, seaweed, etc. Forgetting Iriomote's meager mining, there is four to five million dollars per year to be made in fruits and vegetables. This is a future land for men with vision."

At a large cocktail party given by the Ryukyu Development Loan Corporation (RDLC) (which the U.S. began on "B" yen in the early days), I learned that the return of loans plus payments of interest has made this fund a driving spirit for the growth of the Okinawan economy. Its leaders, referred to as the atomic force of the Ryukyus, are a few young, vigorous, forward-looking men. One of this group said they all were patriotic, and perhaps idealistic a bit, but they claim not to be realists. They know that the presence of the United States and its dollar-boosted economy is here today and will be here tomorrow. But they are striving toward a day away off. Sometime, maybe not in their lifetime, Okinawa may again be a Japanese Prefecture.

As George Kerr indicated in his history, Okinawa in pre-World War II days was considered a fourth-class economic community of Japan. They feel that Japan will again take the reins of its "acknowledged residual sovereignty" and at that time the RDLC hopes it will have brought Okinawa along to such a state that it will be ahead of, instead of dependent upon, Japan. They do not consider the possibility of Japan again pushing Okinawa into the background. Another young man felt that Okinawans have no real say in this destiny. It is to be decided in Tokyo or Washington. Okinawans can only work for self-improvement and strive to rise to the occasion when the day of decision is at hand. I suggested that perhaps this attitude was what once cost Okinawa the mastery of the Asian seas. Why shouldn't one of them take the driver's seat? He said the idea was fruitless because neither Tokyo nor Washington cares what Okinawans think. Why aspire to the unattainable, when they could concentrate on the present and immediate future?

I looked around the room and saw at least two hundred well-dressed young pillars of commerce and industry in a prosperous economy with bold future plans. Twenty years ago not one of them had even a hope of anything better than scratching out a daily sustenance and perhaps learning some skilled trade. With U.S. help and Okinawan perseverance and determination—they have come to their positions of achievement and affluence. Now they need confidence in themselves.

While local self-esteem has grown, it must continue to thrive until some future date when the Okinawan leaders will have "arrived," home-grown, to guide their people to their long-delayed place among the free states of the world.

An enlightened young Ryukyuan, Hajime Kyoda, who returned to Okinawa after studying in America, observed: "I believe in actively seeking good fortune, because it seems that the more we pursue it, the easier getting it becomes." His colleague, Minoru Matayoshi, solemnly prophesies, "With the arm of science, people may jump out from the old, miserable generation and its pessimistic idea. Our generation seems to be this turning point of our history." Later a young Okinawan, in discussing the University of Tokyo consensus, said, "Okinawans have never forgotten that the Japanese treated them as second-class citizens before the war." For many years Ryukyuan men tattooed the backs of their women's hands to prevent their being carted off to Japan by their ardent overlords. On Okinawa today one can still see older women bearing such markings.

On a rainy night in February 1966 before I left Naha, I became first in the long slow line waiting for taxis to leave the Harbor View Club. Behind me were two Okinawan couples about twenty-five years old in impeccable Western dress, animatedly discussing world affairs. When my cab finally appeared I invited them to share it with me. They thanked me and asked if it was my first visit to their island. I told them I had been a "resident" twenty years earlier. (Then I visualized those four sparkling young people as five-year-olds in rags, roaming the streets, with no future ahead of them, eating what could be scraped up from the shambles or begged from "Joe." They have come a light-year in two decades, but with or without external help, *they* had to *want* to—and *do* it.) They refused to let me pay the driver for my share of the ride, wishing it chalked up to "common co-operation between Americans and Okinawans."

The Okinawans of the late 1960s want the best of all possible worlds, but only a few are willing or able to do anything about it. The average Ryukyuan does not honestly care under whose flag he lives. History has beaten out of him any patriotism for his own true and long submerged ethnic individuality. He cares more about knowing, feeling, and believing that he will belong to some substantial entity, whose government will accept him as a full, first-class citizen, where he will be at peace to pursue his day-to-day life, and where he won't have to relearn and realign, once in every generation. Weary of centuries of invasions, incursions, annexation, tributes, wars, and subservience, the local man in the street wants only stability, coupled with the security of a sustained living for himself and family.

How his reasonable desires can be met in the years to come—and be reconciled with the grander aims and aspirations of the larger, stronger factions which surround his island home physically, politically, and emotionally—is the big riddle of the Ryukyus. Since the fourteenth century, the Ryukyus have been the pawn of foreign powers.

Fortunately, today Okinawa boasts a small, new generation of vigorous, enlightened, educated young people who have come of age entirely within the American era. Their way will not be easy. "There is no magic medicine of one dose." But alertly poised and progressive, these young people will, in due course, either achieve their goal, or else produce an even better equipped generation whose success is assured.

# Appendix I

## UNITED STATES MILITARY GOVERNMENT
## RYUKYU ISLANDS

### Extraordinary Proclamation No. 1

### To the people of

### THE ISLANDS OF NANSEI SHOTO AND ADJACENT WATERS SOUTH OF THIRTY DEGREES NORTH LATITUDE

I, WILHELM D. STYER, Lieutenant General, United States Army, Commanding General, United States Army Forces, Western Pacific, having been designated by General of the Army Douglas A. MacArthur, United States Army, Commanding General, United States Army Forces, Pacific, as Military Governor of the Islands of Nansei Shoto and adjacent waters south of thirty (30) degrees north latitude, do hereby proclaim as follows:

#### ARTICLE I

The Military Government of the Islands of Nansei Shoto and adjacent waters south of thirty (30) degrees latitude, formerly under the control of the United States Navy, shall henceforth be under the control of the United States Army.

#### ARTICLE II

The Commanding General, Ryukyus Command, is hereby designated Chief Military Government Officer, and as such is my representative for all matters pertaining to Military Government. He may, in his discretion, delegate his powers and duties to a Deputy Commander for Military Government appointed by him.

### Article III

The provisions of all proclamations, orders, ordinances, regulations, and directives previously issued for the Military Government of the Islands of Nansei Shoto and adjacent waters south of thirty (30) degrees north latitude and not in conflict herewith will continue in full force and effect until such time as they may be changed by me or my duly authorized subordinates.

### Article IV

This proclamation will become effective at 0001 hours on the first day of July, 1946.

W. D. STYER
Lieutenant General
United States Army
Commanding General, United States Army Forces, Western Pacific
Military Governor of the Islands of Nansei Shoto and Adjacent Waters South of Thirty Degrees North Latitude

# Appendix II

## (EXTRACTS) TREATY OF PEACE WITH JAPAN SIGNED SEPTEMBER 8, 1951 ENTERED INTO FORCE APRIL 28, 1952

### CHAPTER II: TERRITORY

#### ARTICLE 2

(a) Japan, recognizing the independence of Korea, renounces all right, title and claim to Korea, including the islands of Quelpart, Port Hamilton and Dagelet.

(b) Japan renounces all right, title and claim to Formosa and the Pescadores.

(c) Japan renounces all right, title and claim to the Kurile Islands and to that portion of Sakhalin and the islands adjacent to it over which Japan acquired sovereignty as a consequence of the Treaty of Portsmouth of September 5, 1905.

(d) Japan renounces all right, title and claim in connection with the League of Nations Mandate System, and accepts the action of the United Nations Security Council of April 2, 1947, extending the trusteeship system to the Pacific Islands formerly under mandate to Japan.

(e) Japan renounces all claim to any right or title to or interest in connection with any part of the antarctic area, whether deriving from the activities of Japanese nationals or otherwise.

(f) Japan renounces all right, title and claim to the Spratly Islands and the Paracel Islands.

#### ARTICLE 3

Japan will concur in any proposal of the United States to the United Nations to place under its trusteeship system, with the United States as the sole administering authority, Nansei Shoto south of 29° north latitude (including the Ryukyu Islands and the Daito Islands), the Nanpo Shoto south of Sofu Gen (including the Bonin Islands, Rosario Island and the Volcano Islands) and

Parece Vela and Marcus Island. Pending the making of such a proposal and affirmative action thereon, the United States will have the right to exercise all and any powers of administration, legislation, and jurisdiction over the territory and inhabitants of these islands, including their territorial waters.

### Article 4

(a) Subject to the provisions of Paragraph (b) of this Article, the disposition of property of Japan and of its nationals in the areas referred to in Article 2, and their claims, including debts, against the authorities presently administering such areas and the residents (including juridical persons) thereof, and the disposition in Japan of property of such authorities and residents, and claims, including debts, of such authorities and residents against Japan and its nationals, shall be the subject of special arrangements between Japan and such authorities. The property of any of the Allied Powers or its nationals in the areas referred to in Article 2 shall, insofar as this has not already been done, be returned by the administering authority in the condition in which it now exists. (The term nationals whenever used in the present Treaty includes juridical persons).

(b) Japan recognizes the validity of disposition of property of Japan and Japanese nationals made by or pursuant to the directives of the United States Military Government in any of the areas referred to in Articles 2 and 3.

(c) Japanese owned submarine cables connecting Japan with territory removed from Japanese control pursuant to the present Treaty shall be equally divided, Japan retaining the Japanese terminal and adjoining half of the cable, and the detached territory the remainder of the cable and connecting terminal facilities.

## CHAPTER V: CLAIMS AND PROPERTY

### Article 19

(a) Japan waives all claims of Japan and its nationals against the Allied Powers and their nationals arising out of the war or out of actions taken because of the existence of a state of war, and waives all claims arising from the presence, operations or actions of forces or authorities of any of the Allied Powers in Japanese territory prior to the coming into force of the present Treaty.

(b) The foregoing waiver includes any claims arising out of actions taken by any of the Allied Powers with respect to Japanese ships between September 1, 1939, and the coming into force of the present Treaty, as well as any claims and debts arising in respect to Japanese prisoners of war and civilian internees in the hands of the Allied Powers, but does not include Japanese claims specifically recognized in the laws of any Allied Power enacted since September 2, 1945.

(d) Japan recognizes the validity of all acts and omissions done during the period of occupation under or in consequence of directives of the occupation authorities or authorized by Japanese law at that time, and will take no action subjecting Allied nationals to civil or criminal liability arising out of such acts or omissions.

# Appendix III

## EXECUTIVE ORDER 10713
## June 5, 1957
## (As Amended by Executive Order 11010, March 19, 1962)
## PROVIDING FOR ADMINISTRATION OF THE RYUKYU ISLANDS

WHEREAS under Article III of the Treaty of Peace with Japan the United States is exercising all and any powers of administration, legislation and jurisdiction over the territory, including territorial waters, and inhabitants of the Ryukyu Islands (the term "Ryukyu Islands," as used in this Order, meaning Nansei Shoto south of 29 degrees north latitude, excluding the islands in the Amami Oshima Group with respect to which all rights and interests of the United States under the said article of the treaty have been relinquished to Japan);

NOW, THEREFORE, by virtue of the authority vested in me by the Constitution, and as President of the United States and Commander-in-Chief of the Armed Forces of the United States, it is ordered as follows:

*Section 1.* Except as the Congress may otherwise provide by law with respect to the Government of the Ryukyu Islands, all administrative, legislative, and jurisdictional powers reposed in the United States by Article III of the Treaty of Peace with Japan shall be exercised in accordance with this Order.

*Section 2.* The said powers shall be exercised by the Secretary of Defense, subject to the direction and control of the President of the United States. In the exercise of this authority the Secretary of Defense shall encourage the development of an effective and responsible Ryukyuan Government, based on democratic principals and supported by a sound financial structure, shall make every effort to improve the welfare and well-being of the inhabitants of the Ryukyu Islands, and shall continue to promote the economic and cultural advancement of the inhabitants. The Secretary of Defense may delegate any function vested in him by this Order to such officials or organizational entities of the Department of Defense as he may designate.

*Section 3.* The Secretary of State shall be responsible for the conduct of relations with foreign countries and international organizations with respect to the Ryukyu Islands.

*Section 4.* (a) There is established, under the jurisdiction of the Secretary of Defense, a civil administration of the Ryukyu Islands, the head of which shall be known as the High Commissioner of the Ryukyu Islands (hereinafter referred to as the "High Commissioner"). The High Commissioner 1) shall be designated by the Secretary of Defense, after consultation with the Secretary of State and with the approval of the President, from among the active duty members of the armed forces of the United States, 2) shall have the powers and perform the duties assigned to him by the Secretary of Defense pursuant to this order.

(b) There shall be under the High Commissioner a civilian official who shall have the title of Civil Administrator. The Civil Administrator shall be designated by the Secretary of Defense, after consultation with the Secretary of State and with the approval of the President, and shall have such powers and perform such duties as may be assigned to him by the High Commissioner.

*Section 5.* There is hereby continued, subject to the provisions of this order, the now existing Ryukyuan central government (hereinafter referred to as the Government of the Ryukyu Islands).

*Section 6.* (a) The legislative power of the Government of the Ryukyu Islands, except as otherwise provided in this order, shall be vested in a legislative body consisting of a single house. Members of the legislative body shall be directly elected by the people of the islands in 1962, and triennially thereafter, for terms of three years.

(b) The territory of the Ryukyu Islands shall continue to be divided into districts, each of which shall elect one member of the legislative body. The present 29 districts are continued, but the number or boundaries of districts may be altered by law enacted by the Government of the Ryukyu Islands with the approval of the High Commissioner. Any redistricting shall be done with due regard to obtaining districts which are relatively compact and contiguous and which have reasonably equal populations.

*Section 7.* The legislative body shall exercise legislative powers which extend only to all subjects of legislation of domestic application. The legislative body shall determine the procedures for judging the selection and qualification of its own members and shall choose therefrom its officers and determine its rules and procedures. Local legislative bodies, the members of which shall be elected by the inhabitants of the respective municipalities in accordance with procedures established by the legislative body of the Government of the Ryukyu Islands, shall be given and shall exercise appropriate municipal legislative powers. The High Commissioner shall report to the Secretary of Defense all laws enacted by the legislative body of the Government of the Ryukyu Islands and the said Secretary shall report the same to the Congress of the United States.

*Section 8.* (a) The executive power of the Government of the Ryukyu Islands shall be vested in a Chief Executive, who shall be a Ryukyuan. The Chief Executive shall have general supervision and control of all executive agencies and instrumentalities of the Government of the Ryukyu Islands and shall faithfully execute the laws and ordinances applicable to the Ryukyu Islands.

(b) (1) The Chief Executive shall be appointed by the High Commissioner on the basis of a nomination which is made by the legislative body herein provided for and is acceptable to the High Commissioner. A Chief Executive so appointed shall serve for the remainder of the term of the legislative body which nominated him and for such reasonable period thereafter as may be necessary for the appointment of a successor pursuant to this paragraph, or, failing such an appointment, pursuant to paragraph (2) of this subsection.

(2) In the event the legislative body does not make an acceptable nomination within a reasonable time as determined by the High Commissioner, or if by reason of other unusual circumstances it is deemed by the High Commissioner to be necessary, he may appoint a Chief Executive without a nomination. The tenure of any Chief Executive appointed pursuant to this paragraph (2) shall be as determined by the High Commissioner.

(c) The head of each municipal government shall be elected by the people of the respective municipality in accordance with procedures established by the legislative body of the Government of the Ryukyu Islands.

*Section 9.* (a) Every bill passed by the legislative body shall, before it becomes law, be presented to the Chief Executive. If the Chief Executive approves a bill he shall sign it, but if not he shall return it, with his objections, to the legislative body within fifteen days after it shall have been presented to him. If a bill is not returned within the specified fifteen day period, it shall become law in like manner as if it had been approved by the Chief Executive, unless the legislative body by adjournment prevents its return, in which case it shall be law if approved by the Chief Executive within forty-five days after it shall have been presented to him; otherwise it shall not be law. When a bill is returned to the legislative body with objections by the Chief Executive, the legislative body may proceed to reconsider it. If, after such reconsideration two-thirds of the legislative body pass it, it shall become law in like manner as if it had been approved by the Chief Executive.

(b) If any bill approved by the legislative body contains several items of appropriation of money, the Chief Executive may object to one or more of such items or any part or parts, portion or portions thereof, while approving the other items, or parts or portions of the bill. In such case, the Chief Executive shall append to the bill, at the time of signing it, a statement of the items, or parts or portions thereof, objected to, and the items, or parts or portions thereof, so objected to shall not take effect. Should the legislative body seek to over-ride such objections of the Chief Executive, the procedures set forth above will apply. In computing any period of days for the foregoing purposes, Sundays and legal holidays shall be excluded.

*Section 10.* Judicial powers in the Ryukyu Islands shall be exercised as follows:

(a) A system of courts, including the civil and criminal courts of original jurisdiction and appellate tribunals, shall be maintained by the Government of the Ryukyu Islands. These courts shall exercise jurisdiction as follows:

(1) Civil jurisdiction in all civil cases, subject to the provisions of paragraphs (b) (1) and (2), below.

(2) Criminal jurisdiction over all persons except (a) members of the United States Forces or the civilian component, (b) employees of the United States Government who are United States nationals, and (c) dependents of the foregoing, provided, nevertheless, that subject to paragraph (c) below, criminal jurisdiction may be exercised by courts of the Government of the Ryukyu Islands over dependents who are Ryukyuans. Criminal jurisdiction may be withdrawn from the courts of the Government of the Ryukyu Islands by the High Commissioner in any case which affects the security, property, or interests of the United States and which is so designated by him.

(b) A system of courts, including civil and criminal courts of original jurisdiction and appellate tribunals, shall be maintained by the Civil Administration. These courts shall exercise jurisdiction as follows:

(1) Civil jurisdiction over any case or controversy of particular importance affecting the security, property, or interests of the United States, as determined by the High Commissioner. Such cases instituted in a court of the Government of the Ryukyu Islands shall be transferred to the appropriate Civil Administration court upon order of the High Commissioner at any time in the proceedings, including final appellate process, prior to the entering of final decree, order or judgment. Cases so transferred may be subject to trial de novo in the discretion of the court of the Civil Administration.

(2) Civil jurisdiction in cases and controversies in which a member of the United States forces or the civilian component thereof, an employee of the U.S. Government who is a United States national, or a dependent of one of the foregoing, unless such dependent is a Ryukyuan, is a party if upon petition of one of the parties to the suit the High Commissioner deems the case to be important in its effect, direct or indirect, on the security of the Islands, on foreign relations or on the security, property or interests of the United States or nationals thereof and determines that the Civil Administration should assume jurisdiction over the case. In this event, such cases instituted in a court of the Government of the Ryukyu Islands shall be transferred to the appropriate Civil Administration court by order of the High Commissioner at any time in the proceedings, including final decree, order or judgment. Cases so transferred may be subject to trial de novo in the discretion of the court of the Civil Administration.

(3) Criminal jurisdiction over (a) the civilian component, (b) employees of the United States Government who are United States nationals, and (c) de-

pendents, excluding Ryukyuans, (i) of the foregoing and (ii) of members of the United States forces.

(4) Criminal jurisdiction in specific cases of particular importance affecting the security, property, or interests of the United States, as determined by the High Commissioner. Such cases instituted in a court of the Government of the Ryukyu Islands may be transferred to the appropriate Civil Administration court upon order of the High Commissioner at any time in the proceedings, including the final appellate process, prior to the entering of final decree, order or judgment. Cases so transferred may be subject to trial de novo in the discretion of the court of the Civil Administration.

(c) Criminal jurisdiction over persons subject to trial by courts-martial under the Uniform Code of Military Justice (10 U.S.C. 801 et seq.) will be exercised by courts other than courts-martial only when the military commander concerned determines not to exercise military jurisdiction under the Uniform Code of Military Justice and specifically indicates to the High Commissioner his approval of referring the case to another court.

(d) The highest appellate court of the Civil Administration shall have jurisdiction to review:

(1) Any case, civil or criminal, tried in the inferior courts of the Civil Administration, whether initiated therein or removed thereto, upon appeal by any party.

(2) Any case, civil or criminal, decided by the highest court of the Government of the Ryukyu Islands having jurisdiction thereof in which is involved

(i) a conflict of decision between the highest court of the Government of the Ryukyu Islands and the highest appellate court of the Civil Administration or

(ii) a question of United States, foreign or international law, including the interpretation of any treaty, act of Congress of the United States, Executive Order of the President of the United States, or of a proclamation, ordinance or order of the High Commissioner upon appeal by any party or, if no such appeal be taken, upon petition, setting forth the special grounds therefor, presented to the court by the chief legal officer of the Civil Administration. The highest appellate court of the Civil Administration shall have power to affirm, modify, set aside or reverse the judgment, order or decree reviewed or to remand the case with such directions for a new trial or for entry of judgment as may be just. In a criminal case, the appellate court may set aside the judgment of conviction, or may commute, reduce (but not increase) or suspend the execution of sentence.

(e) Nothing in this section shall be construed as extending to any court of the Government of the Ryukyu Islands or of the Civil Administration, jurisdiction over the United States Government or any agency thereof unless specific authority has been conferred in the premises by the Congress of the United States.

(f) For the purpose of these provisions the expression

(1) "Members of the United States Forces" shall mean the personnel on active duty belonging to the land, sea or air armed forces of the United States of America whenever in the Ryukyu Islands.

(2) "Civilian component" shall mean the civilian persons of United States nationality who are in the employ of, serving with, or accompanying the United States forces whenever in the Ryukyu Islands.

(3) "Dependents" shall mean the spouse and any child or relative by affinity, consanguinity or adoption when dependent upon the principal for over half of his or her support whenever in the Ryukyu Islands.

Section 11. (a) The High Commissioner may, if such action is deemed necessary for the fulfillment of his mission under this order, promulgate laws, ordinances or regulations. The High Commissioner, if such action is deemed by him to be important in its effect, direct or indirect, on the security of the Ryukyu Islands, or on relations with foreign countries and international organizations with respect to the Ryukyu Islands, or on the foreign relations of the United States, or on the security, property or interests of the United States or nationals thereof, may, in respect of Ryukyuan bills, laws, or officials, as the case may be, (1) veto any bill or any part or portion thereof, (2) annul any law or any part or portion thereof within 45 days after its enactment, and (3) remove any public official from office. The High Commissioner has the power of reprieve, commutation and pardon. The High Commissioner may assume in whole or in part, the exercise of full authority in the islands, if such assumption of authority appears mandatory for security reasons. Exercise of authority conferred on the High Commissioner by this subsection shall be promptly reported, together with the reasons therefor, to the Secretary of Defense who shall inform the Secretary of State.

(b) In carrying out the powers conferred upon him by the provisions of subsection (a) of this section, the High Commissioner shall give all proper weight to the rights of the Ryukyuans and shall, in particular, have proper regard for the provisions of the second sentence of Section 2 of this order.

*Section 12.* In carrying out this order, including Section 11, the High Commissioner shall preserve to persons in the Ryukyu Islands the basic liberties enjoyed by people in democratic countries, including freedom of speech, assembly, petition, religion and press, and security from unreasonable searches and seizures, and from deprivation of life, liberty or property without due process of law.

*Section 13.* The Secretary of Defense may issue such further instructions as may be necessary for the carrying out of this order.

*Section 14.* Except as they may be inconsistent herewith, the proclamations, ordinances, and directives heretofore issued by the existing Civil Administration and its predecessor Military Government agencies shall continue in force and effect until modified, revoked, or superseded under the authority of this order.

No proceeding, either civil or criminal, pending in any court of the Government of the Ryukyu Islands or of the Civil Administration of the Ryukyu Islands on the date of this order shall abate by reason of this order; and any such proceeding shall be conducted and concluded in accordance with laws, ordinances, proclamations, and directives in effect immediately before the date of this order.

*Section 15.* This order shall become effective immediately, but until its provisions shall severally become operative as herein provided, the legislative, executive and judicial functions now vested in the Civil Administration and the Government of the Ryukyu Islands, shall continue to be exercised as now provided by law, ordinance, proclamation or directive, and the incumbents of all offices under the Civil Administration or the Government of the Ryukyu Islands shall continue in office until their successors are appointed or elected and have qualified, unless sooner removed by competent authority.

### Transitional Provisions—Executive Order 11010, March 19, 1962

*Section 3.* (a) This order shall not operate to terminate immediately the tenure of the Chief Executive of the Government of the Ryukyu Islands now in office. That tenure shall terminate when his first successor, appointed under the provisions of Executive Order No. 10713 as amended by this order, enters upon office as Chief Executive or on such other date as may be fixed by the High Commissioner.

(b) The members of the legislative body in office on the date of this order shall continue in office until the termination of their present terms as members.

(c) The amendment of Section 4 of Executive Order No. 10713 made by this order shall become effective on July 1, 1962. All other parts hereof shall become effective on April 1, 1962.

# Appendix IV

## STATEMENT BY THE PRESIDENT OF THE UNITED STATES, MARCH 19, 1962

I have today signed an amendment to Executive Order 10713, dated June 5, 1957, providing for the administration of the Ryukyu Islands. The amendments to the Executive Order, as well as a number of other measures set forth below, are the result of recommendations of the Interdepartmental Task Force appointed last year to investigate current conditions in the Ryukyu Islands and the United States policies and programs in force there.

The work of the Task Force underlines the importance the United States attaches to its military bases in the Ryukyu Islands. The armed strength deployed at these bases is of the greatest importance in maintaining our deterrent power in the face of threats to the peace in the Far East. Our bases in the Ryukyu Islands help us assure our allies in the great arc from Japan through Southeast Asia not only of our willingness but also of our ability to come to their assistance in case of need.

The report of the Task Force examines in detail the problem of reconciling the military imperative for continued United States administration with the desires of the Ryukyuan people to assert their identity as Japanese, to obtain the economic and social welfare benefits available in Japan, and to have a greater voice in the management of their own affairs. The report has also considered in the same context the desire of the Japanese people to maintain close contact with their countrymen in the Ryukyus.

I recognize the Ryukyus to be a part of the Japanese homeland and look forward to the day when the security interests of the free world will permit their restoration to full Japanese sovereignty. In the meantime we face a situation which must be met in a spirit of forbearance and mutual understanding by all concerned. I have directed that a number of specific actions be taken to give expression to this spirit by the United States, to discharge more effectively our responsibilities toward the people of the Ryukyus, and to minimize the stresses that will accompany the anticipated eventual restoration of the Ryukyu Islands to Japanese administration. These actions consist of:

1. Asking the Congress to amend the Price Act (PL 86-629) to remove the present $6 million ceiling on assistance to the Ryukyu Islands.

2. Preparing for submission to the Congress plans for the support of new programs in the Ryukyus to raise the levels of compensation for Ryukyuan employees of the U.S. Forces and the Government of the Ryukyu Islands, and the levels of public health, educational and welfare services so that over a period of years they reach those obtained in comparable areas in Japan.

3. Preparing proposals for the Congress to provide over future years a steady increase in loan funds available for the development of the Ryukyuan economy.

4. Entering into discussions with the Government of Japan with a view to working out precise arrangements to implement a cooperative relationship between the United States and Japan in providing assistance to promote the welfare and well-being of the inhabitants of the Ryukyu Islands and their economic development, as discussed between Prime Minister Ikeda and myself during his visit to Washington last year.

5. Carrying on a continuous review of governmental functions in the Ryukyu Islands to determine when and under what circumstances additional functions that need not be reserved to the United States as administering authority can be delegated to the Government of the Ryukyu Islands.

6. Carrying on a continuous review of such controls as may be thought to limit unnecessarily the private freedoms of inhabitants of the Ryukyu Islands with a view to eliminating all controls which are not essential to the maintenance of the security of the United States military installations in the Ryukyus or of the Islands themselves. The amendments to Executive Order 10713 are designed to accomplish the following purposes:

1. Provide for nomination of the Chief Executive of the Government of the Ryukyu Islands by the Legislature.
2. Restate the veto power of the High Commissioner to emphasize its restricted purposes.
3. Lengthen the terms of the Legislature from two to three years.
4. Permit the Legislature to alter the number and boundaries of election districts.
5. Provide that Civil Administrator shall be a civilian.
6. Make certain technical changes in the provisions for criminal jurisdiction over certain Americans in the Ryukyus.

# Appendix V

## TOKUJI TOKONAMI'S PLAN FOR THE RETURN OF OKINAWA TO JAPANESE SOVEREIGNTY

It was two years ago that I published "A Re-examination of Problems of *Okinawa*" and brought out major problem which I thought would require close study for considering countermeasures in the future. Now I have made this statement upon probing the possible measures to solve these problems. I shall appreciate the candid criticism of all persons who take a serious interest in this subject.

Twenty years now since the end of the war, there is growing a strong desire for the return to Japan of full administrative rights over Okinawa, among all Japanese as well as all inhabitants of Okinawa. In this context we recall the statement by the United States Government to the effect that they recognize the Ryukyus to be a part of the Japanese homeland and look forward to the day when they will be restored to full Japanese sovereignty and also their other statement that they will retain the Ryukyu Islands until the tensions in the Far East relax. Meanwhile, judging from the development of the international situation in that part of the world, the importance of the Ryukyus as a U.S. military base has not diminished in the least in the light of the nuclear experiments by Communist China, and armed conflicts now raging in Indochina, especially in Vietnam.

Nevertheless, the Islanders of Okinawa could hardly bear the continuation of U.S. administration over their Islands until the establishment of peace in the Far East can allow the return of Okinawa to Japan. It is therefore necessary to study the possible measures by which to attain the goal of restoring Okinawa to Japan, while maintaining its mission as the U.S. military base. This is the very reason why I offer here my personal views for the material for discussion.

Regarding immediate measures, in view of the purport of each of the joint communiqués of Prime Minister Kishi and U.S. President Eisenhower, of Prime Minister Ikeda and U.S. President Kennedy, and of Prime Minister Sato and U.S. President Johnson, we should do our utmost to realize the following objectives until the final goal of the return of Okinawa is attained. To this end we hope and expect that the Japan-United States Consultative Committee and the Japan-United States Technical Committee, whose powers have recently been extended, will display positive activity.

*Note 1:* JOINT COMMUNIQUÉ OF PRIME MINISTER KISHI AND PRESIDENT EISENHOWER, JUNE 22, 1957

*The Prime Minister emphasized the strong desire of the Japanese people for the return of administrative control over the Ryukyu and Bonin Islands to Japan. The President reaffirmed the United States position that Japan possesses residual sovereignty over these Islands. He pointed out, however, that so long as the conditions of threat and tension exist in the Far East the United States will find it necessary to continue the present status. He stated that the United States will continue its policy of improving the welfare and well-being of the inhabitants of the Islands and of promoting their economic and cultural advancement.*

*Note 2.* JOINT COMMUNIQUÉ OF PRIME MINISTER IKEDA AND PRESIDENT KENNEDY, JUNE 22, 1961

*The President and the Prime Minister exchanged views on matters relating to the Ryukyu and Bonin Islands, which are under United States administration but in which Japan retains residual sovereignty. The President reaffirmed that the United States would make further efforts to enhance the welfare and well-being of the inhabitants of the Ryukyus and welcomed Japanese cooperation in these efforts. The Prime Minister affirmed that Japan would continue to co-operate with the United States to this end.*

*Note 3.* STATEMENT BY PRESIDENT KENNEDY OF THE UNITED STATES, MARCH 19, 1962 [See Chapter 7]

*Note 4.* JOINT COMMUNIQUÉ OF PRIME MINISTER SATO AND U.S. PRESIDENT JOHNSON, JANUARY 13, 1965

*The President and the Prime Minister recognized the importance of United States military installations on the Ryukyu and Bonin Islands for the security of the Far East. The Prime Minister expressed the desire that, as soon as feasible, the administrative control over these Islands will be restored to Japan and also a deep interest in the expansion of the autonomy of the inhabitants of the Ryukyus and in further promoting their welfare. Appreciating the desire of the government and people of Japan for the restoration of administration to Japan, the President stated that he looks forward to the day when the security interests of the Free World in the Far East will permit the realization of this desire. They confirmed that the United States and Japan should continue substantial economic assistance to the Ryukyu Islands in order to advance further the welfare and well-being of the inhabitants of these Islands. They expressed their satisfaction with the smooth operation of the cooperative arrangements between the United States and Japan concerning assistance to the Ryukyu Islands. They agreed in principle to broaden the functions of the existing Japan-United States Consultative Committee so as to enable the committee to conduct consultations not only on economic assistance to the Ryukyu Islands but also on other matters on which the two countries can cooperate in continuing to promote the well-being of the inhabitants of the Islands. The President agreed to give favorable consideration to an ancestral graves visit by a representative group of former residents of the Bonin Islands.*

1. Extension of autonomy
   a) Utmost efforts will be made so that the autonomy of the inhabitants may be recognized to the widest possible extent with respect to the three powers of legislation, judicature and administration, while restrictions in this respect will be relaxed.

*Note 5. The Execution Order providing for administration of the Ryukyu Islands (the so-called "Presidential Executive Order *"). These matters have already undergone appreciable improvements after the assumption of office of Lt. General Watson II, U.S. High Commissioner of the Ryukyus, but further efforts are intended to be rendered in future along these lines. (Concrete instances are omitted here).*

   b) The current system of nominating the Chief Executive of the Ryukyuan Government will be re-examined.

*Note 6. Matters mentioned in a) and b) require amendment to the Presidential Executive Order of implementation.*

   c) Transfer, to the largest possible extent, of the powers of the U.S. Civil Administration of the Ryukyus to the Ryukyuan Government will be considered.
   d) In short, our basic idea should be to make the self-government or autonomy by the Islanders the general principle, with certain restrictions imposed to prevent the administration of military bases in the Islands from possible interference thereby, instead of to give priority to administration of military bases and subordinating Islanders' autonomy thereto.

2. Improvement of inhabitants' welfare to the prefectural level of the Japanese mainland.
   a) A comparative study will be made of the levels of people's welfare and industry between the Islands and the Japanese mainland and disparities will be filled by an annual plan.
   b) Special emphasis will be placed on education, medical care and other

* Morris Note 4: E. O. 10713.

forms of social security, and agriculture, forestry and fisheries, forestry and river conservancy, and land reclamation by drainage.

3. Japan-U.S. economic cooperation will be drastically expanded and financial capacity of the administrative level of the Japanese mainland will be given.
   a) Financial aid extended so far by undertakings will be increased, but, as this form of assistance is limited in capacity, the following measures will be adopted concurrently:
   b) The basic financial capacity of the Ryukyuan Government is considered to be very weak and therefore Japan-U.S. financial aid like the local allocation tax in force in Japan proper will be afforded.

*Note 7. Amendment to the Price Act.*
*Notes: In Okinawa, as compared with mainland Japan,*
*8. Cost of living is high for income.*
*9. Low income classes are more heavily taxed.*
*10. Educational expenses under the system of educational districts are heavy.*

4. Consideration of the measure of expanding Japanese financial assistance as far as possible and converting from the dollar to the yen economy, thereby to prevent possible economic confusion in the event of the return of Okinawa to Japan.
5. Improvement of administrative capacity
   a) Positive personnel exchange will be made between Okinawa and mainland Japan.
   b) The Nampo Liaison Office of the Japanese Government at Naha, the subordinate organ to the Prime Minister's Office, will be strengthened.
   c) Various kinds of systems and methods of administration will, as far as possible, be made identical with their counterparts in the Japanese mainland, thereby to prepare for the eventual unification with Japan proper.
6. Freer traffic between Okinawa and mainland Japan.
7. Through the aforementioned efforts, possible friction with the mainland at the time of its return thereto will be minimized, while the economic distress in the inhabitants' daily life prior to the return to Japan will be lessened as far as possible, thereby to prepare for the day of return to Japan.
8. Participation in the national administration of Japan.
   a) The proposal that participation in the national government in the homeland at least for the period preceding the day of reversion of Okinawa to Japan should be utilized to serve for the return of Okinawa and improvement of the various conditions there sounds plausible, but, now that Japan has not the administrative rights over Okinawa, participation in Japanese national administration in the true sense of the term is difficult.
   b) It may be suggested that, by amending the Public Offices Election Law for election of Dietmen from Okinawa in the future, on the assumption

of its eventual reversion to Japan, "Okinawa Electoral District" should be specified in the table annexed to such amendment.

c) It is also conceivable that representatives who have no voting right but who are empowered to deliberate and speak at the Diet be sent to the Diet of Japan. But this will require an amendment to the Diet Law.

d) Even under the Diet Law currently in force the opinion of the representative of Okinawa as witness can be heard.

e) It is very feasible that the Diet in the homeland will invite, periodically or from time to time every year, the representatives of the Ryukyuan Legislature and have talks with them.

f) At present close contact is being maintained between the Japanese and Ryukyuan governments and also between the Liberal Democratic Party of Japan and the Democratic Party of Okinawa as brotherly political parties, whilst the Japanese Government is striving to secure full mutual understanding and smooth liaison and coordination of business with the other government, through the Japan-U.S. Consultative Committee and the Japan-U.S. Technical Committee. Yet it will be necessary in future as well to secure closer mutual liaison.

g) In any case, the proposed participation in the national administration is connected with the question of the return of administrative rights to Japan and as such presupposes full mutual understanding between Japan and America.

9. In the Diet there is an opinion favouring the creation of a Special Committee on Okinawa. It may be remarked in this connection that all parties have agreed to the very proposition for the reversion of Okinawa to Japan and they have no objection to it, as illustrated by the several resolutions adopted in both Houses. However, the Government party and the Opposition are sharply divided on the Japan-U.S. Security Treaty which may be considered as the pre-condition to this matter. Thus we cannot expect any fruitful result from the establishment of the proposed Committee, in the light of the current status of operation of the Diet.

10. As may be clear from what I have stated above, problems of Okinawa involve a multitude of matters in respect of which immediate remedial measures should be adopted, and accordingly we should necessarily strive to implement such measures. At the same time, however, it is found essential to study the concrete steps of how to accelerate and realize the return of Okinawa to Japan by people, whether government or private, in Japan, in America, and in Okinawa, respectively.

    I shall express my personal views in matters in respect of which countermeasures should be studied:

1. It is essential to deepen our understanding of the peculiar features of the U.S. military bases in Okinawa.

   a) Bases in Okinawa are not only necessary for securing the structure of the Japan-U.S. Security Treaty, but also constitute bases under U.S.-Korea, U.S.-Philippine and U.S.-Chinese Mutual Defense Treaties. Furthermore, they form the defense center in the whole region of the Far East.

b) In Okinawa there are military and supply bases for the following units: **

Land—The 9th Corps; the 30th Air-Defense Artillery Brigade (nikes and hawks); the 173rd Air-borne Brigade; the 1st Special Force Group.

Sea —The 7th Fleet; the 4th Patrol Squadron; the 3rd Marine Division; the 16th Marine Air Group.

Air —The 313rd Air Division (including tactical missile groups—Mace B).

Total strength of about 60,000 persons.

In other words, in terms of atomic weapons, Okinawa forms the base for polaris submarines, Mace B, and B-57 bombers.

*Note 11. The total area of military lands accounts for 8.77 per cent (207.9 million m²) of that of Okinawa and the Ryukyus (including the main Island, Iwojima,*** and Torishima Islands) 13.88 per cent of same.*

c) In the light of the above, Okinawa possesses sufficient power not only of retaliation but also of attack against aggression by a foreign country. Thus, needless to say, Japan is serving to secure the peace in the Far East. Meanwhile, Communist China experimented with nuclear explosion some time ago and her nuclear armament is believed to be a question of time, but this possibility will not present a great immediate threat to our nation.

d) The fact that Okinawa is a nuclear base does not increase the possibility that Okinawa will fall a victim to nuclear retaliation especially in case of an emergency. Moreover, America could make nuclear retaliation by other methods if Okinawa base should be destroyed, and thus an attack, if made against Okinawa, will not produce much effect.

e) In view of the peculiarities of bases in Okinawa, even in case Okinawa returns, in its present condition, to full Japanese sovereignty, if the agreement on bases under the Security Treaty remains applicable, bases in Okinawa may not perform their functions satisfactorily.

2. In the circumstances, special conditions must be imposed for securing the functions as military bases. In other words, Islanders' cooperation setup will be required particularly in respect of the following matters, unlike in the case of military bases on the homeland:

** Morris Note 2: As of April 1965.

*** Morris Note 3: This must be Ie Shima; Iwo Jima is in the Bonin (Ogasawara) Group.

a) Protection of military secrets.
b) Some of the public utilities, such as water service, electricity, roads, and harbor facilities, are in joint military and civilian use, and some guarantee should be provided so that satisfactory execution of military purposes may not be interfered with.
c) With respect to the provision of labor within the bases and for works connected with military authorities some exception will be made so that the accomplishment of business may not be hindered.
d) In case of an emergency, extension of control by military authorities will be recognized.
e) Cooperation setup between Japan and Islanders will be established so that America may not feel anxiety over the maintenance of bases in Okinawa.

3. Reversion of Okinawa to Japan and United Nations Charter
   a) As the United States does not propose the placing of Okinawa under its trusteeship system under Article 3 of the Treaty of Peace with Japan, the continuation of American administrative control over Okinawa in the present condition is considered to be a provisional measure. Accordingly, administrative rights over Okinawa should be restored to Japan as early as possible.

*Note 12. No revision of the San Francisco Peace Treaty will be necessary, because the return to Japan is possible by virtue of the Japanese-U.S. Agreement (December 25, 1963) as instanced by the return of Amami Oshima Islands.*

   b) However, this is not a contravention of Article 78 of U.N. Charter as alleged by the Socialist Party, but is subject to Article 77 thereof. On this account appeal to the United Nations for restitution of Okinawa will be meaningless.

*Note 13. Article 78 of U.N. Charter—"Relationship between members of the United Nations shall be based on respect for the principle of sovereign equality."*

*Note 14. Article 77 of U.N. Charter—"The trusteeship system shall apply to such territories in the following categories as may be placed thereunder by means of trusteeship agreements: Territories which may be detached from enemy states as a result of the Second World War."*

   c) Needless to say, the United States has no intention of placing Okinawa under its trusteeship and states manifestly that it has no intention of making it its territory.
   d) Okinawa is not a colony, and accordingly does not fall under the United Nations' resolution opposing colonies.

4. Can we await the reversion of Okinawa to Japan until the extinction of the need of military bases?
   a) As there is a necessity for Okinawa to perform its mission as a military

base for a considerable length of time in the future, positive cooperation on the part of Islanders is needed.

b) Islanders' cooperation for the maintenance of military bases can be given full play by the return of administrative rights.

c) The Socialists and the Communists who both oppose the Japan-U.S. security system are, needless to say, in opposition to the continuance of military bases and refuse to cooperate in it.

5. Reversion to Japan by separation of military bases from administrative rights.

a) If the continuance of military bases in Okinawa is necessary for some time to come, administration over Islanders in general will be left, as far as possible, to their autonomy, to enable the military bases to perform their mission with full cooperation of Islanders. This measure should be carried a step further and such portion of U.S. administration will be delegated to Japan or such portion of administrative rights will be restored to Japan.

b) In case administrative rights are delegated or partially returned to Japan, it will be necessary to divide administrative districts into those for inhabitants in general and those for military bases. For that matter,

(1) Powers concerning maintenance of districts for military bases and of military bases will be retained by the High Commissioner.

(2) Whereas, administrative districts for inhabitants in general will be made administrative districts of the Ryukyuan Government.

*Note 15. Division of administrative districts into those for military bases and those for general administrative districts is considered to be useful in making a distinction in administrative terms after the restitution of administrative rights.*

c) Next, with respect to districts for military bases and their allied affairs, America's administrative power continues to be recognized, but the administrative districts of the Ryukyuan Government will be placed under Japanese administrative control, thereby to realize the return of such rights to Japan.

d) The Ryukyus, on their reversion to Japan, will be returned to Japan by a Japan-U.S. Treaty concerning the restitution and subject to the Constitution of Japan. Especially as the requirement under the treaty, Okinawa will be treated tentatively as Japan's special administrative district. Special administration will be effected to meet the military needs, while, as to districts for military bases, American administrative control over them will be recognized for the time being. Consequently, as a general rule, laws and regulations identical with those on the homeland of Japan will apply in Okinawa, whereas, as to military relations, special treatment will be recognized.

*Note 16. Municipal law of Japan will apply as a general rule, but certain exceptions will be granted. For example, certain control over military bases more peculiar than that under the Japan-U.S. Security Treaty will be recognized.*

Note 17. *Special provision will be made for maintenance of military secrets, public peace, labor and operation of public utilities, in an emergency.*

Note 18. *The employees by the military authorities totaled 54,983 or 6 per cent of the whole population as of September 1961.*

e) The Socialist Party maintains that military bases are inseparable from administrative rights, but if we assume that the bases are necessary for some time to come, the reversion to Japan will be impossible for that period of time. Moreover, the Socialists deny the Japan-U.S. security system, declaring that bases are unnecessary, closing their eyes to the actual circumstances. Their argument, thus, is entirely detached from the reality and should be considered an unfeasible opinion.

f) Military bases in Okinawa cover a considerably large area, but even so, it does not follow that administrative rights over the whole area of it should be retained. With the cooperation setup of Islanders in general it will be possible to specify the pertinent districts. Particularly, isolated Islands have hardly anything to do with the bases.

Note 19. *As a provisional step, a joint control scheme of Japan, America and Okinawa will be introduced and America will be made to have general responsibility for administrative rights, which will then be restored to Japan.*

g) As to the Bonin Islands, where there are only half-blood inhabitants, the restitution of their administrative right may be considered according to their necessity as military bases.

6. Okinawa in relation to the Constitution of Japan

a) The military bases in Okinawa are marked by the aforementioned peculiarities, and, as a matter of course, their potential power is by far the greater than the self-defensive power as stipulated in Article 9 of our Constitution. It is therefore constitutionally impossible for Japan to assume charge of the bases in Okinawa nor is this financially practicable. Viewed in this light, the contention that the return of Okinawa to Japan will be possible only upon re-armament by virtue of a revision of the Constitution is not acceptable.

b) Consequently, if the return of the Islands to Japan is contemplated on the premise of the existence of bases, such bases must be excluded from the scope of application of the Constitution.

c) The Socialist Party takes the view that even now the Japanese Constitution is applicable to Okinawa. But, since the United States has the right to exercise administrative control over the Islands by virtue of Article 3 of the San Francisco Peace Treaty, our Constitution naturally is inapplicable there.

d) Since the Constitution is not applicable to Okinawa, it is natural that

Article 9 thereof should not be applicable to it, and this renders it possible for Okinawa to be an atomic base. Indeed, under the prevailing international situation, Okinawa's mission as a military base will be performed by its nuclear armament.

7. Okinawa in relation to the Security Treaty

a) On the application of Article V, paragraph 1, of the Security Treaty

Article V, paragraph 1, of the Security Treaty states that each party recognizes that an armed attack against either Party in the territories under the administration of Japan would be dangerous to its own place and safety and declares that it would act to meet the common danger in accordance with its constitutional provisions and processes.

*Note 20. If, in case administrative rights over Okinawa are restituted to Japan, Okinawa enters into war under U.S.-Korea, U.S.-Philippine, and U.S.-China Mutual Defense Treaties, Japan will naturally be entangled in war. The reversion of Okinawa to Japan will have an effect on Japan as if she would have concluded a mutual defense treaty with the Republic of Korea, with the Philippines and with China, respectively. Therefore, it is necessary to state expressly in a Japan-U.S. Agreement to be concluded in the event of the return to Japan of administrative rights over Okinawa that the provisions of the Security Treaty will not apply.*

b) Okinawa in relation to "Agreed Minute to the Security Treaty"

With respect to Okinawa, the Japanese side states in "Agreed Minute to the Treaty of Mutual Cooperation and Security" that ". . . Japan possesses residual sovereignty over these Islands. If an armed attack occurs or is threatened against these Islands, the two countries will of course consult together closely under Article IV of the Treaty of Mutual Cooperation and Security. In the event of an armed attack, it is the intention of the Government of Japan to explore with the United States measures which it might be able to take for the welfare of the Islanders."

Whereas, the American side makes it clear that "in the event of an armed attack against these Islands, the United States Government will consult at once with the Government of Japan and intends to take the necessary measures for the defense of these Islands, and to do its utmost to secure the welfare of the Islands."

This clarifies the point that, while in the case contemplated in the preceding paragraph, Japan will not intervene in a war in a manner of chain-reaction, she will take steps, such as those for relief and protection which she is naturally bound to do as the homeland.

c) Consultation under Article IV of the Security Treaty

Article IV of the Security Treaty states that "The Parties will consult together from time to time regarding the implementation of this Treaty, and, at the request of either Party, wherever the security of Japan or International peace and security in the Far East is threatened." However, this has nothing whatever to do with the question of whether administrative rights are returned or not, and accordingly consultation should be held on the assumption of matters concerning Article IV.

d) The question of application of the Security Treaty apparently has no direct connection with Okinawa at the moment, while, as regards the effective period of the Security Treaty, it is mentioned in Article X, paragraph 1, of the Security Treaty that "this Treaty shall remain in force until in the opinion of the Government of Japan and the United States of America there shall have come into force such United Nations arrangements as will satisfactorily provide for the maintenance of international peace and security in the Japan area." Whereas in paragraph 2 of the same Article it is stated that "However, after the Treaty has been in force for ten years, either party may give notice to the other Party of its intention to terminate the Treaty, in which case the Treaty shall terminate one year after such notice has been given." In 1970 paragraph 2 will terminate at one year's notice. Consequently, as to the situation after 1970, there arises a question whether the Treaty should be made to continue in force as it stands now for a certain period, or the Treaty should be placed in a somewhat uncertain condition in which it may be terminated at one year's notice.

Of course, we recognize the necessity to have the Treaty continue in force for maintaining the system of Japan-U.S. security and cooperation, while, simultaneously, we should keep up our cooperation in securing bases after 1970 as well.

e) Both the Socialists and the Communists are in opposition to the Security Treaty, as noted above. They expect 1970 to be the time for revision of the Security Treaty and in an effort to do away with the Treaty, are staging a campaign against revision of the Security Treaty, while carrying on a movement for the restitution of Okinawa to Japan. We should exercise every possible precaution so that people may not be misled by the movements directed by the Socialists and Communists.

8. Okinawa in relation to Northern Territory of Japan

a) By virtue of Article 3 of the San Francisco Peace Treaty, Okinawa is under U.S. administrative control, while Shikotan and Habomai Islands belong to Hokkaido, as recognized by the Japan-Soviet joint declaration. Kunashiri and Etrofu Islands are the proper territory of Japan to which Japan has renounced all title under Article 2 of the Peace Treaty. They should be restituted to Japanese sovereignty under Matsumoto-Gromyko correspondence and thus they are now under unlawful possession of Soviet Russia.

b) Therefore, from a purely theoretical point of view, higher priority should be given to the restitution of the northern territory, but the restoration of administrative rights over the Ryukyus and the Bonin Islands serves to show all the more clearly the unlawfulness of Soviet control over our northern territory and also to accelerate its restitution to Japanese sovereignty.

Note 21. *Now 890,000 of our compatriots are in Okinawa; in the Bonin Islands are living mixed blood islanders; and all Japanese inhabitants of the northern territory have been repatriated to the homeland.*

c) Soviet Russia makes a gesture as if she would consider the restoration of the northern territory on the condition of the restoration of Okinawa and the Bonin Islands. However, she will lose that pretext upon the return to Japan of administrative rights over Okinawa. Therefore the earliest possible return to Japan of administrative rights over Okinawa is desired. In summary, the road to Okinawa's reversion to Japan is:

a) As the immediate step, closer connection and concert will be established between Okinawa and the homeland of Japan, while efforts will be made to deepen Japan-U.S. mutual understanding, to extend local autonomy, to improve people's livelihood, and to increase financial aid, up to the levels of their counterparts in the homeland.

b) For the time being, Japanese people in the homeland and inhabitants of Okinawa will duly adjust the cooperation setup as far as possible, in view of the importance of the mission of Okinawa as a military base.

c) It is necessary to restitute such portions of U.S. administrative rights as concern the inhabitants and their livelihood which have nothing to do with the military bases, so that full cooperation of the people in the homeland and Islanders may be assured.

d) To that end, the restitution of such rights will be realized, in principle, by a relevant Japan-U.S. treaty. As to the portions related to military bases, a condition may be attached that certain rights be reserved by America lest the proper functions of military bases should be interfered with.

e) In that case, Okinawa will be, in principle, subject to all laws in force in Japan. But, actually, from its relation to military bases and other matters, in some cases all such laws cannot be made applicable on the same footing as in the homeland and in others Okinawa should be treated as the special administrative district where laws different from those in force in the homeland will apply.

f) In relation to U.S. forces, some administrative agreement different in substance from that under the Japan-U.S. Security Treaty will be concluded.

g) By realizing early reversion to Japan through the aforementioned process, closer cooperation between the Japanese people and Islanders regarding bases in Okinawa will be established and the Japan-U.S. security setup will be strengthened and tightened and thereby the realization of the return to Japan of her northern territory may be accelerated.

Note 22. *There is an argument that Okinawa should be returned to Japan unconditionally and then an agreement regarding military bases should be concluded with America. But, in the event Okinawa is restored to the homeland, a Japan-U.S. special agreement, when con-concluded thereafter, will not be considered dependable by America. Nor is it feasible as an actual political contention.*

h) With respect to the Bonin Islands, half-blood Islanders have been allowed to return to live in the Islands after the war's ending. However, so long as there is no military inconvenience, they should be restored to Japanese sovereignty in the same way as Okinawa and treated similarly.

i) Thus, friendly relations between Japan and America will be further strengthened and will thereby contribute better to the promotion of the peace in Asia.

# Bibliography

Appleman, Roy E., *Okinawa: The Last Battle,* Department of the Army, Washington, 1948.

Ishikawa, Kiyoharu, *A Bibliography of Material About the Ryukyu Islands (Okinawa) in English Language,* Naha, University of the Ryukyus, November, 1964.

Kerr, George H., *Okinawa: The History of an Island People,* Rutland, Vermont, Charles E. Tuttle Co., 1958.

King, Col. Norman D., *Ryukyu Islands* (bibliography), Washington, Department of the Army Pamphlet, 550–4, March 1967.

Kluckhohn, Jane, and Lueders, E. G., *Through Okinawan Eyes,* Albuquerque, University of New Mexico Press, March 1951.

Morison, Samuel Eliot, *Victory in the Pacific,* vol. 14 of History of United States Naval Operations in World War II, Boston, Little, Brown & Co., 1960.

Osborn, Fairfield, ed., *The Pacific World,* New York, W. W. Norton, 1944.

Sneider, Vern J., *The Teahouse of the August Moon,* New York, G. P. Putnam's Sons.

# Index